D0891859

Beliefs and Holy Places

Beliefs and Holy Places

A Spiritual Geography of the Pimería Alta

James S. Griffith

The University of Arizona Press
Tucson & London

The University of Arizona Press
Copyright © 1992
Arizona Board of Regents
All Rights Reserved
♾ This book is printed on acid-free, archival-quality paper.
Manufactured in the United States of America.

97 96 95 94 93 92   6 5 4 3 2 1

Library of Congress Cataloging-in-Publication Data

Griffith, James S.
  Beliefs and holy places :   a spiritual geography of the
Pimería Alta / James S. Griffith.
     p.   cm.
  Includes bibliographical references and index.
  ISBN 0-8165-1261-2 (alk. paper)
  1. Primería Alta (Mexico and Ariz.)—Religious life and customs.
  2. Shrines—Primería Alta (Mexico and Ariz.).   3. Religion and
geography.   I. Title.
BL2527.S68G75   1992   91-26425
291.3'5'097217—dc20   CIP

British Library Cataloguing-in-Publication Data
A catalogue record for this book is available from the British library.

Contents

Illustrations

Acknowledgments

Any book whose scope is this broad is of necessity the collaborative work of many people. Few of my trips of learning in the Pimería Alta have been made alone; a comprehensive list of all my companions, guides, and mentors would be impracticable to compile. However, certain names stand out, one in particular. Richard Morales has traveled long with me and taught me much. Companion on numerous trips in Sonora and Arizona, he shared my search for information concerning *la corúa* and Juan Soldado, and has greatly increased my understanding of San Francisco. Much that is accurate and respectful in this book is due to my long association with this good man.

I first heard of la corúa from Olga Ruiz of Imuris, Sonora. Pete Castillo of Marana, and Carmen Villa Prezelski, Luis Armando Salazar, and Tom Sheridan of Tucson all shared their knowledge of that huge serpent. Barre Tolkein of Utah State University suggested parallels between O'odham lore about snakes and sucking monsters and similar beliefs from elsewhere in Native North America.

Danny Lopez of Big Fields Village and Blaine Juan of San Simon have increased my understanding of O'odham traditions. Willard Anita, then chairman of Gu Achi District, took time from a busy schedule to escort me to the Children's Shrine and explain that sacred place to me. Ethnobotanist Gary Nabhan shared information concerning the nehbig, as well as other valuable ideas. Julian Hayden of Tucson gave me much to think about concerning various kinds of shrines, both in Pima country and on the far western desert.

I have had many good companions on my trips to Magdalena. Among these, Bernard Fontana, Lee Larson, Charles Polzer, S.J., John Schaefer, Frank Urquides, and Antonio Federico stand out in my memory. Gary Nabhan and anthropologists Bob Thomas and Tom Sheridan discussed their experiences at Chuwhiy Guwsk with me. Father Keiran McCarty, O.F.M., helped me with historical details. Artura Carrillo Strong enlightened me on the uses of certain printed prayers.

Charles Carrillo and Yvonne Lange of Santa Fe enlightened me on problems of iconography concerning both San Francisco and the Santo Niño de Atocha. Diane L. Stevens of the Taylor Museum at the Colorado Springs Fine Arts Center sent me a photograph of that institution's copy of the Currier and Ives print of San Francisco. Helena E. Wright of the Division of Graphic Arts of the National Museum of American History explained the dating of Currier and Ives prints. My *compadre* Peter Morse of Honolulu provided advice and assistance as well.

The late Ted Rios of San Xavier Village accompanied me on many visits to churches and chapels on the Papago Reservation. He taught me much, limited only by my imperfect ability to learn. Daniel Matson generously shared his memories of the desert missions in the 1940s and took a memorable trip to Gunsight village with me. The late Fathers Lambert Fremdling, O.F.M., Regis Rohder, O.F.M., and Theodore Williges, O.F.M., took time from their vital work in the early 1970s to tell me of the churches they had built twenty years before. Bernard Fontana served as director of that long ago dissertation and has been friend, neighbor, and field companion ever since.

Lalo Guerrero and a host of others have told me stories of el Tiradito. Randall Legler remembered for me how the shrine looked in the 1920s, and Jim Elliott introduced me to some early written descriptions. Pete Castillo, Ramon Machado, Richard Morales, and Antonio Federico are among those who have shared their knowledge of ghosts and el Tejano with me. Margaret Redondo shared her family traditions of the seige of Caborca.

Acknowledgments

I have had many companions on my trips of investigation into the baroque art and architecture of Sonora. The late Tom Naylor, Bernard Fontana, Leah and Oscar Ward, Ed and Mary Catherine Ronstadt, Father Charles Polzer, S.J., Mardith Schuetz-Miller, and many other companions of the Southwest Missions Research Center's Kino Mission Tours have contributed much. Robert Quinn of the University of Arizona Art Department introduced me to the glories of the baroque styles of New Spain, and Arquitecto Jorge Olvera of Mexico City took me ever farther toward an understanding of those vital styles.

The late Edward Spicer of the University of Arizona taught me much by word and action. His hand is on all my work in subtle ways.

Anyone who works in the folklore of Southern Arizona owes an incalculable debt to Frances Gillmor who founded the Arizona Folklore Archive and to Byrd Howell Granger who continued it through the 1960s and 1970s, and to many students and other collectors who have enriched that wonderful resource over the years. I especially wish to mention Doris Seibold of Patagonia, whose collected legends of Santa Cruz County provide a perfect starting place for any further study in the region. Acknowledgment must also be made of the many people of Arizona and Sonora who have taken time to help all these amateur and professional folklorists, for without them there would be neither archive nor book.

Donna Howell accompanied me on fieldtrips to Sonora, the Papaguería, and elsewhere in Arizona, and introduced me to the Rincon and Leon Ranch cemeteries. She edited the first versions of this manuscript and gave much good advice, some of which was heeded.

Bernard Fontana and the late Robert K. Thomas, both anthropologists at the University of Arizona, read the manuscript and offered valuable suggestions. My wife Loma and my children Kelly and David shared much of the fieldwork and its attendant inconveniences for more than twenty years. Each has taken an active interest in the work and contributed to it. John Shaefer generously allowed me to use his photographs.

All these people and others whom I have not named contributed much that is of value within these pages; any errors of fact and interpretation are my own.

ix

Finally, I wish to dedicate this book to the people of the Pimería Alta—O'odham, Yaqui, Mexicano, and Anglo—whose lives and beliefs are reflected, I hope accurately and respectfully, in its pages. By keeping faith with their various heritages they have enriched my life incalculably.

Jim Griffith

Introduction: Many Journeys

This book is about a region, some of the peoples who live in that region, and traditional relationships that tie people to places within that region. The region is the Pimería Alta, or central Arizona–Sonora Borderlands. The peoples in question—Tohono O'odham, Yaquis, and Mexicans—were once part of the Spanish Empire. Each of their cultures has been molded to some degree by that historical fact. They express their relationships with the land in many ways—through belief, legend, custom, and even art and architecture. Although the story reaches far back into the past, this is not a history book. It deals with living cultural traditions that exist alongside the mainstream American culture with which most of us are most familiar. Although these traditions continue to exist with relatively little attention from the cultural mainstream, they affect the lives of thousands of people.

As I write this, it is fall on the Sonoran Desert. The summer heat and rains are over, and it is once more comfortable to be out-of-doors all day long. September and October on the desert are much like April and May elsewhere—they are months of increased outdoor activity, including traveling. For many Mexicans and Indians in the area, this renewed mobility takes the form of a pilgrimage to the old mission community of Magdalena de Kino, Sonora, some sixty miles south of the Mexico–United States border. Thousands of

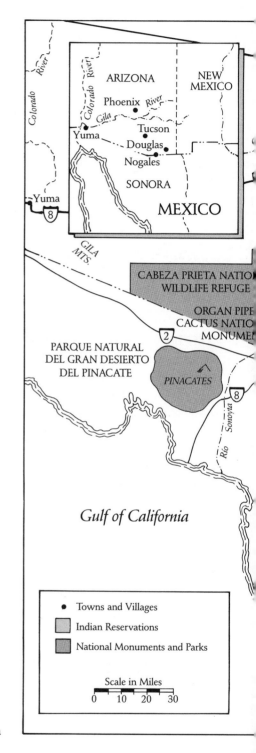

Legend

- ● Towns and Villages
- Indian Reservations
- National Monuments and Parks

Scale in Miles
0 10 20 30

Map of the Pimaría Alta

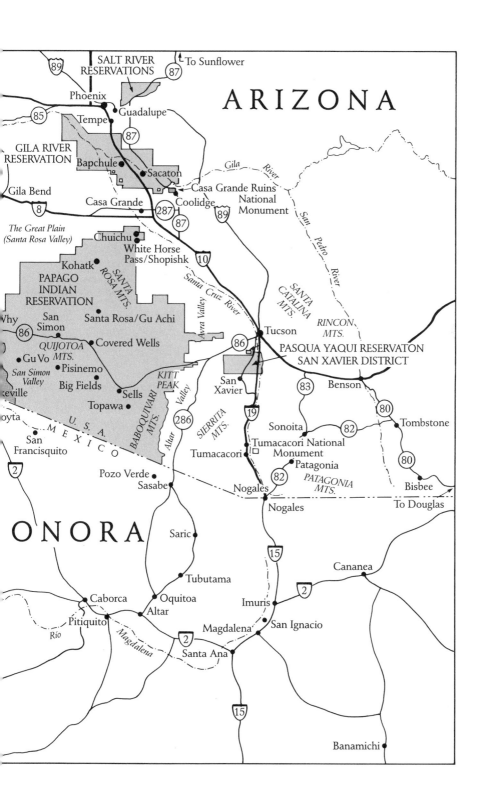

people from all over Arizona and Sonora travel there for the great fiesta de San Francisco, which takes place each year on October 4.

On their journey, pilgrims to Magdalena are constantly surrounded by reminders of those who have come this way before them. Roadside crosses mark sites where travelers met sudden death; small shrines and chapels commemorate favors asked of God and the saints. In Magdalena itself, visitors to the church pass the exposed grave of Father Eusebio Francisco Kino, the Jesuit missionary who brought the Catholic religion and European culture to this whole region. The statue of Saint Francis Xavier, which is the visible focus of the pilgrimage, is believed by some to have been brought to Magdalena by Kino before his death in 1711. The legends told about saint and statue call to mind the three-hundred-year history of Europeans in this region. For Mexican pilgrims, the trip can be a kind of reaffirmation of their traditional culture—an imported culture which has put down strong roots in its new desert home.

For a Tohono O'odham family on its way to Magdalena the experience would call to mind different stories, a different history. Such a family might start out from a village on their reservation west of Tucson. On their way, they would travel through a country familiar through dozens of ancient stories. They would surely catch a glimpse of Baboquivari Mountain, center of the O'odham universe and dwelling place of I'itoi, the Creator and Elder Brother of the Tohono O'odham. Depending on their point of origin, they might pass near the place where the Flood Children were sacrificed generations ago to avert a flood, or even Quito Wa:k, where I'itoi killed a monster that had been sucking whole villages into its maw. Returning from their pilgrimage with religious pictures and statues purchased in Magdalena, they would probably install these sacred objects in a small chapel, which appears to be a Catholic structure but which is actually the result of a complex blending of native and Christian beliefs and practices.

Yaqui Indians also go to Magdalena. They go from Tucson and other Arizona towns, from their ancestral villages on Sonora's Río Yaqui, and from Hermosillo and other Sonoran cities where they have settled over the years. They, too, have their own traditional concepts of who San Francisco is and how he should be honored.

Some may bring musical instruments and dance regalia, and perform the deer and pascola dances for their saint—dances that blend Yaqui and European heritages and reflect a strong traditional relationship between people and the creatures of the desert.

What of the folks called Anglo Americans, the people, like me, who represent the mainstream culture north of the border? A few of us do indeed go to Magdalena, hear and retell the legends and stories connected with San Francisco, Baboquivari, and I'itoi, and understand something concerning the Yaquis and their dances, but in my experience there is a difference. For most of us, the beliefs, customs, rituals, and relationships that are the subject of this book are alien, things that we may learn about, and even come to value highly, but to which we come as outsiders. I certainly am such an outsider, and perhaps the story of how I came to an understanding of this region and its traditions is an appropriate way to begin.

I have been living in and near Tucson, Arizona, for more than thirty years. One of the things I did, as I slowly came to know the region and its people, was to redefine again and again just where it was that I lived. At first, I was in *the Southwest*, a region defined through its relationship to the rest of the United States. Then, as I came to know the area better, I lived in *Arizona*, one of the fifty states. But Arizona is a state of many regions in its own right, so perhaps I lived in *Pima County,* or even *Tucson*. Those places weren't large enough, however. They are defined politically, and the region I was beginning to learn about sprawled across several political boundaries. I was even beginning to discover that the area immediately south of the International Border had a lot of natural and cultural history in common with my home. Perhaps I lived in a binational area, defined some way other than politically.

For a while, therefore, *the Sonoran Desert* seemed to be the proper term. It covers much of southern Arizona and northern Sonora, and has a distinctive topography, fauna, and flora. However, the phrase describes the region in terms of natural history, and I was and am primarily interested in people, their history, and the ways in which their contemporary cultures reflect that history. "The Arizona-Sonora Borderlands" as a definition filled the bill fairly well, but it didn't give any sense of the region's culture and history. So I finally borrowed an expression from the early Spanish chronicles and decided that I lived in the *Pimería Alta*.

The Pimería Alta, or Upper Pima Country, is the region in which Father Eusebio Francisco Kino labored from 1687 until his death in 1711. In present-day terms, it stretches from the Gila River on the north to Mexican International Highway 2 on the south, and from the valleys of the San Pedro and Magdalena rivers on the east to a bit west of Ajo. For Father Kino it was a cultural description: it demarked the area occupied by the northernmost grouping of people who called themselves *O'odham,* and spoke mutually intelligible languages of the group that contemporary linguists call "Piman." This "Upper Pima Country" or "The Land of the Northern Piman Speakers" is still a meaningful cultural region in the 1990s. Its inhabitants still seem to share a common history and to some extent a common traditional culture. This is despite the fact that the O'odham have been compressed into a small part of their former land, which is now divided between two nations that didn't even exist in Father Kino's lifetime.

The Pimería Alta is a varied land. From the eastern oak and grass country westward through the range of mesquites and saguaros to the sparse bushes of the Colorado River, the country slopes downhill, getting hotter and drier as it does so. The slope is a gradual one, interrupted by mountain ranges running roughly from north to south. Separating these ranges are valleys. The ones to the east—the Magdalena, the San Pedro, the Santa Cruz—contained flowing rivers in Kino's day. A century of pumping in the Santa Cruz Valley has lowered the water table so that the river no longer flows past Tucson in 1990 as it once did. West of the Santa Cruz, the rivers are only potential watercourses. Dry for most of the year, they fill with roaring torrents of muddy water after heavy summer rains.

The river valleys are the traditional highways of the eastern Pimería Alta and the sites of settled communities as well. In the dry country to the west, human occupation was dependent on other kinds of permanent water sources: dripping springs in the mountains, or basins in the rock where the precious fluid was caught and preserved from one rainfall to the next. There were O'odham even in the barren, volcanic Pinacate region to the west of the present-day border town of Sonoyta, Sonora. They lived in small communities and were prepared to move over wide areas in search of food and water. These were people we now call the Sand Papagos. Their descendants still live among the Tohono O'odham, although their traditional way of life has been largely a thing of the past for almost a hundred years.

The present-day Pimería Alta has changed greatly over the past century. Railroads, paved highways, and airports link it with the rest of the world. An imported, high-technology civilization supports huge populations on electrically pumped underground water. Population centers have grown immensely, while many of the truly marginal areas, such as the country of the Sand Papagos, no longer support human occupation. But the human past of the region can still be traced: in historical records, in still-occupied settlements that were here three centuries ago, and in the traditions that still persist within the living cultures of the Pimería.

The people with whom this book is most concerned belong to three general cultural groupings. First, there are the original occupants of the Pimería Alta—the Tohono O'odham, formerly called the Papago Indians. Although most have by now moved to the north of the International Border, a few still reside in the Sonoran portion of their traditional homeland. Beginning in the seventeenth century, increasing numbers of Spaniards and, later on, Mexicans came to live here and call this region theirs. The presence of their descendants, and of other, more recently arrived bearers of Mexican culture does much to give this region its character. Finally, large numbers of Yaqui Indians arrived in southern Arizona as political refugees during the late nineteenth century. They brought with them their own cultural blend of native and European ideas and ways of doing things, and have made an indelible cultural mark on their new home.

There is another important set of nineteenth-century arrivals: the people called "Anglos" in regional English. Their culture differs in one basic way from those with which this book is concerned. Its roots are in northeastern North America and northern Europe. This breaks a centuries-old pattern of cultural diffusion into our region from Mexico. The cultural patterns with which this book is concerned, be they aboriginal or transplanted from southern Europe by way of Mexico, all have strong ties to the south. Anglo-American culture, regionally important though it now is, stands outside this set of relationships, and therefore outside the scope of this book.

As I began to learn my way around the Pimería Alta, most of my first reactions to what I saw were immediate and aesthetic. I was overwhelmed by the noise and activity of the annual fiesta of San Francisco in Magdalena, Sonora, for instance, and intrigued by the many still-standing mission churches of the region, from San Xavier del Bac to La Purísima Concepción in Caborca, Sonora. I was captivated by the beauty and understated intensity of the Yaqui Easter ceremonies. Later on, I visited the twentieth-century missions and folk-Catholic chapels of the Papago Reservation and set out to learn why those buildings looked the way they did. Yaqui and O'odham music and dance, grave markers, house shrines, and roadside crosses all engaged my attention. In each of these cases, my first reaction was an emotional and aesthetic response to what I saw and heard; later I learned something of the rich backgrounds of belief, tradition, and history that lay just beneath the surface. This book is an end product of those several journeys of learning, reaction, and explanation—journeys into the region's traditional Indian and Mexican cultures, and the ways in which those cultures relate to specific places. A rich network of supernaturally sanctioned relationships exists between people and places in the Pimería Alta. Many older rural Mexicans and Mexican Americans believe that our springs are watched over by what appears to be a descendant of the old Middle American Plumed Serpent. I'itoi, the Creator and Elder Brother of the Tohono O'odham, is thought by some O'odham to live today in his cave on Baboquivari Mountain, just as he has done for centuries. Places where he intervened in the problems of the Desert People can still be seen, and their stories persist in the minds of the People whom he created.

A composite San Francisco, owing parts of his nature to Saint Francis Xavier, Saint Francis of Assisi, and Father Kino, is prayed to in Magdalena, Sonora, by many Mexicans and Mexican Americans, O'odham, and Yaquis. He responds to their needs in his own way. Tohono O'odham and Yaqui Indians build chapels and carry on native Christian ceremonies that owe as much to America as they do to Europe. The dead are remembered, and their presence is still felt by some in the places where they lived, died, and are buried. Shrines and places of petition flourish. Finally, many of these places are visually united by a particular art style, the baroque.

All these beliefs, customs, legends, and art forms have their roots deep in the past. Some of those roots seem to reach back to a time when one of the main cultural influences on our region was the trader-priests from the high cultures of pre-Hispanic central Mexico; others lie in the Catholic missionary efforts of seventeenth- and eighteenth-century New Spain. Taken together, these relationships and their stories tie past and present together with a complex web of belief, legend, and art.

A few terms need to be explained before we start on our journey. I shall use "the Pimería Alta" and "Central Arizona-Sonora Borderlands" interchangeably to refer to the region under discussion. The natives of this region, called "Pimas" by the Spaniards, have long called themselves "O'odham"—The People—in their own language. Those O'odham who live in the desert lands to the west of Tucson were for years called the Papago Indians. Recently, the tribe took as its official name a term in its own language—Tohono O'odham, or "The Desert People." I shall tend to use "Papago" when talking about the past, and "Tohono O'odham" when discussing the present.

The portion of the traditional lands of the Tohono O'odham that has been set aside for their use by the United States government is the Papago Indian Reservation; the political entity that occupies the reservation is the Tohono O'odham Nation, but I will also speak of the Tohono O'odham Nation as synonymous with the Papago Indian Reservation. In other words, it is a physical place as well as a political entity. The Papago Indian Reservation occupies 2.5 million acres of desert between Tucson and Ajo. It is part of a much larger area, historically called the Papaguería, or "Land of the Papagos." The reservation occupies the space from the ridge of the Baboquivari Mountains west to the Ajo Mountains and from the International Border to just south of Interstate 10. There are also detached districts of the Tohono O'odham Nation at Gila Bend and San Xavier, and a small parcel of land—Tohono O'odham Tract—at Florence.

Scattered over the valleys and mountains of this desert country are some seventy villages and one town, Sells, which is the capital of the Tohono O'odham Nation.

The reservation is only a part of the traditional lands of the Tohono O'odham, which extended west past the Ajo Mountains and south into Sonora. For this larger area I shall use the traditional Spanish word, *Papaguería.*

The Spanish language is spoken by Mexicans in Sonora and by Mexican Americans in Arizona. I shall use each term where it is appropriate, and also *Mexicanos* where I wish to refer to participants in the regional culture on both sides of the border. This is a term of self-reference preferred by many traditional Mexican Americans now in the fifties or older. "Chicano" as a term for Mexican Americans has come into widespread use within the past twenty years. Many of the people who prefer to refer to themselves as Chicanos are comparatively young urban dwellers who are often politically active. I shall use "Chicano" when referring to members of this group.

I know of no really good term for the people who, like myself, represent the mainstream of American national culture. The conventional word is "Anglos," but that brings with it a certain degree of confusion. If "Anglos" stands for "Anglo-Americans," where does that leave descendants of immigrants from western Europe, Africa, and Asia? The common word in local Spanish is "Americanos"; but many find that term, with its apparent claim of exclusive Americanism, offensive. The Spanish word *estadounidenses*—"United Statesers"—is unfamiliar and unwieldy. For the purposes of this book, I shall use the traditional "Americanos" as well as the conventional "Anglos," while acknowledging the drawbacks of each.

This book is written primarily for the people who, like me, find themselves living in this part of the world and are curious about some of its traditions. It gets complicated at times for a perfectly simple reason: human culture is often very complex indeed. It moves from legend to art form to belief to practice for the same reason: this is the real world I am trying to describe, and real life is not easily compartmentalized.

Finally, although I constantly refer to the past in these pages, the subject matter of this book is definitely a thing of the present. Like any other part of living culture, these beliefs and practices are dynamic links between past and future. They are stable rather than static; their general outlines have persisted for a long time, while their details keep changing to reflect changes in the world of the peoples whose cultural property they are. There is no way of knowing what the future holds; for the present, the legends, customs, and beliefs discussed in the ensuing pages are a very real part of the cultural environment of the Pimería Alta and give this region much of its distinctive character.

Beliefs and Holy Places

1. Meeting la Corúa

July 7, 1983, was a warm day in Northern Sonora. I was with my friend Richard Morales, visiting craftspeople whose work we had previously encountered at the important regional pilgrimage town of Magdalena de Kino, some sixty miles south of the Arizona-Sonora border, along Mexico's International Highway 15. Magdalena's annual Fiesta de San Francisco provides an occasion for the manufacture and sale of painted glass frames intended for holy pictures and family portraits. We were gathering information on these frames and the people who make and use them, in preparation for an exhibition to be held later that year in Nogales, Arizona.[1]

We were on the outskirts of the eighteenth-century mission town of Imuris at the house of Olga Ruiz, a woman whom we knew from several visits to the fiesta. At fiesta time, Olga usually sets up a stand at the northwest corner of Magdalena's Plaza Monumental. There she sells medicinal and other herbs as well as the painted frames which were the object of our interest that afternoon. We had done our interview, taken several photographs while she painted one of the frames, and purchased a couple of frames from her. Now we were sitting in front of her house, drinking coffee and visiting.

The summer rains had already started, and the concrete ford and the footbridge that cross the Río Magdalena just west of Imuris had washed out. The river was passable for our pickup, however, and we drove to Olga's house on the low ground across the river from the colonial town. Olga belongs to a social class locally called *pajareros* ("bird catchers"). Pajareros typically make their living in a number of ways: trapping and selling wild birds, for instance, and making bird cages to hold them; gathering and selling wild foods and medicines; picking whatever commercial crops might be in season; and catering to the needs of religious pilgrims to Magdalena by making frames and other objects of glass. On this day, Olga and her husband were preparing to go off into the mountains for a few weeks to harvest *bellotas,* the edible wild acorns (*Quercus emoryi*) that are an important seasonal snack food for many dwellers of the Sonoran Desert. In fact, their stake-bed truck was loaded and waiting by the house when we arrived. We were discussing the impending trip and congratulating ourselves that we had shown up before they departed.

Olga mentioned that they would be camped by a certain spring. There was another spring nearby where they had formerly camped, she told us, but someone had killed the *corúa* that lived there, and the spring had dried up. Richard and I looked at each other, then asked her to repeat what she had said. The spring dried up when someone killed its corúa, we were told. When we asked the next question—what is a corúa—she replied that a corúa is a big snake that lives in springs of water and protects them. If the corúa is killed, the spring disappears.

Richard and I discussed *la corúa* on the drive back to Tucson later in the day. Richard, who was born and brought up in the farming community of Marana, north of Tucson, thought he remembered the word being used for a kind of irrigation pipe that leads the waters over a wash or an arroyo. He decided to ask some of the old-timers he knew about *la corúa*, particularly his father-in-law, Pete Castillo, a countryman born in Caborca, Sonora, in the early years of this century.

Richard called a few days later with his news. The corúa, according to Pete, is the snake—the BIG snake—that lives in springs and protects them. It is harmless and has a round mouth without teeth. It also has a cross between its eyes, on its forehead. If you kill it, the spring it lives in will dry up. As Richard put it to me, "If you kill the corúa, you lose your water rights." Another member by marriage of the same family, Frank Urquides, remembered that when he was little he had been warned not to play after dark or in irrigation ditches, lest the corúa "get him."

For my part, I had been looking up snake and water terms in Horacio Sobarzo's *Vocabulario Sonorense*. I found that "corúa" was a regional word for boa constrictor and that it derives from a Yaqui Indian word meaning large, thick snake. I also found that the root of the word, *co*, seems to mean "snake" in many languages of the Uto-Aztecan family to which Yaqui belongs, and that the same root appears in the Aztec word *quetzalcoatl*, the name of the great feathered serpent deity who was involved with the winds and with water. One of the still standing towns on the Río Sonora, Sobarzo writes, is Bacoachi; in the Opata language, this is said by Sobarzo to mean "the place of the water serpent." There is a tradition that on this site there was a sanctuary dedicated to an enormous water snake.[2]

Still browsing through Sobarzo's *Vocabulario*, I found another word, *alicante*. This word has two meanings locally. It is an above-ground irrigation channel, built of stone and mortar. It is also the local name for a small racer snake. The word is also used in Spain, where, by contrast, it refers to vipers.[3]

As Richard and I pursued this topic, we discovered that most of the older people to whom we talked knew about the corúa. Some, like the mother of one friend, didn't recognize the name but knew all about a large snake that protects water sources. She told her daughter that an aunt had seen the one that lived in the Tanque Verde to the northeast of Tucson. Subsequently, the snake had been killed and the spring had dried up.

Another friend, Leo Armando Salazar, originally from Tres Alamos, north of Benson in the San Pedro Valley, remembered hearing his uncles telling him about la corúa. There were two corúas, he thought, a male and a female. The female had long hair reaching down its back. The male, which lived in Kuyper Springs, had two long fangs or tusks that it used to clean the veins of water. One occasionally would see a corúa sunning itself on the rocks. It is harmless; however, Salazar seemed to feel that it was best not to see or be seen by one. He told a story about some vaqueros who saw a corúa remove its fangs and swim around in the water of a pond behind an earthen dam. One of the vaqueros hid the fangs, and when the corúa couldn't find them, it killed itself. Shortly after the incident, the dam was washed away in a heavy rainstorm.

Another association between snakes and water came to light when Richard Morales visited his uncle Samuel Morales in San Luis del Río Colorado, Sonora, across the border from Yuma. It was just after the heavy floods of October 1983; in a discussion of this event, Sr. Morales remarked that they had received *una media culebra* ("a half serpent") of water. When Richard asked him how much water a whole serpent would be, he answered that he had never seen that much but that this storm was definitely una media culebra. Back in Marana, Richard's father-in-law Pete Castillo agreed with this estimate; the storm certainly brought a media culebra of water with it.

Culebra or *culebra de agua* is also a local term for a severe wind and rain storm involving a funnel cloud. Rain from a culebra de agua is said to fall in sheets, rather than drops. A ceremony of prayer formerly used to avert one of these is called *matando la culebra* ("killing the serpent"). This ceremony involved special prayers that were recited by an elderly, respected, local woman. Upon being asked to perform the ritual, she would do so, standing outside her house and facing the storm. In some versions of the ceremony, she would hold a knife in her hand. At the end of the ceremony, she would make the sign of the cross and go back indoors.[4]

A legend concerning a culebra de agua is still told in the old mission community of Oquitoa, Sonora, located in the Altar Valley some fifty miles south of the International Border. The story concerns the Franciscan missionary Joaquín Olizarra, who served Oquitoa in the first decade of the nineteenth century, and who is remembered as a man of great faith and piety. One day Oquitoa was threatened by a culebra de agua, described as a serpent-shaped cloud with the potential of destroying the entire village. Father Olizarra walked out of doors, and, facing the cloud, made the sign of the cross. The culebra dispersed and the village was saved.[5]

6

Finally, a long wisp of highly localized rain of the sort that one can often see in the summertime across the valley is often called *una cola de culebra* "a snake's tail." This term is also used in other parts of Spanish America.

Near the village of Cucurpe in Sonora's San Miguel Valley, anthropologist Thomas Sheridan collected data concerning la corúa, which according to his informants is a sort of boa constrictor. It is very long and thick and can attract its prey to itself through some mysterious means, said by some to involve its sweat or its breath. However, it does not bite and can even be stroked. If you kill one at a water hole, the water will dry up.[6] Although the Cucurpe area is now occupied by mestizos, it was originally an Opata Indian village and the site of a Jesuit mission to that people. Cucurpe is located about twenty miles east of Magdalena, just outside the Pimería Alta.

The O'odham still live within the boundaries of their land, the Pimería Alta. They, too, know of large, water-dwelling serpents. Old-time Tohono O'odham believed in the existence of a big snake called *nehbig*. It lived in springs and was so powerful that it attracted lightning to itself. It was considered a thing to be respected.[7] "Nehbig" is also the name of a monster that destroyed people and villages near the Sonoran O'odham village of Quito Wa:k by sucking or inhaling them into its mouth. It was finally dispatched by I'itoi, Elder Brother and Creator of the Tohono O'odham. In one version of the nehbig legend, the animal's death throes caused the water to splash out of the pond in which it lived.

The Tepecano of Azqueltan, Jalisco, are the southernmost branch of O'odham speakers. They formerly told of large, serpentlike creatures called *chanes*. Chanes lived in streams and ponds, and were invisible, "except in rainy weather, when they appeared as great arcs or bows in the sky, striped with colors, head in one spring and tail in the other, as they visited. But ordinarily they were invisible, though their forms were well-known. They had the bodies of serpents with horns like cattle. They were to be treated reverently, as they had the power of sickening all those who disregarded them."[8]

Finally, again from slightly outside our area, there is a Yaqui belief concerning a big snake with a cross on its forehead that lives in a large water hole under a hill in the valley of Sonora's Río Yaqui, some 300 miles south of the Arizona-Sonora border. This monster, which can suck animals and humans into its mouth with its breath, was once a Yaqui *maestro* or Catholic prayer leader named Acencio. As a result of wicked deeds committed while he was alive, Acencio was transformed after death into a monstrous serpent. Using prayers, the people chased him into the cave he has occupied ever since.[9]

While all these legends and beliefs link serpents with water in one way or another, the material concerning the nehbig, the Cucurpe corúa, and the monster who was once Acencio add something extra: the belief that these creatures attract their prey by suckling or breathing in. Legends concerning a Sucking or Swallowing Monster that was killed by a local hero are found among many North American tribes; the specifically O'odham version of this widespread legend will be discussed in chapter 2.

Snake stories may be found in our regional literature as well. In his book *Texas Cowboys*, describing his experiences in eastern Arizona early in this century, Dane Coolidge tells of hearing a story from an old Mexican farmer about a "big black snake down in Sonora that had a golden cross on its head. It lived in a cave on the mountain and the people offered it milk and young chickens and worshiped it like a god."[10] No water here, but the size of the snake and the cross on its head are strongly reminiscent of both the corúa beliefs and the Yaqui legend of Acencio, the evil maestro. In fact, Coolidge's yarn may well be a version of the latter legend. European-descended Southwesterners have for a long time been telling stories about Indians who worship a huge snake in a cave. A literary use of this theme occurs in Willa Cather's *Death Comes for the Archbishop*.[11]

Closer to home is a published account of Joe Clark and Jesús Castro, early pioneers near Oracle, Arizona, who killed a huge rattlesnake near a spring in Peppersauce Canyon, some forty miles northwest of Tucson. They are said to have delayed killing it for a while, as they were concerned that some Indians might have worshiped it as the guardian of the spring.[12] The question occurs of where they might have gotten the idea that local Indians would do such a thing.

A Very Old Snake Indeed

There certainly seems to be a belief among some local Indians and Mexicans in certain connections between snakes and water. One of these involves some sort of large serpent with supernatural powers that guards springs of water. The animal seems to be harmless; I suspect that Frank Urquides' family simply used the threat of the corúa to keep him from harm in response to a traditional Mexican pattern of scaring one's kids into safety, rather than out of any belief in the actual malevolence of the reptile. In much the same way, other friends have been told by their parents that the pictures of sphinxlike animals that decorate old-style sewing machines were creatures which would carry off children who pestered their mothers too much.

Other connections between snakes and water are concentrated in two areas: irrigation and severe rainstorms with a strong potential for flooding. Faced with this complex and multifaceted set of snake-water associations, one is tempted to search in neighboring regions for similar beliefs. In this case, one needs only to look as far as Mesoamerica and the deity Quetzalcoatl, or the Plumed Serpent.

As is so often the case when one deals with alien religious systems, there is a real danger of oversimplifying the Aztec cosmography. Quetzalcoatl was much more than a plumed serpent connected with water. While his name can mean "plumed serpent," it can also mean "heavenly twin." He was god of the winds, god of the morning, god of twins and monsters, and the planet Venus, among other aspects and manifestations. Aztec religion was the sophisticated end product of centuries of philosophical speculation among the religious specialists of central Mexico's high cultures and is extremely difficult for a person steeped in European traditions to grasp fully. The fact remains, however, that one of Quetzalcoatl's aspects was that of a large, plumed serpent, and that this particular deity was involved with water.[13] (Another god connected with water was Tlaloc; he is often portrayed with large, round eyes and long fangs. It is tempting to see traces of Tlaloc in the stories of the corúa in Kuyper Springs who cleans the veins of water with its fangs.)

How did this belief in a water serpent, which seems to be related

9

to the religion and cosmography of the high cultures of Central Mexico, come into this desert region so far to the north of its area of origin? One answer is suggested by the late archaeologist Charles Di Peso in his report on excavations at the huge archaeological site of Paquimé, near Casas Grandes in the Mexican state of Chihuahua. Casas Grandes is located about 65 miles as the crow flies south of the U.S.-Mexican border, and about 40 miles east of the Sonora-Chihuahua line. For those not traveling by crow, it can be reached by Mexican Highway 2 from the border crossing at Douglas–Agua Prieta, a distance of about 135 miles.[14] Di Peso's contention, supported by a good deal of impressive evidence, is that the ruin he calls Paquimé was a sort of staging area for a deliberate attempt at trade and proselytization that were carried on by immigrants from Central Mexico's high cultures.

He feels this took place roughly between the years A.D. 1060 and 1340, and that many of the characteristics of what we think of as historic Southwestern Indian culture were in fact brought deliberately from Mexico. From the south, believed Di Peso, came such gods as Tezcatlipoca, Quetzalcoatl, and Huitzilopochtli, along with such practices as large-scale irrigation agriculture, the ceremonial ballgame, human sacrifice, and the ritual use of macaw feathers (as well as the actual macaws to provide the feathers). From the north came precious materials such as turquoise and iron pyrites, both important items of ceremonial use in ancient Mexico. These and other materials, according to Di Peso, were traded to the south, to the high cultures of the Valley of Mexico. The city of Paquimé flourished for almost three centuries as a religious and economic center, finally succumbing to decay, and in the mid-fourteenth century, to destruction by enemies.[15]

This is Di Peso's view, and he states it elegantly and persuasively in the first three volumes of his monumental site report. Many other archaeologists do not agree with his interpretations of the material, and most particularly with his early dating of the various phases of occupation at the huge site he excavated. But he is one of the few recent scholars to attempt an historical synthesis and explanation for the native cultures of what is now the southwestern United States and northwest Mexico.

10

According to Di Peso, the cult devoted to Quetzalcoatl is the most visible of the various Mesoamerican religions to arrive at Paquimé. Quetzalcoatl's image in his manifestation as the plumed serpent was painted on pottery, engraved on shell, and even piled out of dirt and stones to form a huge effigy mound at Casas Grandes itself. Serpent motifs appear on pottery, on shell jewelry, and in rock art in many parts of the prehistoric Southwest, as well as in and near Paquimé.[16]

The importance of this figure among Native Americans of the American Southwest is not confined to the past. Contemporary Pueblo Indians know about a great horned water serpent that lives in bodies of water. According to the Hopi, Water Serpent came from the Red Land of the South and is the patron of the Water Corn Clan who also derive from that land. Water Serpent can cause floods, earthquakes, and landslides. He figures in the ceremonial art of Hopi, where he is called *Palelekon*, and of Zuni, where his name is *Kolowi:zi*.[17] In the New Mexico pueblo of Santa Ana, the priest in charge of the irrigation ditch prays and makes offerings to Water Serpent.[18]

Di Peso's theories may well explain the knowledge concerning a water serpent among the native peoples along what is now the central portion of the Arizona-Sonora border. Another explanation is that these beliefs are a part of the general belief system associated with the Uto-Aztecan language family, and need no elaborate theories of trade and proselytization to explain their presence over the entire area occupied by Uto-Aztecan speakers. Either of these suggestions would go far to explain the presence of water-serpent lore among the native peoples of our region.

The individuals who have told me about la corúa and the culebra de agua, however, are not Indians but Mexicanos. How did the beliefs make the leap from one culture into another, unrelated tradition? There seem to be at least two possible answers. In the first place, many of my informants claim local Indian ancestry. It is perfectly possible that some knowledge of this creature came into local Mexican culture from native Sonoran and Arizona traditions. There is another possibility. Spaniards mated with Indian women in Central Mexico from the early sixteenth century on, and many families must have carried knowledge of some of the deities of traditional Mexican religion, not as a serious challenge to the Christian belief system, but, like the knowledge of la corúa in contemporary Arizona and Sonora, simply as additional bits of information in a complex mestizo world view. If these families came to the region that is now Sonora and Arizona, they would have brought their knowledge of the Water Serpent along with them. And so the corúa may have entered our region in the wake of the Spaniards. No matter how they may have gotten here, the traditional associations between snakes and water in the Pimería Alta serve as reminders that the cultural region we call the American Southwest has been for centuries not the Southwest at all, but rather the far Northwest.

Similar water serpents appear in contemporary folk belief in other parts of Mesoamerica. In Tlayacapan, Hidalgo, people tell of *acoatl* or Culebra de Agua (Water Serpent), a dangerous water spout which "hangs down from the heavens like a snake, lashing and blasting the earth with wind and rain."[19] In Tecospa, Mexico, the Aztec name of the leader of the rain spirits is *Yeyecoatl,* or "Wind Serpent." His Spanish name is Culebra de Agua.[20] Far to the south in Mitla, Oaxaca, Elsie Clews Parsons collected a belief reminiscent of the corúa of the Pimería Alta. A female serpent named Mother of the Water lived in the Lake of White Water. When the serpent was accidentally killed, the lake dried up.[21]

A central Mexican belief in an animal that seems to combine aspects of la corúa with aspects of the sucking monster legend referred to above is given in Fray Bernardino de Sahagún's monumental *General History of the Things of New Spain,* a compilation of information he collected from surviving Aztecs in the years just after the conquest of Mexico. Of the *acoatl* or *tlilcoatl,* Sahagún's informants said:

> It is a water-dweller; it lies in the mud: cylindrical, thick—a fathom in girth; long, very long, extremely long. It is large-headed, big-headed; bearded; black, very black; glistening; fiery-eyed; fork-tailed. In craggy waters, in water caverns [it makes] its dwelling-place. Its food is fish. It is one which attracts people with its breath; it drowns people. When the acoatl sees its victim, "It follows one, runs, slithers, goes

like the wind, flies, coils itself, hisses, blows; it strikes one, attracts one with its breath, drowns one; it swallows things; it swallows one whole; it coils itself." [22]

These few examples by no means exhaust the Water Serpent lore of twentieth-century Mexico. Rather, they serve as evidence that such lore, similar to that of the Pimería Alta, is widespread throughout contemporary Mesoamerica.

La corúa stands apart from European Christian cultural tradition in a curious and possibly revealing way. Christianity has its own potent serpent symbols, which are neither neutral nor benevolent. It is difficult to detect in the passive corúa, silently guarding its springs and dying when its fangs are hidden, any trace of the ancient Enemy of Mankind who played such a destructive role in the Garden of Eden. Whatever la corúa is, however it came to be embedded in our regional culture, it is a creature of the New World rather than an importation from the Old.

Although knowledge of la corúa is certainly a part of our regional cultural scene at the moment, it seems to be tenuous and confined to the oldest generations, especially in Arizona. I suspect that its time remaining with us will not be very long. For most people in the urbanized 1990s, water comes out of pipes rather than from springs, and stories of the big serpent that guards the water sources have become increasingly irrelevant for the younger generations. Ten or twenty years in Arizona, perhaps double that in Sonora, and the written word may well be the only place to go for traces of this particular link with our distant past.

2. A Mountain and a Shrine

Southwest of Tucson, in the middle of the rugged western wall of the Altar Valley, stands one of southern Arizona's great landmarks—a mountain named Baboquivari. Clearly visible for miles, Baboquivari occupies the middle of the mountain range of the same name. A sharp, high peak, it dominates the valleys to the east and west of it. In a very real sense, Baboquivari is at the center of the Tohono O'odham universe. It can be seen from virtually every part of the Papaguería: from nearly every Tohono O'odham village in the United States and Mexico. It is an exhilarating experience to be driving along near Casa Grande, in the far northwest corner of the Tohono O'odham Nation, and glimpse the familiar outlines of Baboquivari, some eighty miles to the southeast, jutting up between two nearer hills.

Its name is an English version of a Spanish attempt at rendering the original O'odham name, *waw kiwulk,* or Constricted Hill. This name was apparently given because from some angles the peak looks as though it had been squeezed in the middle; as one O'odham friend put it, "just the way you would squeeze a piece of wet clay." It has had other names as well: Father Kino's traveling companion Juan Mateo Manje likened it to a castle sitting on a rock but decided to name it "Noah's Ark."[1] For undocumented aliens making their weary way on foot towards the jobs of central Arizona it is *el*

14

Tambor, "the drum." But for most English-speaking Arizonans it is Baboquivari, or simply "Babo."

Such familiarity may be a bit misplaced. Baboquivari, at 7,730 feet above sea level and generously equipped with vertical faces, has been a favorite of mountaineers at least since Professor Robert Forbes of the University of Arizona made the first recorded ascent in 1898. (Years later he celebrated his eightieth birthday by climbing it again.)[2] At least one person has died scaling its steep sides. Even more importantly, Baboquivari deserves to be mentioned with respect because it is the home of I'itoi, Elder Brother and creator of the Tohono O'odham.

I'itoi was among the first three beings to be created, along with Buzzard and Coyote. It was I'itoi who then created people. After people had lived in this region for a long time, I'itoi got into a fight with a powerful personage named Siwani, who lived to the north of the desert, near where the Pimas or River People live nowadays. Siwani killed I'itoi one night, but at dawn he came back to life. Four nights in a row Siwani killed him, and the last time he stayed dead. The flesh rotted away from his bones, and the bones themselves were scattered. After many years had passed, however, I'itoi returned as a little old man, although he had been a young man when Siwani killed him. I'itoi gathered people to help him in his struggle against Siwani. He went to villages in the East, the North, the West, and the South, asking for help. Apparently whatever responses he received in these regions were insufficient, for he went on from the South to ask for help from the people who lived Below, in the underworld. These responded, and with their assistance he defeated Siwani. Afterwards, the various peoples who had helped I'itoi chose different parts of the new land they had conquered. Those who had been hunters chose the desert and became ancestors of today's Tohono O'odham.[3]

These and other accounts of the very distant past are not confined to the Tohono O'odham. The Akimel O'odham, or River People who still live along the Gila and Salt rivers to the north of Tucson know of I'itoi and tell many of the same stories concerning him . . . except that they call him Se'e'e. In the far western portions of the Papaguería he has another name: Montezuma. How the His-

15

Baboquivari Mountain from the West. I'itoi's cave is on
one of the spurs running down from the main peak. Photo by
John P. Schaefer.

panicized name of the last ruler of the Mexica or Aztecs came to be
bestowed upon the Elder Brother of the O'odham has never been
explained. Legends of a Montezuma who will return someday to
bring peace and prosperity to his Indian people are common over
much of the southwestern United States, and indeed many western
O'odham believed that their Montezuma would one day return.[4]

As the story goes among the Tohono O'odham, I'itoi went to
live in a cave on the west side of waw kiwulk, Baboquivari Mountain, sometime after his defeat of Siwani. There he stayed, and
there, according to some, he still lives. Only on those occasions

16

when his help has been desperately needed has he come out and mingled with the rest of creation.

One such occasion was when a monster called a *nehbig* came out from underground near the village of Quito Wa:k, in what is now Sonora, between the towns of Caborca and Sonoyta, far to the west of Baboquivari. One O'odham friend described the nehbig to me as being like a whale, except that it lay on the ground, inhaling strongly. It sucked things, people, even whole villages down its throat, simply by breathing in. Affairs reached crisis proportions, and the villagers decided to send for help to I'itoi. A messenger ran to I'itoi's home below Baboquivari and explained the problem. When I'itoi came out of his cave, he was a little old man, all bent over, with white hair. He agreed to help, and sent the runner back to prepare for his arrival.

Four days later I'itoi arrived at the village, this time in the guise of a strong, young man. The villagers, acting on his instructions, had gathered black rocks from a certain hill and had cut four long greasewood poles. The rocks may have been obsidian, for I'itoi made a large knife out of them. He took this knife and the four long poles and went to where the nehbig was. Like everything else within range of its breath, I'itoi was sucked down the nehbig's throat. As he went in, he propped the beast's mouth and throat open with the greasewood poles. Reaching the nehbig's heart, he cut it out with his knife and ran back out of the throat, pulling the poles out as he went. The nehbig disposed of, he went back to his home on Baboquivari.[5]

This is how the story has been told in the eastern portion of the Tohono O'odham Nation. A slightly different version was collected in the village of Quito Wa:k in the 1920s by anthropologist Edward H. Davis. This has the nehbig living in a huge lake of water that had been left over from a great flood. When Montezuma, as I'itoi is called locally, killed the nehbig, the monster "thrashed and threw his great body around until, in his dying agony, he had splashed all the water out of the pool, since which time there has been no water in that place."[6]

The villagers kept the nehbig's heart. It was in two portions, a male and female. These were put in special baskets and kept in caves. The male heart is believed to have been stolen some time around 1900, but the female portion is said to still exist.[7] If this is true, it is kept safe in a cave somewhere near Organ Pipe Cactus National Monument and cared for by the residents of a nearby village.

Some O'odham believe that other traces of the nehbig may be seen in the region near Quito Wa:k. Davis was told in 1920 that a calcarious crust on the surface of the dry lake bed where the nehbig had supposedly lived was in fact the creature's skin. And according to ethnobotanist Gary Nabhan, O'odham have explained a series of collapsed sinkholes all along the border from Sasabe west to near Sonoyta as places where the nehbig came up for air. There is a site near Quito Wa:k where the fossilized bones of large extinct mammals have been uncovered. These are believed by at least some O'odham in the area to be nehbig bones.[8] The stories about the nehbig have parallels among many of the native peoples of North America. Tales of a sucking monster who is killed by a hero who allows himself to be swallowed by the beast in order to kill it have been reported from Greenland to Alaska, and from the Arctic Circle to the Mexican border. Although the details may differ, the general pattern remains quite recognizable.[9] Among the Nez Perce in the state of Washington, for example, it is Coyote who was building a salmon ladder when he became aware of the Swallowing Monster. He went to where the huge animal lay and entered its mouth, meeting on his way down its throat many people and animals who were its previous victims. When he succeeded in cutting the monster's heart out, Coyote set loose all the living victims he found inside the beast, and then revived all those who had died. He finally distributed parts of the monster to different regions.[10]

Back in the Pimería Alta, other stories are told in which I'itoi left his cave in order to help the People in times of need. Over in the eastern portion of the Papaguería, a young woman was weaving a sleeping mat when a red kickball came into the clearing where she was sitting. She concealed the ball under her skirt, and when a young man came in, looking for his ball, she told him that she hadn't seen it. It was a special ball, however, which the sun had made out of red dust, and when she finally relented and tried to produce it from under her skirt, it was nowhere to be found. It had gone into her womb, and nine months later she gave birth to a baby girl with animal claws on her hands and feet. This child was called *Ho'ok*. [11]

As Ho'ok grew older and fiercer, people became scared that she would harm the other children, and they went to I'itoi's home on Baboquivari to ask him for help. I'itoi, who appeared as a tiny old man, spoke with Ho'ok. He showed her a mirage to the south of where she was, telling her it was her father, who was the sun. Ho'ok went to the south to look for her father. When she had traveled south all the way into Mexico, she saw the mirage again. This time it was behind her, far to the north. So she turned around and went north again until she came to a cave in the mountains. Here she lived, killing wild animals for food and dressing herself in their skins.

As time wore on, Ho'ok started visiting the nearby O'odham village of Pozo Verde and carrying off little children, which she would kill and eat. Once again the people went to I'itoi and asked for help. Knowing that Ho'ok enjoyed dancing, I'itoi invited her to a big ceremony and dance at a specially prepared ground near the village. He also brought special cigarettes which would make her sleepy. These he gave to Ho'ok to smoke during the course of the dance. For four days and nights the dance went on. Several times Ho'ok got sleepy and tried to go back to her cave, but each time the people hid in the bushes along her path and shook their dance rattles, knowing she was afraid of rattlesnakes. Each time she would go back and start dancing again. Finally, after four days and nights, Ho'ok fell into a deep sleep. I'itoi carried her to her cave, where the people had already prepared a great quantity of firewood. He put her inside the cave, lit a huge bonfire, and sealed the cave entrance. Ho'ok woke up screaming from the heat and pain, and hurled herself against the cave ceiling, splitting it with her head and making a great crack. At this I'itoi jumped on top of the rock above the cave and sealed the crack with his foot. Ho'ok died in the fire. Some of the smoke from the fire is said to have escaped through the crack in the roof of the cave and turned into a blue hawk, but how I'itoi dealt with that menace is another story. [12]

The village of Pozo Verde is in Sonora, just west of the border town of Sasabe. People there can still tell the story of Ho'ok and her cave—in fact, the version I have just told was adapted from one collected in Pozo Verde in the late 1970s. The smoke-blackened cave where she met her fiery death is still visible near the village, as is I'itoi's footprint on the rock above it. About a mile north of Pozo Verde is a large clearing surrounded by a rock wall, and here villagers believe the dance to have taken place. It is still used as a shrine.

When Father Kino and Juan Mateo Manje visited Pozo Verde in February of 1699, they were told the same story of Ho'ok and her fiery end, which Manje dutifully set down in his journal, with the note that he did not know whether it was a fable.[13] And the story has passed beyond the O'odham. In 1956, I heard a version from a Mexican *vaquero* in a bar in Sasabe, Arizona. The Ho'ok was not named, but simply referred to as a witch who ate children. I'itoi did not enter into the narrative either, and the protagonists were simply the witch on one side and the villagers on the other. In fact, I don't remember the narrator mentioning that this was an Indian story; it simply went with the place. He, too, told me that the cave where the witch died, *bien quemada*, or "well-burned," as he put it, was still visible.

The story of the Ho'ok is also known by the Tohono O'odham's cousins, the River People. They, too, tell how she wandered through the desert and finally found a place to live in a cave, and they place the cave in the south end of the Baboquivari range, near the village of Pozo Verde. There are places associated with her and her wanderings in Pima country, just as there are in the Papaguería.[14]

As was the case with the legends of the nehbig, the story of the Ho'ok is not unique to the O'odham. Tales of a witch or old woman who devours children have been collected from several tribes. The tale is not limited to this continent, however; the German story of Hansel and Gretl who went into the forest and who barely escaped being cooked and eaten by a witch should be familiar to most readers of this book. It is possible to speculate as to whether this similarity of stories is due to parallel cultural evolution or whether the child-devouring witches of North America are, in fact, reflections of European stories which have been learned and passed along by members of various Indian groups. Although I have no solid answer to the question, I personally incline to the former explanation.

The most recent occasion on which I'itoi is said to have come out of his cave to render aid was in the late nineteenth century, when a railroad was being constructed across Papago country. I'itoi led the wild animals away from the proposed route to a place of safety.[15] But for at least some O'odham, he is still there, in his cave.

The cave is certainly still there. Tohono O'odham and others visit from time to time and leave offerings. When naturalist Gary Nabhan went there around 1980, he found a jar of saguaro cactus syrup and a green frog effigy on the floor, and key chains, rosary beads, and shoelaces hanging from the ceiling. Other offerings included medallions, bullets, cigarettes, and chewing gum. I'itoi Ki, I'itoi's House, was hard to find and not easy to squeeze into, but it apparently was still an important place for many O'odham. For Nabhan, it was a cave on the edge of something large, deep, and unknown; a place where one could come in contact with some of the hidden things of this world and receive their blessing.[16]

I'itoi's presence in his cave became a more than academic consideration in January 1983, when then Secretary of the Interior James Watt removed 2,065 acres on the east slope of Baboquivari from further consideration as a federally protected wilderness area. This effectively opened the tract to mineral exploration, and potentially to mining activities. One article in the local press on the potential impact of this move mentioned both I'itoi's home and the peak's popularity among mountain climbers and hikers.[17] At its February 1983 meeting, the Papago Tribal Council passed a resolution demanding that the eastern portion of the mountain be made part of the Papago Reservation.[18]

Among the reasons given in the resolution for this move, the Council mentioned that "Papagos believe Baboquivari Mountain to be the home of the creator, I'itoi, and the center of mother earth." It was further noted that "Papagos believe that desecration of the site could lead to the destruction of the Papago people and the universe." Within a few weeks of this action, Tribal Council representative Harriet Toro had taken the resolution to Washington, D.C.

21

She reported that "congressional officials reacted favorably." However, she mentioned to a reporter for the tribal newspaper that some younger Papagos were "willing to go out and take weapons with them if it comes to the point of development."[19]

On April 15, 1983, Secretary Watt redesignated the entire tract as a wilderness study area. A representative of the Bureau of Land Management's Arizona office was described as saying that the decision was made "because of the land's importance to the Indians and because no mining companies have expressed interest in surveying the area." Secretary Watt resigned from office over a totally unrelated matter on October 9, 1983. I am not aware that the issue of mineral exploration for Baboquivari has arisen since.[20]

This is not I'itoi's only traditional home; there is a natural lava tube in the Pinacate Mountains to the south and west of Sonoyta, Sonora, where he is believed to have dwelt. The Norwegian explorer Carl Lumholtz visited the site in January 1910, in the company of an elderly Papago medicine man. The party left offerings for I'itoi: an arrow, a prayer stick with a small eagle feather attached to it, a bunch of yucca fiber, blue glass beads from a necklace, and some cigarettes "for the god's personal use." Each offering had its purpose: the yucca fiber, for instance, was to request favorable winds for the expedition.[21] As recently as the 1950s, offerings were left there. But according to astronomer William Hartmann in his book *Desert Heart,* by the 1970s there were no offerings to be found at the site. One of the reasons for this falling into disuse is not hard to come by: few O'odham now go west of Sonoyta. The people whose country that once was, the Hia Ced O'odham or Sand Papagos, have moved north and east to the United States, to the villages and towns in and around the Papago Reservation.[22]

The Children's Shrine

The Children's Shrine is another sacred place in the Tohono O'odham Nation. One version of its story says that many years ago, in that portion of the past which is only accessible through remembered legends, a farmer whose fields were near the village of Gu

The Children's Shrine, looking west. Photo by James S. Griffith,
March 1970.

Achi (now called Santa Rosa on the maps) noticed that an animal
was eating his melons and beans before they could be harvested.
This went on for some time, and the farmer identified the thief's
tracks as those of a badger. One morning the farmer saw the badger
and chased it into the dry riverbed, where it began digging a hole.
Even though it is forbidden even to touch a badger, the angry farmer
dug after this one, intending to kill it.

Suddenly water (in some versions of the story, a great wind,
followed by water) came gushing forth from the hole. The farmer
became frightened by the volume of the water and the roaring noise
it made and ran to the village for help. The villagers were scared as

23

well and consulted their local medicine men, who said that if something were not done to stop the water, the whole country would be flooded and everyone would be drowned. Four medicine men tried to find a solution to the problem. The first put a small sea bird into the hole, and the water receded a little. The next placed a larger bird, a crane, into the water, and the third man a sea turtle. Each time, the water receded slightly, but still kept coming out of the hole. The fourth medicine man told the villagers that in order to stop the water, they must sacrifice four children, two boys and two girls. All Tohono O'odham belong to one of two huge kinship groupings: the Buzzard People and the Coyote People. One boy and one girl were to be chosen from each of these groups. The villagers grieved and protested, but the medicine man remained firm in his statement that the sacrifice of the four children, the "best and handsomest in the village," was the only path by which disaster could be avoided.

The villagers finally agreed, and the four children were chosen. The grandmother of one of the boys who had been chosen hid her grandson in a rolled-up sleeping mat. Another boy was chosen to take his place. The four children were taken to the place where the water gushed out. They were dressed in special clothing, and their faces were painted. All the time, the village elders were chanting to them, telling them what they had to do in order to save the people. They were slowly lowered down the hole, and the waters subsided as they went down. When the water and the children had completely disappeared, the villagers placed a flat rock over the hole and other stones on top of it. They placed two ocotillo stalks at each of the four directions. Farther back from these the site was surrounded by a circle of peeled ocotillo stalks, with an opening in each of the four directions. When the villagers went back to the village, the woman who had hidden her grandson unrolled the sleeping mat where he had lain. All she found was some green scum of the sort that is left when standing water recedes. This version of the legend was collected in the early 1960s in Quijotoa Village. Other versions exist. Only recently I heard from an O'odham man who lives near Santa Rosa that because the people quarreled among themselves, I'itoi became angry and stamped his foot on the ground, causing the earth to crack. Out of this crack came the flood waters. Still another version seems to have circulated primarily among Anglo Americans in the early 1940s. In this variation, three children were sacrificed to avert a drought. I suspect that this radical departure from the norm, as I understand it, is an Anglo reworking of the O'odham original. After all, droughts seem more understandable in a desert than floods, and three is as significant a number for Europeans as four is for Native Americans.[23]

Over the centuries, the shrine has been cared for and regularly renewed by the Santa Rosa villagers. New ocotillo stalks are set around the central rock pile and the old stalks placed on two huge piles to the north and south of the shrine itself. These neat piles of disintegrating ocotillo stalks, which measure approximately five feet high by ten or twelve feet long, testify to the length of time the shrine has been maintained. They looked much the same in January 1990 as they do in photographs taken of the shrine in the 1940s.[24]

My wife and I visited the Children's Shrine on January 4, 1990. The site is now fenced to protect it from vandalism, and people wishing to visit it must first get permission from the Gu Achi District Office. Inside the protective fences and gates, it remains much as it has been. Within the circle of peeled ocotillo stalks, a few offerings—an artificial flower and some colored pebbles—lay on the central heap of stones. Outside the circle, to the north and the south, lay the long piles of discarded ocotillo stalks. The stalks around the rock pile still looked fresh and bright tan in color; I later learned that the shrine had been renewed about six months before.

Beyond the double circles of new and discarded stalks were more offerings. Brightly colored toys and trinkets were scattered over a couple of square feet of desert just west of the shrine. There were plastic combs and toothbrushes, small Teddy bears of various materials, a white plastic cross, a bead necklace, and much, much more.

About twenty feet east of the shrine, a short, east-west stretch had been cleared of creosote bushes and tufts of grass. In it were eight flat, gray stones, each flanked with a pair of short, peeled ocotillo stalks. This, according to tradition, is where the medicine men sat while they deliberated what should be done to halt the flood.

(According to the O'odham who told me this, the deliberations were actually carried out by four pairs of medicine men. Thus the eight flat rocks.)

There was something special about the atmosphere that day at the Children's Shrine. It was a very quiet place, even though it lies within sight of two well-traveled paved roads. Neither my wife nor I felt the need to speak other than quietly, or move other than slowly. Whatever happened there all that time ago, augmented by the centuries of reverence, offerings, and renewal, seems to have left its mark. This is indeed a holy place, a place with its own kind of power.

The shrine is renewed every four years in a four-day ceremony. The old stalks are respectfully removed and added to the pile, and new ones are substituted for them. The pile of stones is dismantled, the individual stones are cleaned, and the pile reassembled. This is also a time for asking the Flood Children for crops, and for placing flat pieces of wood representing different crops in the shrine. After the work of renewal comes an all-night dance, at which it is believed that the sacrificed children join in, sensed but unseen by the living.[25]

The O'odham are not the only people in the American Southwest to have such a legend of child sacrifice in order to save the earth from flooding. Among the Hopis and Zunis it is believed that at one point in the distant past, Water Serpent caused a flood and was given children in sacrifice. The children were told "to go down into the waters to meet their 'uncle'" in order to check the flood.[26] Thus the Tohono O'odham legend of the Flood Children may be connected in some way with regional beliefs in Water Serpent. If knowledge of Water Serpent was indeed brought to what is now the American Southwest from Mesoamerica, that land where human sacrifice was deemed necessary to maintain the rhythm of the universe, it is easy to speculate that the Southwestern idea of sacrificing children to avert catastrophe might have a similar origin.

The legend of the Flood Children lives on in another visible way. There is a popular Tohono O'odham dance called the *chelkona*—the Skipping and Scraping Dance. Once used in a context of intervillage competitions, the chelkona is a current favorite of exhibition dance teams who present shortened versions of O'odham dances at powwows, festivals, and other multicultural occasions. The dancers are either boys and girls or young men and women. The girls usually wear long white dresses; the boys may be bare to the waist or wear white shirts. Both groups have their faces painted, usually with white clay. The boys carry images of birds; the girls hold flat, triangular cloud images. The two lines move in a complex series of patterns, paralleling, joining, and intersecting each other.[27]

One O'odham organizer of a chelkona dance group explained to me that the dance, or possibly a specific set of songs for the dance, commemorates a certain event. After the sacrifice of the Flood Children, I'itoi took them on a journey to show them the world they had helped save. At one point on this journey they went to the sea coast. My friend described the children skipping through the shallows above the breaking waves, with birds flying overhead and the sun glinting on the ocean spray, and said that the lines of dancers in some of their movements re-enacted to that moment.

Some of the songs used for the chelkona reflect this legend. Here are the lyrics of the first three songs of a set of eight which were sung at a chelkona performance given at Gu Achi village on May 13, 1972. The performers were students from the Papago Club of Phoenix Indian School, under the direction of elders from Gu Achi and Quijotoa villages.[28]

Song 1

Green I'itoi came from the East.
Little green I'itoi came from the East.
And there he stood up and saw it.
Therefore the spreading land got green.

Song 2

Now you come running! The children come running!
Now you come running! The children come running!
They don't know the place where they arrived.
From there they dance zigzagged.

Song 3

The ocean lies far away.
The ocean lies far away.
There they arrive and see

White birds there in
(The water side by side).

Although the predominant mode of O'odham ritual poetry and rhetoric is allusive rather than descriptive, these verses indeed seem to refer to I'itoi's journey with the Flood Children, and in fact, were so described by individuals participating in the dance. The song set goes on to enumerate other places. There are Black Mountain, Foam Mountain, "Gourd Carrying" Mountain, a "Big Road," and finally the village of Gu Achi.

Names on the Land

Each of the different peoples who live in the Pimería Alta uses distinctive philosophies when it comes to bestowing names on the land. Anglo Americans, living in an officially secular democracy, have honored individuals, be they national figures, "discoverers," or persons of local stature. Thus we have Washington Camp to the east of Nogales, honoring our first president; Coronado National Forest, commemorating a famous Spanish explorer; and Mount Wrightson, in memory of a local mining engineer who met a violent death in 1859. Spaniards and Mexicans, on the other hand, tended to name places after Catholic Christian figures and concepts, as in the case of the Santa Catalina (St. Catherine) and Santa Rita (Saint Rita) Mountains as well as the Santa Cruz (Holy Cross) River. This practice of naming—or dedicating—a place in honor of some saint of member of the Holy Family was a real part of the process of converting a pagan land into a Christian one. Not all Spanish language place names in our region were assigned thus, however. Some were descriptive, as in the Rincon ("Corner") Mountains and the ranch (later the twin cities) of Nogales, or "Walnut Trees."[29]

O'odham names are descriptive. Gu Achi means "Big Narrow Ridge." *Gu Oidak* means "Big Fields," *Quijotoa* "Carrying-basket Mountain," and *Cowlik* "Little Hill." These names describe permanent features of the landscape; others reflect some incident or temporary condition. And so there are villages named *Pan Tak,* meaning "Coyote Sitting" and *Sil Nakya,* "Hanging Saddle."[30] A place in the valley west of the Baboquivari Mountains is called *Ho'ok Muerta*, or "Dead Witch" in a mixture of Spanish and O'odham. This, according to some, is where I'itoi told Ho'ok to look for her father; others feel it is where the dance was held that led to her death.[31] These are all names of places within the modern boundaries of the Tohono O'odham Nation. That O'odham speakers once lived far beyond the limits of what is now their reservation is attested to by such place names as Tubac and Tumacacori in Arizona, and Caborca, Oquitoa, and Cibuta in Sonora.

These names—local, descriptive, and sometimes mythic names in the O'odham language—refer to no other place in the world, and to no experiences other than those of the O'odham. They stand in stark contrast to the other, imported names of the Pimería Alta, which serve to tie this land to other places and to philosophies and religions which had their birth and development elsewhere. Some O'odham place names have changed, almost beyond recognition. A small village on the west bank of the Santa Cruz River was called *Chuk Shon*—"Black Base"—on account of the black rock covering a nearby hill. When the Spaniards established a mission there they pronounced it as best they could—"Tucson"—with the accent on the second syllable. Later on the settlement became part of the United States and was dominated by English speakers. The spelling of its name remained as it had been in Spanish days, but the pronunciation changed to accommodate the English-speaking tongue. Now the accent has shifted and the hard "c" is gone, and I live near a place called "TOO-sahn." And the Black Mountain that gave its name to the village was later called Sentinel Peak, and is now "A" Mountain.

All these details reveal the changing relationships between the O'odham and their place, the Pimería Alta. That this is their land in a very real sense is attested to by the legends and stories related in this chapter. I'itoi created people out of the dirt in this particular part of the world, and the ancestors of the Desert People came from the Underworld to occupy this specific place. As a friend once put it to me, when a Papago dies he returns to the earth he was created from in a very specific way. For the Tohono O'odham, this region is both the Garden of Eden and the Promised Land, rolled into one. No other living people can claim Baboquivari as the center of their world; no other living people can claim the events that took place there and at the Children's Shrine. This land belongs to the Tohono O'odham, and we have just seen a very small part of the documentation of their title.

3.   A Saint and His People

The town of Magdalena de Kino is just west of Mexico's International Highway 15, about sixty miles south of the twin border cities of Nogales, Arizona, and Nogales, Sonora. Magdalena is a growing community of perhaps forty thousand people. Its prosperity comes mostly from trade and agriculture, and it serves as a commercial center for a wide stretch of rich farming and ranching country. But Magdalena de Kino has something in addition to this, something special that draws thousands of visitors each year. This is the devotion to San Francisco, centering around a statue in a small chapel attached to Magdalena's parish church. This church is on the south side of the town's huge Plaza Monumental, which occupies the site of the tiny mission community from which the modern town has grown.

Perhaps the best time to experience the regional importance of San Francisco—the problem of exactly which San Francisco we are dealing with shall be ignored for the moment—is to visit Magdalena on October 4, the date of the annual Fiesta de San Francisco. Streets and plazas on the west side of the town are lined with temporary booths in which a bewildering variety of food, drink, jewelry, trinkets, medicinal herbs, blankets, kitchenwares, holy pictures, and candles is offered for sale. On the south edge of the Plaza Monumental, between three and five hundred people are waiting to enter a side chapel of the church in a line that seems never to get any shorter during the course of the day.[1]

Musicians stroll around beer gardens in the smaller of the town's two plazas and visit the local bars, entertaining patrons at a fixed fee per song. A group of Yaqui ceremonial dancers and musicians may be performing in front of the church, while just to the west of the main plaza a traveling carnival, complete with rides and games of chance and skill, has been set up. Everywhere there are people— people praying, people in church, people buying and selling, eating and drinking, sleeping, arriving, and leaving. They seem to be of all sorts: Mexicans, Mexican Americans, and a few Anglo Americans; Tohono O'odham and Yaqui Indians from Arizona; Yaquis and Mayos from Sonora. The level area along the railroad tracks to the west of town has been converted into a temporary village of brush shelters, and every hotel room, spare bed, and backyard in the entire town seems to have its temporary occupants.

This is no recent phenomenon; in 1851, John Russell Bartlett of the United States and Mexico Boundary Commission visited Magdalena at fiesta time. He found the town's population to be increased by more than 10,000 pilgrims, and the streets lined with booths selling foods and liquor. There was dancing to an orchestra that played polkas and waltzes, and widespread and enthusiastic gambling.[2] With the exception of the public gambling, which has been reduced to a few shell games, the fiesta in 1990 maintains all the features Bartlett saw in 1851.

To explain this huge annual celebration, we must go back in time to the days when the Pimería Alta was the northwestern frontier of New Spain. The story centers around the lives of three men, two of whom died long before Europeans arrived in this region. The first is Father Eusebio Francisco Kino, the Jesuit missionary who labored in the Pimería Alta between 1683 and his death in 1711, and who lies buried in the Magdalena plaza. The second is Saint Francis Xavier, a Spanish Basque who died off the coast of China in 1552, and whose body lies in the former Portuguese colony of Goa, on India's west coast. The third is Saint Francis of Assisi, a medieval

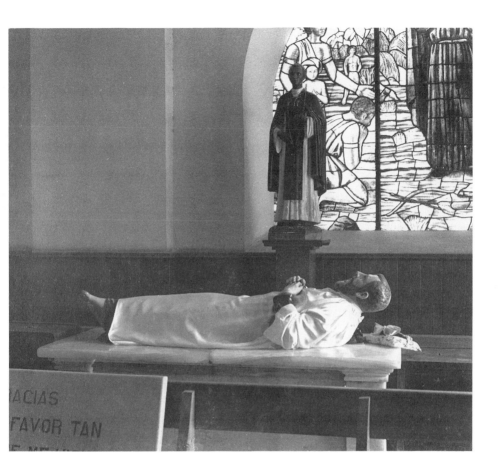

The reclining statue of San Francisco Xavier in Magdalena, Sonora. The statue's carved black cassock is visible at the wrists and ankles, below the white cloth overgarment. The objects under the statue's head are either offerings or things which have been temporarily left by their owners for the purpose of acquiring supernatural power from their proximity to the statue. The stained-glass window in the background depicts Saint Francis' missionary work in the Far East; the statue represents San Martín de Porres. The plaque on the lower left thanks the saint for a favor. Photo by James S. Griffith, 1983.

Italian who founded the Order of Friars Minor or Franciscans. All three have touched our region in a number of ways; the presence of all three is still strongly felt.

Three Principal Actors

Magdalena's main plaza is located on the western edge of town, near the place where the Rio Magdalena flows for most of the year, watering the fields that have supported this and other nearby settlements since long before the days of Columbus. It is a huge open space ringed with trees and grass and with a paved sunken courtyard in its center. In the middle of this sunken space is a fountain. Two buildings stand within the plaza, at its north and south borders.

On the south side of the plaza is the church dedicated to St. Mary Magdalene, patroness of the town since the founding of its mission in the 1690s. It was built in the early 1830s and has since been extensively repaired and redecorated.[3] An "L"-shaped building with the altar at the meeting of the two naves, it seems to have little about it that distinguishes it from hundreds of other churches in Mexico. Until, that is, one notices a small rectangular chapel to the southwest side, in the angle of the "L." Its doors open to the outside rather than into the church, which gives it an air of being subtly detached from the structure that enfolds it. If one watches for a while on any day of the year, one sees a steady stream of people entering and leaving.

Inside the chapel, resting on a rectangular platform some six feet long by three feet wide and about three feet high, is the life-sized statue of a man. He is bearded, and dressed in a black cassock. He lies on his back with his hands joined in prayer and his feet crossed. The statue represents a corpse—the corpse of St. Francis Xavier— San Francisco Xavier in Spanish.

Born in 1506 near Pamplona, Francis Xavier studied at the University of Paris, where he became a follower of St. Ignatius Loyola, founder of the Society of Jesus (also known as the Jesuit Order). He was ordained in 1537, and four years later he went to the Orient as a missionary. Here he stayed the rest of his life, working in India, the East Indies, and Japan before dying in 1552 as he was embarking on a mission to China. Popularly called "the Apostle to the Indies," he was canonized in 1662 and is the patron saint of missionaries. His day in the Catholic calendar is December 3.[4]

After his death, Francis Xavier's body was sent for burial to the then Portuguese colony of Goa, where it still lies in state in the church of Bom Jesus. When the body arrived in Goa it was in an excellent state of preservation, a fact taken for evidence of the intense spiritual quality of the man who had occupied it. It is for that reason that one of the acceptable representations of this particular saint is as a corpse—the way he appears in the chapel in Magdalena.[5]

On the north side of the Plaza Monumental, across from the church, is a small structure consisting of a dome supported by four arches. Centered below the dome is a smaller dome, this one about seven feet high, with four rectangular windows let into its sides. Peering through one of the windows, the visitor looks into an excavated area several feet below the present ground level. The stone footings of an old wall run diagonally across the space. In the center of the excavated area, flanked by small piles of human bones, lies the skeleton of a man. This is all that remains of Father Eusebio Francisco Kino, S.J., Apostle to the Pimas and the first European to establish a permanent presence in this desert country.

Eusebio Kino was born in 1645 in the mountain village of Segno, in the Italian Tyrol. His family name was originally Chini, and there are still Chinis in Segno. He was educated at Jesuit colleges, first in nearby Trent, and later at Hall, near the Austrian city of Innsbruck. In 1663 he suffered from a life-threatening illness and promised his patron saint, St. Francis Xavier, that if he recovered he would join the Jesuits and spend his life as a missionary. He did recover and swiftly embarked on the rigorous training of a Jesuit. This training lasted until 1677 and included mathematics, astronomy, and cartography—skills that were considered potentially useful to missionaries, especially in the Far East, where Kino hoped to follow his patron. This was not to be, however, and Father Kino was sent to

Mexico where he worked as a missionary in Baja California for several years. It was not until 1687 that he began what was to become his life's work—the evangelization of the Pimería Alta.[6]

Kino was an indefatigable traveler and worker. He made expeditions over much of what is now southern Arizona and northern Sonora, visiting Indian villages, preaching, saying Mass, and establishing missions. In all, he began twenty missions, many of them at villages that are still occupied. San Xavier, Magdalena, Caborca—these and many others are the living testimonials to Kino's zeal, energy, and genius.

What Kino did at these places was *found missions*—he started programs for converting the inhabitants into Christian subjects of the Spanish Empire. This is different from building churches, an activity that could take place several years after the mission was founded. That Father Kino also built churches at many of these same villages is true, but the fact is that with very few exceptions little or nothing remains of these buildings. The existing colonial mission churches of the Pimería Alta were for the most part built a century later, after the Jesuits had left the area and had been replaced by members of the Order of Friars Minor, or Franciscans.

The missions Kino established were in already existing villages. This was not always the case in New Spain. Elsewhere the missionaries would establish missions at new locations and then induce the native population to come and live at them. But here in the Sonoran Desert almost every spot capable of supporting human life was doing so already, and so Kino and his followers started their missions in existing villages.

Kino worked in the Pimería Alta until March 1711, when he rode into Magdalena to dedicate a new chapel to his patron, San Francisco Xavier. He fell suddenly ill and died near midnight on March 15, 1711. He was buried beneath the floor of the chapel he had come to dedicate. There he rested until May 19, 1966, when his remains were discovered by an international team of archaeologists.

This discovery came about in the following manner. In 1965, a statue of Father Kino was unveiled as Arizona's contribution to the National Hall of Statuary in the Capitol Building in Washington, D.C. Looking for a way in which Mexico could honor this pioneer whose field of work spanned two modern nations, the president of Mexico commissioned Professor Wigberto Jimenez Moreno, then director of the Department of Historical Investigation of the National Museum of Anthropology and History, to find Kino's remains. He it was who assembled the team which discovered Father Kino's burial site. This discovery led to the construction of the Plaza Monumental as a proper setting for his remains, and to the addition of the honorific "de Kino" to Magdalena's name.[7]

The third actor in this complex story, Saint Francis of Assisi, was born into a wealthy Italian merchant family in Assisi in 1181. Francis lived a life of luxury until 1205, when he experienced a vision of Christ which changed his entire life. He henceforth devoted himself to a life of poverty, of care for the poor and sick and for lowly animals, and of preaching. The religious Order of Friars Minor, commonly known as the Franciscans, was founded from among the ranks of his followers. He died in Assisi in 1226 and was canonized in 1228. His feast day is October 4.[8]

St. Francis of Assisi is remembered for his extreme poverty and humility and for his almost unique vision (for a European) of the unity of all life, even including his "Sister Death." For this latter reason he was recently named patron saint of ecologists.[9] Twentieth-century representations of the saint show him accompanied by birds and small animals. Older statues and pictures, however, depict him as an ascetic and often portray the ecstatic moment when he received the stigmata, or Wounds of Christ, on his hands and feet.

It was the Franciscans who were called to work in the missions of the Pimería Alta after 1767, when the Jesuits were expelled from the whole of Spanish America. This expulsion, which was planned and executed by the Spanish military under conditions of great secrecy, was ordered by the Spanish Crown for reasons that were mainly political. Arriving in the Pimería Alta in 1768, the Franciscans stayed until 1843, when the last friar died. By that time the region had become part of a new political entity called Mexico. The Franciscans built most of the colonial churches now visible in the Pimería Alta. In 1895, Franciscans returned to the northern part of the Pimería, where they still maintain a presence among the O'odham of Arizona.[10]

A Composite Saint

Although the statue in the side chapel represents San Francisco Xavier, the huge annual fiesta held in his honor does not occur on his day at all, but rather on October 4, the day assigned to Saint Francis of Assisi. This was apparently not so in 1832, when the present church was dedicated on December 3, San Francisco Xavier's day.[11] But at some time after that, probably under the direction of a Franciscan priest, the date was changed. It has been suggested that this was done as part of an attempt to get the dedication of the feast changed to the Franciscan saint.[12] Although that may well be the case, I know of no positive evidence for the assumption.

There are other Franciscan qualities to the Magdalena San Francisco as well. Although the statue in the church is portrayed as wearing a black cassock (sometimes with a white cloth garment slipped on over it), most of the smaller statues available for sale to pilgrims on the plaza are dressed in the brown robes of the Franciscan Order. Curiously enough, these brown habits were not used by the Franciscans at the time of their mission work in the Pimería Alta. They did not become the official Franciscan garb until an 1897 proclamation by Pope Leo XIII.[13] The habits of the earlier Franciscans in the Pimería Alta were gray in color; elsewhere in New Spain they were blue.[14] Not only are the popular statues of San Francisco Xavier clothed in the brown robes of modern Franciscans, this is also the color of the *habitos* or habits which are sold in the plaza and worn by some of the faithful as outward signs of indebtedness to the saint for favors rendered, and by others who hope for a miraculous cure.

There is yet another complication: especially since the discovery and exposure of Father Kino's remains, many visitors to Magdalena seem to have gotten the understandable impression that the statue of the dead man in the church is a representation of the dead man whose bones are visible in the plaza. Some pilgrims to Magdalena believe in a San Francisco who worked in this region and died here. He was buried in Magdalena and both his bones and his statue are on view in the main plaza.[15]

So it is that the San Francisco who is venerated and visited in Magdalena de Kino is neither San Francisco Xavier nor San Francisco of Assisi, but a composite saint made up of elements from both, with some characteristics of Father Eusebio Francisco Kino as well. And the complexity doesn't end there.

A saint in Roman Catholic belief is someone whose exemplary Christian life caused him or her to be taken upon death directly into the presence of God. Sainthood is determined by the Church in a complicated procedure which includes the processes of beatification and canonization, for each of which stages two distinct and fully authenticated miracles are required, among other evidence that the individual concerned is, in fact, in heaven. It is believed that, being in the presence of God and understanding the suffering of the human condition, saints can and do intercede on behalf of human petitioners. One prays to a particular saint, and the saint, if so minded, petitions God on one's behalf.[16]

In conversation with pilgrims to the shrine of San Francisco at Magdalena, however, it is possible to get the impression that in this case things don't work in quite that way. I hear little about San Francisco interceding on the behalf of petitioners, and a good deal about his own miraculous powers. It is easy to get the impression that, for some at least, it is the composite saint himself who does the curing or performs the requested miracle. Furthermore, the arrangement between petitioner and saint is believed to be reciprocal; San Francisco expects something in return for his help.

A phrase I constantly hear in connection with San Francisco goes on the order of: *"San Francisco es un santo muy milagroso, pero a la vez es un santo muy cobrador, y lo que debes, pagas."* ("Saint Francis is a very miraculous saint, but at the same time he is a saint who exacts his price, and what you owe, you pay.") What this means is that if you are granted a miracle by San Francisco and have promised to act in exchange, he will collect from you in one way or another, whether or not you keep your promise. One common belief is that he will collect with fire, by burning your house or your car with you or a family member inside. Alternatives involve death through sickness or some sort of accident. But it is considered foolhardy in the extreme to make a promise to San Francisco and not intend to keep it.

One morning in the mid-1980s I received a phone call from my friend Richard Morales, companion on many trips, including several informal pilgrimages to Magdalena. He had read horrible news in the morning paper: a vaquero and fine craftsman whom we had both visited a few weeks before had just died of smoke inhalation in a bunkhouse fire in the ranch where he worked. Knowing that the man had a reputation as a heavy drinker, I suggested in the course of our conversation that he might have gotten hold of a bottle of liquor and fallen asleep with a lighted cigarette in his hand. In precisely the same tone of speculation, Richard responded, "Jim, I wonder if he owed San Francisco anything." Not a comfortable thought. It was Richard whom I heard in Magdalena being interviewed about the fiesta by reporters from a regional TV station. The question was asked, "Why do you come to Magdalena?" The response: "To be honest with you, it's out of fear." And no wonder, if the alternative is a fiery death.

The promises made to San Francisco may take many forms. One of the most popular is a vow to walk to Magdalena from the border at Nogales, just before the día de San Francisco on October 4. The heaviest summer heats have dissipated. The days are in the mid-90s and the nights are cool, but it is still a long, exhausting walk which takes at least two days. Forty years ago the trip was made along the railroad tracks; now many pilgrims choose to walk along the edge of the international highway, with cars and trucks zooming by constantly—a somewhat risky business at best.[17]

Other vows, or *mandas,* as they are called in Spanish, may involve presenting the saint with a *milagro,* or small metal reproduction of the part of the body which has been afflicted. Milagros are stamped out by the hundreds and are for sale in many of the shops that cluster along the south and west sides of the plaza by the church; more expensive ones are made to order by local jewelers. One may also promise to purchase a habito and wear it for a prescribed number of days. It should be emphasized that all these acts may be done as acts of petition, as well as acts of thanksgiving.

Stories are occasionally told of individuals who trick San Francisco with their promises. I have heard, for instance, of a man who promised to go on his knees to Magdalena from the mining town of Cananea, some one hundred miles to the east. This he did, sure enough . . . but he was kneeling on a mattress in the back of his pickup truck![18] This sort of activity is considered a bit risky, however, and most foot travel to Magdalena involves real sacrifice and discomfort, if not actual suffering. In 1989 I saw two young men running along the road to Magdalena. They would run as far as they could, be picked up in a car by friends and driven a ways, then run some more. And in 1971 I saw a young man doing the same thing . . . barefoot. He left bloody footprints on the asphalt.

Early October isn't the only time of the year that pilgrims visit San Francisco. Every time I have gone to Magdalena with Mexican American friends, we have gone first to the chapel to pay our respects to San Francisco. Other possibilities might be discussed on the drive down, but somehow the final decision is always the same—first things first. Visitors to the saint walk through the plaza towards the church, perhaps pausing to buy a votive candle or two, and then file into the side chapel where San Francisco lies. There is almost always one or two people in line to see the saint, as well as a beggar or two seated outside by the door, hoping to benefit from the religious feelings of the pilgrims.

Once inside the chapel, visitors approach San Francisco by way of his feet. Most people touch or even kiss the statue's feet, hands, and face, crossing themselves at least once in the process. Many then try to lift the statue's head. The belief underlying this action is that if San Francisco allows you to lift his head, you are "all right" with him; if not, you are in serious trouble. Friends have told me of seeing strong men try and fail to lift the saint's head, and then fall to their knees in prayer, with tears rolling down their cheeks, begging the saint to soften his heart toward them. Usually the story ends when the narrator tells of leaving the chapel shortly after witnessing a second, equally futile attempt.

One woman I know visited the saint on his feast day and slipped her hand under his head to lift him. She says he was a good deal heavier than she had expected and that while she was summoning all her strength for the task, a man near the door whispered in English, "Both hands, lady, both hands!" Although I have never seen anyone try and fail to lift the saint, I have certainly experienced what seemed like a weight difference of many pounds between one visit and another—a difference remarked upon by many people with whom I have discussed San Francisco.

Two published accounts collected by high-school students in Patagonia in the 1940s tell of people going to confession after failing to lift San Francisco, and subsequently succeeding.[19] Neither confession nor any other contact with the official Catholic Church has been mentioned in any of the unsuccessful head-lifting stories I have been told. The matter these days seems to be strictly between the saint and his devotees, just as it really seems to be San Francisco who does the curing and works the miracles.

Two other stories published in the same Patagonia collection have no parallel in anything I have heard personally. They concern people who came into sudden good fortune and decided to share it with San Francisco. In one case a man discovered buried treasure and tried to give a portion to the saint[20]; in the other, a woman made a cushion for San Francisco and left it at the chapel.[21] The man was unable to leave the chapel unless he took his money back with him, while the woman found the cushion when she returned home. I have not heard stories like these told concerning San Francisco, and the friends I have mentioned them to do not recognize them. While these narratives may appear to concern the saint's generosity to deserving individuals, there is another possible interpretation: they may also tell of his rejecting a petition or payment from someone of whom he did not approve.

One would think that stories of miraculous cures attributed to San Francisco's intervention would be common. Curiously enough, I haven't heard many. There are two in the archives, both collected by high-school students. One is from the Patagonia area, while the other is from Safford. The Safford narrative is a straightforward one of the collector's great-grandmother praying to San Francisco, recovering from what seemed to be a mortal illness, and going on pilgrimage to Magdalena shortly thereafter.[22] The Patagonia tale is more complicated: it involves a little girl who sank in quicksand. Her mother didn't believe in religion but was prevailed upon by some neighbors to pray for help to San Francisco. As soon as she did so, there was a knock on the door and her daughter returned. When the mother took her child to church to thank the saint for his intervention, the little girl pointed out the statue as being of the man who pulled her out of the quicksand and brought her home.[23]

When I first arrived in southern Arizona I heard a joke in Spanish which seems to relate to the problem of San Francisco's identity, as well as to a certain unbending quality which seems to be a personality trait of the Magdalena saint. A man fell out of an airplane, and as he fell, he cried out to San Francisco to help him. A gigantic hand appeared out of nowhere and caught the man up, while a voice boomed out, "Which San Francisco?" The man fell on his knees in the palm of the huge hand and started praying: "Thank you San Francisco of Assisi for having come to my aid in the moment of. . . ." As the hand tipped over, dumping him out into space once more, the voice boomed out, "Pity."

The Pimería Alta is a region of long-lasting customs and well-established continuities. The question has naturally arisen in my mind of whether or not there is any evidence that Magdalena was some sort of ceremonial center before Father Kino's arrival on the Sonoran scene. There seems not to be. I know of no missionary accounts that would lead toward such a conclusion. When the bi-national archaeological team was excavating the plaza in search of Kino's San Francisco chapel, they did find a stone-lined pit or cyst containing a shell from the Gulf of California and three stone axes.[24] This was apparently some sort of offering, but one offering does not a pilgrimage make. And so the matter must rest in the realm of speculation, with no solid evidence for or against the suggestion.

So here in Magdalena we have a Saint Francis who partakes of characteristics of Saint Francis of Assisi, Saint Francis Xavier, and Eusebio Francisco Kino, S. J. He is the object of constant visits and a huge annual fiesta and pilgrimage. He is believed to work miracles on his own, and to exact payment of some kind from those whom he has helped. There is a feeling that he watches over a large part of the Sonoran Desert. In some ways he acts more like a local deity than a Catholic saint, although there is no evidence that there was a powerful local deity worshipped in Magdalena before Father Kino's day.

43

A Remarkable Statue

The visible focus for all this belief and ritual activity is the reclining statue of San Francisco Xavier in the side chapel of the Magdalena parish church. Many Mexicanos in Sonora and Arizona believe that the original statue was brought to Magdalena by Kino himself. It was not, however, intended by him for that mission, but rather for the mission at San Xavier del Bac, some twelve miles south of present-day Tucson, Arizona. Kino had started to build a church at this village in 1700—a church that was never finished. According to a legend collected in Magdalena in the 1960s, Father Kino was bringing the statue through town on the back of a mule, on his way to San Xavier. When the mule reached Magdalena, however, it refused to go any farther. It simply stood as though rooted to the ground. When the statue was unloaded, the mule moved around freely, but as soon as the statue was once more placed on its back, it refused to budge. This was taken as a sign that the statue desired to stay in Magdalena, and so there it remained. The same story was heard in Magdalena in 1851 by John Bartlett of the United States–Mexico Boundary Commission. After almost 140 years, it seems still to be going strong.[25]

A story collected by a Patagonia high-school student in the 1940s combines this theme with a tradition of Father Kino's burial in Magdalena. Papago Indians were carrying San Francisco's body through Magdalena on donkeys when the corpse fell off and could not be lifted back onto the pack animal. They buried the body in Magdalena, built a church over it, and placed a statue of the saint in the church. Now Papagos go to Magdalena every year on pilgrimage.[26]

Tales such as these are what folklorists call *legends*—narratives that are believed and told as the truth by at least some members of the community in which they have currency. Not all the legends I will retell concerning the San Francisco statue can have "really happened." In fact, several are mutually contradictory. Many of the details may be hard for contemporary, mainstream Americans to believe, but they are nonetheless important documents that illuminate, not a series of actions that took place in the past, but a community's beliefs concerning what happened. These particular legends constitute doorways into the universe of popular Mexican and Mexican-American belief concerning San Francisco, and, by extension, concerning the way things work in this world. To the extent that these beliefs are acted on, they influence reality and indeed become reality.

There is another important reclining statue of San Francisco Xavier in the region. The eighteenth-century mission church of San Xavier del Bac, located just south of Tucson, was built by Franciscans, next to the site of a 1762 Jesuit church. Left without a resident priest in 1831, the mission came once again under the care of the Order of Friars Minor in 1913, and has been administered by them ever since. It is still maintained as a mission to the O'odham community of Bac, or Wa:k as it is spelled in contemporary O'odham orthography. Although the church is dedicated to San Francisco Xavier, and although most of its religious statuary seems to have been in place since the building's dedication in 1797, the reclining San Francisco is a comparatively recent addition.

The statue rests in an ornate box in San Xavier's west transept. It is carved of wood and represents a bearded man lying on his back. His right arm is missing; his left arm consists of a wooden hand and forearm, with a strip of cloth for an upper arm. This allows the whole arm to be moved easily. Bruises and wounds from scourging are represented on the forearm, and there are lines of blood on the neck and in front of the ears. All this evidence suggests that the statue was originally intended to represent Christ rather than Saint Francis Xavier. The blood on the head and neck could be from the crown of thorns, while cloth upper arms would allow the statue to be hung on and removed from a cross. Marks on the wrist where the wood is worn away suggest that it was indeed tied to something with strips of cloth. The only evidence against this interpretation is the fact that the remaining hand shows no traces of the conventional nail hole through which Christ was attached to the cross, and the fact that the arm does not seem to match the body. The statue's legs are missing, having been sawed off just below the hips. Stylistically, the statue appears to date from the late-eighteenth or early nineteenth century.[27]

The oldest photographs of San Xavier's west transept date from around 1880 and show the statue where it is today, lying in a wood-

The San Francisco statue at San Xavier mission. The saint is covered with offerings: photos, hospital bracelets, and milagros. Photo by James S. Griffith, May 1991.

framed case that has been covered with white cloth on three sides. White curtains have been parted to reveal the statue.[28] There is a tradition that this statue originally came from the mission church at Tumacacori, some thirty miles south of San Xavier in the Santa Cruz Valley. Tumacacori, whose mission had been established by Father Kino, was abandoned in December 1848, after a particularly severe Apache attack. Its residents fled north, bringing with them to San Xavier the saints from their abandoned church. Five of these statues were returned to Tumacacori in 1973 and may now be seen in the museum at Tumacacori National Monument.[29] One of these statues, representing San Cayetano, appears beside the reclining statue in early photographs.

A San Xavier O'odham tradition has the reclining statue coming from Tumacacori, but in a slightly more mysterious way. According to this story, the statue was found near San Xavier in the bed of the Santa Cruz River, where it had apparently floated down from Tumacacori.[30] This is not the only regional legend in which a San Francisco statue seems to take a hand in determining where it will stay. We have already seen the legends explaining the coming of San Francisco to Magdalena; the statue at the Sonoran O'odham village of Chuwhiy Guwsk, which will be discussed below, is likewise said to have appeared suddenly on the site of its future dwelling place. Similar stories are told concerning miraculous statues in Spain and elsewhere in Western Europe.[31] There is a tradition among the Franciscan friars stationed at San Xavier involving one Father Tiburtius Wand, a famous missionary who was stationed at San Xavier in the 1920s. He wished to create some sort of an alternative to the trip to Magdalena, which in those days of wagon transportation could take upwards of a month. In his view, Papagos went to Magdalena, got drunk and otherwise spent their money, and needed some motivation to stay at home. He therefore "recycled" the damaged statue of Christ into a reclining San Francisco and placed it in the elaborate case in which it lies, which was taken from the first motorized hearse to serve the San Xavier community.[32]

If this story is true, the question remains of what function the statue was serving before Father Tiburtius' time. It may well have been a representation of the Entombed Christ, a common devotional figure in eighteenth century Hispanic Catholicism.[33] The fact that it seems originally to have been carved as a Christ figure, and has apparently lain at San Xavier since 1880 beneath a statue depicting the suffering Christ, certainly suggests that possibility.

The statue at San Xavier, while it apparently has not fulfilled Father Tiburtius' hopes of changing the pilgrimage habits of the O'odham, has gained a considerable local devotion over the years. It is usually covered with offerings of metal milagros, hospital bracelets, photos of individuals needing special attention from the saint, and even notes pinned to the blankets that cover it. These coverings are often specially made for the statue, as are the lace and satin pillows one frequently finds slipped under the statue's head. On a typical weekend one can see Mexican-American pilgrims walking from Tucson to San Xavier to visit San Francisco. They often carry staffs as badges of their pilgrimage.

The feast day for this San Francisco is October 4, the actual feast of St. Francis of Assisi, and the day on which Magdalena's reclining statue is honored. The statue lies in state in front of the main altar for a day, and then is carried in evening procession around the plaza to the accompaniment of music and fireworks. There is another statue of San Francisco Xavier in the church—the patronal statue over the main altar. This one is a standing representation of the saint, and it is feasted on December 3, the day of San Francisco Xavier. This presence in the same church of two separate versions of the same saint, each with his own feast day, has led to some interesting explanations. A Mexican-American friend remarked to me one December 3 that it was the feast day of *San Francisco parado*—the "standing St. Francis." October 4, on the other hand, was *el día de San Francisco acostado*—"the day of the reclining St. Francis." Meanwhile, the humble St. Francis of Assisi, whose day October 4 actually is, has become forgotten and uncelebrated by many in the Pimería Alta.

Just as they do in Magdalena, pilgrims visiting the San Francisco at San Xavier often try to lift the statue's head. One of my Chicana friends told me that when she was a girl living in Tucson, her mother would take the whole family to Mass at San Xavier Mission every month or so. After Mass, the children would be lined up and made to visit the reclining statue of San Francisco, each one lifting the statue's head in turn. When my friend asked her mother the reason for this, she was told that the saint did not permit girls to lift his head if they had lost their virginity.

The feeling that the reclining statues at San Xavier and Magdalena are somehow related comes out in several legends. One Tucson man told me that he had heard in his family that each statue actually "belonged" in—or was originally intended for—the other church. However, each time an exchange was attempted, something happened to prevent it. The river would be up and therefore impassible, or the axle of the *carreta* carrying the statue would break, or the burros would go lame. At any rate, for one reason or another it was never possible to complete the exchange.

The account told by another family was that the San Francisco now at Magdalena was originally at San Xavier, while the San Xavier San Francisco was originally in Magdalena. One night, the two statues changed places. That, according to this particular account, is why the San Francisco at San Xavier has no legs—he walked the whole way and wore them off.

A rather complex story involving Magdalena, San Xavier, and San Francisco (presumably the city in California) was collected for the Arizona Folklore Archives in 1960. Here it is as the student collector submitted it.

> San Xavier
>
> They were taking San Francisco from San Francisco to Magdalena in an exchange between the two churches. When they got to Tucson they stopped to rest. They were not able to move San Francisco from that spot. All the men together could not move him. The fathers said it was because he wanted to stay there. So the church was built on that spot and named San Xavier. Afterwards they got the saint from Magdalena, whose name is San Francisco de Oases, and that one did pass by very well on its way to San Francisco.
>
> (My grandmother did not know of any miracles San Francisco de Xavier has done, although she has heard that he has. But she did know of two that were done for her grandfather and her father by San Francisco de Oases who was at that time in Magdalena.)[34]

Here again the statue takes a hand in determining where it will stay. "San Francisco de Oasis" seems to be a regional corruption of "San Francisco de Asís," or St. Francis of Assisi. I have heard it used thus in the old Jesuit mission community of San Javier in Baja California. And it is a perfectly logical pronunciation for a desert country.

Finally, a woman in Imuris, Sonora, told me that the statue presently at San Xavier is the original statue from Magdalena. It had been sold by a Magdalena priest years ago to the "Presidente de Arizona." Her explanation of that was that "some Mexicans will sell *anything."* The presidente had the image placed in the church at San Xavier del Bac as a part of a strategy designed to keep the local Papagos from coming on pilgrimage to Magdalena, becoming drunk, and getting rolled and robbed. This echoes the Franciscan tale concerning Father Tiburtius and the statue at San Xavier.

A final set of legends concerning the statue in Magdalena deals its adventures during the 1930s and 1940s. As the Mexican Revolution of 1910 moved slowly toward resolution in the 1920s and 1930s, religious strife became a part of the national experience. On one side were devout, traditional Catholics; on the other were social idealists who viewed the Church and its beliefs as an obstacle to reform. Farther south, in the west coast states of Jalisco and Colima, there was actual, bloody conflict between the two sides. President Alvaro Obregón was shot to death in 1928 by a young assassin who cried out "Viva Cristo Rey" (Long Live Christ the King) as he did his deed. In Sonora, the leftist regime of Plutarco Elías Calles actively discouraged and even attempted to suppress many Catholic practices.

In September of 1934, Sonoran government officials ordered that the saints' images, including that of San Francisco, be removed from the church in Magdalena and carried to the capital city of Hermosillo. There they were burned in the furnaces of the *Cervecería Sonora*—the Sonora Brewery. The church building itself was converted to secular uses, becoming a meeting place, library, and dance hall. This state of affairs seems to have lasted for about a decade before the building was restored to its religious function.

Many stories circulate among Magdalena's Catholics concerning the terrible fates that overtook the men and women who were involved with this act of desecration. A saddle maker who had advocated the removal of San Francisco from the church is said to have injured his arm in an automobile accident. After going in vain to several doctors, he finally permitted his wife, who was a religious woman, to pray for his restoration to health at the altar stone where San Francisco's image had lain. His arm was restored, with no further medical treatment. Another advocate of the saint's removal, a schoolteacher, was said to have gone insane after the burning of the image. As her illness was mental, nothing could be done for her, and she was thought to have remained in that state in 1949, when the tale of her fate was collected by a student at the University of Arizona.[35]

In 1988 I spoke with a woman from Magdalena who told me that she had witnessed a fatal automobile accident in the 1950s. The man who had driven the truck that carried the statue of San Francisco from Magdalena to its place of immolation in Hermosillo's Cervecería Sonora was struck and instantly killed on the streets of Magdalena . . . by a truck belonging to the Cervecería Sonora! Just in case I wasn't following her, she then explained that the man had carried San Francisco from Magdalena to the cervecería in a truck in order to destroy him, and that San Francisco had retaliated by sending a truck from the cervecería to Magdalena to destroy *him*.

There are some in Magdalena who refuse to believe that the statue was ever really burned. For them, the story of what really happened runs as follows: When the priest at Magdalena heard of the impending desecration of the church, he summoned a group of faithful Papago Indians and smuggled San Francisco's statue out of the church and into their care. They took it to one of their villages in Sonora, near the U.S. border, where they kept it for several years, until it was safe to return it to Magdalena.

My friend Richard Morales knows a man who claimed to have seen the statue during its supposed exile among the Papagos. He was at an Indian village near the border (the village was unnamed in the story) around 1940, trading for mules. Those were the days when one could buy really good mules from the Papagos living along the border. When the trade was consummated, the Indian with whom he was doing business said to him, "¿No quieres saludar a tu santo?" (Don't you want to greet your saint?)

"¿Qué santo?" (What saint?), the buyer asked.

"Tu eres de Magdalena, ¿no? ¿No quieres saludar a San Francisco?" (You're from Magdalena, aren't you? Don't you want to greet San Francisco?) came the reply.

He was led into a small chapel, where he found what he believed—and still believes—to have been the San Francisco statue from Magdalena. For many people, stories such as this are proof that the statue was never burned.

There is a possible explanation for these stories. Just south of the International Border, some forty miles east of Sonoyta, Sonora, is the Tohono O'odham village of San Francisquito, or *Chuwhiy Guwsk* (Jackrabbit Falls Down). There has been a reclining statue of San Francisco in a small chapel in that village since at least the early 1940s. According to a 1950 article in *The Kiva* it had been purchased about six years previously for $180 from a man living south of Magdalena.[36] It may be that this image was the one seen by Richard's friend in the O'odham village and that its presence in San Francisquito provided evidence to the faithful that their beloved statue in Magdalena was not really destroyed.

In the late 1940s the statue's arrival in Chuwhiy Guwsk was already shrouded in legend and mystery. The following narrative has been condensed from one collected around 1950.

The statue was originally in a church in a small village near Magdalena but disappeared from that church in a mysterious fashion and reappeared in some bushes on the site of present-day Magdalena. After men and burros were unable to move the statue, a church was built around it. Much later, during the Revolution, the figure disappeared again. It was rediscovered in the early 1940s by an old man who found it buried in some soft dirt under his kitchen floor, near the Magdalena church. With the help of an Indian woman (tribe unspecified), he cleaned the statue and painted clothes on it to replace its original garments, which had rotted away. People came to the old man's house to view the figure for the rest of that day and part of the night. The local priest was said to be very angry when he heard of the discovery of the statue.

The following day the figure was missing again. This time it was discovered at the little Papago village of Chuwhiy Guwsk. A woman heard strange noises in the storehouse behind her home. Fearing that an animal had gotten in, she entered and found the statue of San Francisco from Magdalena. She could find no tracks near the statue. Frightened, she told a very old man about her experience. He didn't believe her at first, saying it must have been a vision. When she finally persuaded him to see the statue for himself, he said that a church must be built on that very spot. The church was built and is the one standing at Chuwhiy Guwsk.[37]

The altar of the chapel at Chuwhiy Guwsk (San Francisquito), Sonora. It is interesting that, while all the pictures of the older statue (like the one resting on the right end of the altar) show San Francisco with his head to the viewer's left, all contemporary altars I have seen have the statue lying with his head to the right. Photo by James S. Griffith, March 1990.

The church and its statue still remain at Chuwhiy Guwsk, and are the focus of an annual pilgrimage and fiesta that draws Tohono O'odham from many villages in southern Arizona. When I visited the village in March 1990, I took a close look at the life-sized statue lying in front of the altar. It did not sufficiently resemble the pre-1934 Magdalena statue as it appears in photographs to suggest that it is indeed the original statue, rescued from the clutches of the Sonoran government.

Ethnobotanist Gary Nabhan suggests that the arrival of the statue in Chuwhiy Guwsk and the establishment of the pilgrimage to that village were O'odham responses to the unavailability of San Francisco in any visitable form in his original site. Papagos have always been major participants in the annual pilgrimage to Magdalena; when that pilgrimage was denied them after the destruction of its focal image, they simply instituted another. This seems to be borne out by a statement Nabhan heard in Chuwhiy Guwsk to the effect that San Francisco had "gone into hiding to escape the Mexican authorities and had reemerged there to be among the O'odham people again."[38]

At some time in the 1940s a statue of San Francisco was once again placed in the side chapel at the Magdalena church. For some, it was a new statue, carved to replace the one that had been destroyed. For others, it was the old statue, repaired and recarved, and returned from its hiding place. Whichever it was, it is said to have been carved (or refurbished) in Nogales, Sonora, by an itinerant sculptor who is remembered only by his nickname, "el Tiguas."

When the statue was finished and ready to be taken to Magdalena, people weren't quite sure it was safe to do so. So el Tiguas asked for and received permission to place the statue temporarily on trestles in the front office of a Nogales, Sonora, newspaper. There it stayed for a while, until the newspaperman involved noticed that elderly ladies were coming into his office, praying to San Francisco, and leaving offerings of money with the statue. These offerings were later pocketed by the sculptor. This outraged the newspaperman, who, although he did not believe in the saints, believed even less in what he considered to be cynical exploitation of those who did believe. The next time el Tiguas entered the office, he was met by an irate newspaperman, who pointed a finger at the door. "Tiguas," he thundered. "Tu y tu santo—¡afuera!" (Tiguas—you and your saint—Get out!) Shortly thereafter, the statue was moved to Magdalena.[39]

This by no means exhausts all the legends concerning the statues of San Francisco. In fact, every time I discuss the subject with a new Mexicano acquaintance, I hear a new legend, or a distinctive variant of a familiar one. Furthermore, everyone I talk with knows at least one San Francisco legend.

54

As numerous as they may be, the legends cluster around certain themes. One group seeks to explain why a church dedicated to St. Mary Magdalene has a miraculous statue of Saint Francis Xavier, while the mission church dedicated to that saint—San Xavier—has a statue of less importance. Others focus on the relationship between the two reclining statues. Yet another set of legends deals with what must have been an extremely traumatic series of events for Sonora's Catholics: the removal of the sacred images from the Magdalena church and the closing of the church itself as a place of Catholic worship. The same set of events seems to have spurred the establishment of the San Francisco statue and pilgrimage at Chuwhiy Guwsk, as well as many of the legends surrounding that establishment.

This regional, composite saint is such a familiar figure in his homeland that families and individuals take his story and make of it what they wish. San Francisco has become a part of the regional culture of the Pimería Alta, providing assistance when needed but also serving as a subject for a bewildering variety of stories, a focal point for the creative storytelling impulses of a people.

That is not to say that the stories are original to this saint and region. Most of the San Francisco legends I have heard have strong parallels elsewhere in Mexico, as well as in Western Europe, especially Spain. They tie the Pimería Alta to the rest of Christendom while at the same time asserting its uniqueness as a region.

No matter what some of the faithful may believe, it appears to me that the statue of San Francisco from Magdalena really was burned in the furnaces of the Cervecería Sonora. The pictorial representations sold in the stores that cater to pilgrims in Magdalena all seem to be taken from a photograph of the statue as it was before the 1930s. The saint is shown as a bearded man, dressed in Mass vestments. (This was until recently the way Roman Catholic priests were buried.) His hands are folded in prayer with their fingers interlaced. His knees are slightly bent and his feet crossed. He is flanked by two ornate vases holding what appear to be chrysanthemums. Hanging behind him is a richly embroidered or brocaded cloth. Not only has the setting for the statue completely changed, the statue simply does not appear to be the one that is in the chapel now.

When I first started noticing these pictures in the early 1960s, they were actual postcard-sized photographic prints, done on glossy paper by a firm in Mexico City. After the black-and-white prints were made, they were tinted by hand with green, blue, red, orange, and other colors. Since the mid-1980s, these hand-tinted photos have been replaced in the stores by color reproductions of a painting which seems to have been based on the original black-and-white photograph.

This, or a similar photograph, seems to have been used as a model for a metal engraving of the statue that was apparently executed in Mexico City. Although many of the details in the engraving are different from the photograph, the two are similar enough that the photo may have served as a rough model for an artist who was accustomed to supplying many of his own details. The plate was signed by José Guadalupe Posada, the great Mexican popular engraver who worked in Mexico City for the Arroyo Vanegas printing firm and died in 1913.[40] It is labeled "SAN FRANCISCO JAVIER DE MAGDALENA SONORA." I have not found this print reproduced or mentioned in any catalogue of Posada's work. I have seen copies of it for sale as devotional pictures (as opposed to art objects) in the Magdalena plaza as recently as 1987.

The famous New York firm of Currier and Ives also made an image of Magdalena's San Francisco. I have not been able to discover anything about the circumstances of its production, but from internal evidence it seems to have been made between 1874 and 1890.[41] It is entitled "MILAGROSA IMAGEN DE SN. FRANCISCO JAVIER. Que se venera en la Iglesia Parroquial de la villa de la Magdalena. SONORA" (Miraculous statue of St. Francis Xavier which is venerated in the parish church of the town of Magdalena, Sonora).[42]

It shows the saint reclining in an open-fronted casket that is flanked by kneeling angels bearing candelabra. The saint is bearded and his hands are folded; his feet are not crossed. He is wearing a white garment covered by a rich cloak that is hung over his shoulders. Over the casket hover twelve cherub heads in a cloud. The statue certainly does not appear to be the same as that shown in the old photographs or in the Posada print. These images of Magdalena's San Francisco, like the legends recounted earlier, are evidence of the regional importance of this unique composite saint. Like the legends, they tie the Arizona-Sonora borderlands to other parts of the world, while at the same time affirming the regional importance of the devotion.

The Painted Frames

There is a cottage industry of artisans that functions for the benefit of Magdalena's pilgrims. About five individuals in Magdalena and nearby Imuris spend at least some of their time making and selling painted glass frames for holy pictures. Olga Ruiz, the original source of my knowledge of la corúa, is one of these individuals. Most are of the social class locally called pajareros; that is to say, they are poor people, frequently regarded as outsiders by the communities on the edges of which they live. They make their living by turning their hands to a variety of traditional crafts and skills. In the area around Magdalena, one of these crafts involves the production of painted glass frames.[43]

A typical frame is made from a sheet of glass measuring approximately eight by ten inches. The glass is painted on its underside, with a space left at the top or along one side for the holy picture. The typical frame has a background color applied in opaque paint, and floral or geometric designs put on in translucent colors. A sheet of crumpled tinfoil is inserted behind the glass, giving a wonderful shimmering, glittering quality to the translucent colors. The whole frame is then backed with either tin or cardboard. If tin is used for the backing, it is fastened permanently onto the glass plate by a tin molding around the edge of the frame. If the backing material is cardboard, it is clipped to the glass with bits of tin. This allows the purchaser to insert his or her own picture in the frame. The frames that are permanently backed with tin come with pictures already inserted.

Most of the paintings on the frames consist of one, two, or three brilliantly colored flowers done in the translucent colors against solid, opaque backgrounds. Frequently a scroll across one corner bears the word RECUERDO, Spanish for "souvenir" or "memento." For this reason a 1983 exhibition of the frames was entitled "Glittering Recuerdos." From this title a false impression has spread among some non-Spanish speakers that "recuerdo" is the proper name for the frames, which actually are called *cuadritos* or "little pictures" by their makers. Each year's crop of frames is slightly different from the last, as the artists try to produce something new, exciting, and marketable. In 1989 fewer craftspeople than before seemed to be selling the frames at the fiesta but those who were had added butterflies and birds to their repertoire of decorative motifs. One prolific artist, Jesús León of Imuris, was experimenting with the Mexican eagle, serpent, and cactus on some of his frames. A few of the artists also make glass and tin crosses and boxes using the same techniques.

The origins of this dynamic local art form are difficult to discover. Reverse painting on glass, called "tinsel painting" by some collectors, was a popular middle-class domestic craft in the United States in the period just after the Civil War. Whole pictures were created using the technique, with still lifes and landscapes among the most popular themes.[44] Coming closer to home, reverse glass painting has been used for picture frames in northern New Mexico since the late nineteenth century, along with the similar technique of putting the glass over some patterned material like wallpaper.[45] Frames similar to the New Mexico ones have also been found in the state of Oaxaca, in southern Mexico. In far-off Cajamarca, Peru, a wide range of objects from coasters to mirror frames is done in reverse-painted glass, in what is felt to be a craft survival from colonial times.

None of this tells us exactly how the technique arrived in Magdalena. I have found no evidence for its use there before the 1950s. In 1967 I photographed Jesús León's workbench at a Magdalena fiesta. According to those photographs, he was at that time engaged in using convex plastic frames with tiny dried flowers inserted under them. However, the craftspeople I have talked with have told me that they have done the reverse painting all their lives. For now, the history of this art form in Magdalena remains shrouded in mystery, like so many aspects of this region's popular culture.

Most of the frames are sold to Tohono O'odham who come to Magdalena at the time of the annual October 4 fiesta. The artists consider them to be their major customers and in fact explain the rather gaudy appearance of the frames with the traditional cultural stereotype that "Indians like bright colors." The uses to which the O'odham put the frames and the pictures they contain will be discussed in the next chapter. They are not by any means the only purchasers, however. I have seen the frames on Mexican and Yaqui altars in Arizona.

Anglo Americans are also becoming a small but growing part of the market. For most of them the motivation is probably a bit different from that of the Mexicans and Indians I have talked with, who feel that they are buying pretty frames to put around their holy pictures or family photographs. In contrast, many of the Americanos look on themselves as collecting folk art. In my case, for example, the frames are catalogued and added to a collection which may eventually go into a public institution; I regard them as data in addition to enjoying them for other reasons. For many, myself included, they are visible, tangible objects which when hung on the wall remind us of some pleasing or interesting aspect of regional culture. In a sense they have changed from being decorative settings for spiritual and family icons into being icons themselves. Rather than making a beloved religious or family picture still more beautiful, they have become symbols of a specific place—the old Pimería Alta.

A Diversity of Peoples

All four of the Pimería's major ethnic groups—O'odham, Yaquis, Mexicanos, and Americanos—come to the fiesta de San Francisco in early October. Each group has its own understanding of the fiesta and of the saint in whose honor the feast is celebrated. The beliefs concerning San Francisco that I have discussed so far were collected mostly from Mexicanos. For O'odham, San Francisco seems to be a different person. In fact, many older, traditional O'odham seem to equate San Francisco with God. Two Franciscan missionaries have told me stories of experiences that they had in the 1940s. One was visiting a sick child in the village of Chuichu, just south of Casa Grande. The little boy had a cross shaved in his hair, a cross that was filled with mud made with holy water from Magdalena. The priest noticed a picture of San Francisco hanging in the room and asked who the picture represented. "It's God," replied an elderly Papago man.[46]

The other priest was at San Xavier, and was approached by a puzzled older man from one of the villages out on the desert. There was something, he said, that he had been worrying about, and he thought Father would be able to help him. It was true, wasn't it, that San Francisco and God were the same?[47]

When evaluating stories such as these two, it must be kept in mind that we are dealing with an oral tradition. This means that there is no "correct" version and that, while the O'odham elders with whom the priests had spoken may well have believed that San Francisco and God were the same individual, all O'odham may not have shared those beliefs. The other thing to remember is that oral traditions are dynamic and that these conversations took place in the 1940s. O'odham concepts of San Francisco may well have changed in the almost fifty years since the two priests spoke with the elders.

Several stories concerning San Francisco were told recently to naturalist Gary Nabhan, as he was walking on an extended pilgrimage from the Gila River through the main part of the Tohono O'odham Nation on his way to Magdalena, Sonora. Each one seems to portray a holy figure who shared qualities with Saint Francis of Assisi. In one case, birds and donkeys sang to warn the people when an earthquake rocked a chapel. This story certainly fits the personality of the Franciscan saint who saw unity in all life and who is associated in legend and art with birds and other small animals. Nabhan was also told of a young woman who had been taken from her village and raped by Mexican soldiers. She was found in the desert and brought to safety by a man wearing a humble, stained robe, a person who was identified by the storyteller as San Francisco, surely the poverty-loving saint of Assisi.[48]

When Nabhan visited the Sonoran O'odham village of Chuwhiy Guwsk on October 4, 1989, he chatted with several O'odham concerning the identity of San Francisco. The consensus of opinion seemed to be that, no matter what priests and others might say, the

San Francisco whose day is celebrated in October is a different person from San Xavier, whose day is in December. All this evidence suggests that O'odham beliefs concerning the saints, and most particularly San Francisco, are complex, and we academic outsiders are just beginning to learn about those beliefs.

Yaquis know of San Francisco as well. The first days of October see Yaquis from Arizona and Sonora arriving in Magdalena. Some years deer and pascola dancers and musicians can be seen performing for the saint outside the chapel and then earning extra money by playing and dancing for the general public in the streets and bars. The Yaquis from Sonora are easily identified by their traditional dress. The women wear long, full skirts of brightly colored material, adorned with rows of lace ruffles, while many of the men have straw cowboy hats, embroidered western shirts, and bright neckerchiefs.

In the early 1940s, anthropologist Ruth Warner Giddings was told that among the Yaqui dancers honoring San Francisco at his fiesta were the members of the Bow Leaders' Society—the Coyote dancers. They were described as dancing to a song that "praises San Francisco as a great Yaqui soldier who was able to kill a very powerful bird called *kupahe*." Another Coyote song refers to San Francisco in the army. San Pedro borrowed his bow and pulled on it until it broke. Another Coyote song which was sung in public as recently as 1987 refers to a similar story, but with St. John pulling St. Francis' bow.[49]

This soldierly San Francisco seems unlike the saint as he is understood by O'odham or Mexicanos. It seems probable that, just as Yaquis have a specifically Yaqui understanding of many other aspects of the universe, so in Magdalena they encounter a San Francisco who is a uniquely Yaqui conception.

For Anglos, San Francisco seems to be tied to the country in a slightly different way than that perceived by Mexicans. Rather than a powerful regional figure, he seems to be understood as an actor in a powerful regional story. Anglos visit the fiesta at Magdalena, but even those who are not studying or practicing in the fields of folklore or anthropology do so with a certain sense of visiting someone else's cultural occasion. Americanos go to Magdalena because it

61

is interesting, or fun, or possibly a combination of the two. Few in my experience do so for the very Mexicano motivations of keeping faith, requesting supernatural assistance, or even fear of supernatural reprisals. Here is another way to put it: Most Anglos I know go to Magdalena in early October to experience the fiesta; Yaquis, O'odham, and Mexicanos go to be a part of the fiesta.

Back to the Fiesta

The first impression I always have when I arrive at the fiesta is of the tremendous complexity of the event. Two large plazas and their surrounding streets are full of people, a condition that intensifies toward the evening of October 3, vigil of the feast day itself. (In Sonora, religious feasts are often celebrated more intensely on the night before the feast—the vigil—than they are on the actual day.) Not only have people come from all over southern Arizona and northern Sonora for the fiesta, many people have come from even farther away in order to cater to the pilgrims' needs.

There are blanket salesmen, for instance, from places like Hermosillo and Mexicali. They park battered vans in the streets near the plaza, stack blankets on a trestle table, and proceed to sell their wares. This they do while wearing small microphones around their necks. They will assemble several blankets and bedspreads into a bargain package, salting their talk all the while with a wonderful running flow of jokes, wisecracks, and other humor. These experienced traditional pitchmen do not like to be photographed or taped. Their constant patter, bellowed out over low-fidelity amplification, adds a nerve-racking flavor to the festive scene.

Other merchants come from many parts of Mexico. I became friends with one such man in the 1960s, and we visited regularly in Magdalena at fiesta time until his death some fifteen years later. His name was José Moya, and his home was on the outskirts of the city of Durango, in the western Mexican state of the same name. He would travel from fiesta to fiesta on an annual circuit that stretched from the American to the Guatemalan border. Over the course of our visits together, I learned something about his work. Sr. Moya may be taken to represent a large number of traveling merchants who visit Magdalena on an annual basis. He traveled by bus, making occasional trips to Mexico City to replenish his suitcases of merchandise—ribbons, cheap jewelry, religious medals, combs, and other novelties. He varied his purchases according to the town he was planning to visit, knowing from experience what sold in different parts of Mexico. I know he spoke a few words of Yaqui and Papago (as well as fluent English, learned while working in Chicago in the 1940s); he probably was able to "get along" in several other native languages as well. His knowledge of local religious customs was broad and essential to his trade. I visited with him in his booth at fiestas in Chihuahua, northern and southern Sonora, and Sinaloa, and was constantly impressed by his understanding and explanations of the regional culture in each location.

Arriving in Magdalena with his wife, he would rent a space on the main plaza from the town authorities. He tried to keep the same space each year. He would also purchase wood and canvas with which to construct his stall. Here he would live with his wife until it was time to leave, sleeping in the back of the temporary structure and eating food cooked by his wife over a small brazier.

After Magdalena he would go for a few weeks to Hermosillo and then on to Aduana, a small colonial mining town near Alamos in the southern part of Sonora. After that community's annual fiesta of the Virgin of Balbanera was over, he would move on to Guasave, Sinaloa, for yet another fiesta, and so on into southern Mexico, traveling from fair to fair, fiesta to fiesta. By Christmastime he would be back in Durango, selling toys from a temporary stall on the street. Then he would take a vacation, which he once described to me as a time in which he had nothing to do but read books. Just after Easter, he would be on the road again. After his death, his wife carried on the family business until her death a few years later. In 1990 a nephew operated a similar stand at a different place on the Magdalena plaza.

Healing plays an important part in the rationale behind many visits to Magdalena. Olga Ruiz, whom we met in chapter 1, sells medicinal herbs as well as glass paintings. Some of the herbs she gathers herself, the rest she buys from others. Her herbs are displayed in small sacks. Many are identified with handwritten labels;

upon request she will explain the proper uses of each one. There are other herb sellers as well, some of whom represent national firms. Their displays are differently organized, with the herbs done up in small, sealed packets and provided with printed labels complete with instructions.

I once saw a medicine pitchman pushing his wares from a small table he had set up on a side street. He had several jars on the table containing horrible-looking worms in formaldehyde, and was lecturing to an enthralled audience on the dangers of drinking unpurified water. Amoebas were his topic of the moment, and he went on at length about their dangers. Finally, at the climax of his talk, he held up a jar of rather murky water. Holding a desk-type magnifying glass in front of it, he exhorted his audience to look at the amoebas. And the audience was dutifully looking when I walked away.

On October 1, 1989, I noticed a ring of spectators on the lawn on the northeast corner of the plaza. They surrounded two people: a standing man and a woman seated with a large constrictor-type snake draped around her neck. The woman was blindfolded with a red bandanna handkerchief, and quietly fondled the snake's head to keep it from moving off. She remained thus while I watched her. Earlier she had made psychic readings as a means of attracting a crowd for her partner's sales pitch. A fellow spectator told me that she had said that a man standing behind her in the audience had a machine in his hand, and sure enough he was wearing a wristwatch. Now, however, she sat quietly, while her partner explained the virtues of some small, yellowish, pyramidal crystals that could be used to alleviate many kinds of medical and other problems.

He suggested to the spectators that they rub the crystals over their bodies when they were at home at night, then soak them in water, then sprinkle the water on the doorstep in the sign of the cross. He gave them a prayer to repeat and told them not to pray with excessive grief, for God was a God of love, and disliked that sort of thing. He was still talking when I left.[50]

Also in 1989, I found a kind of printed prayer, new to me, for sale in the plaza. I was very familiar with one sort of prayer or novena: it is written in florid Spanish and addressed to a specific saint in the Roman Catholic calendar or to a member of the Holy Family.

Sometimes such leaflets contain simple prayers and sometimes whole novenas, with a ritual to be followed over the course of nine days. They are common adjuncts of popular Catholicism in Mexico, turned out by printing houses in centers such as Guadalajara and shipped all over the Republic. The ones I encountered in 1989 did not fit into this traditional Catholic pattern.

Many were addressed to some aspect of Death. Most Holy Death, the Secret of the Most Holy Death, and the Holy Corpse were all objects of printed petitions. Other mysterious figures like the Seven Nudes, the Just Black Judge, and Don Diego Duende (a *duende* is a spirit—frequently an evil spirit or goblin) appeared in the texts. Each of the pamphlets was illustrated with a line drawing of some kind, often of an articulated, living skeleton. All of the petitions had to do with gaining power over other people. Sometimes this was expressed in terms of making someone love the petitioner; other pamphlets merely spoke of power and domination in general terms.

Suspecting that these printed cards might be related to another comparatively recent arrival on the border—the drug trade—I sent copies of them to Arturo Carrillo Strong, author of *El Corrido de Co-caine,* a book of interviews with Sonora and Arizona *mafiosos.* (*Mafioso* is the popular word in regional Spanish for a person who is involved in the drug trade. It does not necessarily imply membership in the Mafia.) He took them to an ex-mafioso he knew, who recognized several and said that my hunch was correct. Men involved in the drug trade, he told Strong, are often very religious individuals. However, they know better than to ask God, the Virgin, and the Saints for help in such projects as defeating the opposition or ensuring the safe arrival of a drug shipment. They turn, rather, to the devil, who is reputed to look more favorably on that sort of activity.[51] Incidentally, I did not find similar material when I visited the fiesta in October 1990.

Magdalena serves not only as a focus for local belief and legend but as a point of contact between this region and the outside world. New ideas and devotions can and do enter by way of Magdalena's popular fiesta, which not only attracts people from the Pimería Alta but from many other parts of Mexico. Most of the pilgrims to Magdalena are from within this region; many of the people who provide them with services are from the outside world. And so Magdalena is the site for the continuation of a process of mediation between the regional and the international, a process that has been going on since Father Eusebio Francisco Kino started work here about three hundred years ago.

The painted frames I mentioned earlier can serve to illustrate one way in which this process of mediation functions. Local Magdalena artists create reverse paintings on glass using a technique which may well be related in some way to a middle-class craft that was popular in the mid-nineteenth-century United States. Into the frames they have created they insert commercially made holy pictures belonging to an international religious tradition—Roman Catholicism—and printed in Mexico City. At a fiesta dedicated to a purely local composite saint they sell these pictures to Tohono O'odham—descendants of the people Father Kino rode into this country to convert. And the O'odham take them back to their desert villages where they use them in a kind of Catholicism that is uniquely theirs. The next chapter will deal with this specifically Papago form of native Christianity and the places associated with it.

4. Native Christianities

West of Tucson, the desert stretches some two hundred miles to the Colorado River. The country consists of long, dry valleys running roughly northwest-southeast and separated by rugged mountain ranges. Normally these valleys contain dry washes; it is only after heavy summer rains that they run with water. As one moves westward, the mesquites, paloverdes, and saguaros of the Sonoran Desert gradually thin out as the country gets progressively drier. By the time one reaches the Colorado, little vegetation can be seen save scattered clumps of bursage and other hardy shrubs. Arizona Highway 86 crosses the first one hundred miles or so of this region, from Tucson to the old mining town of Ajo. For most of these miles, the highway takes the traveler through the Tohono O'odham Nation.

A typical old-time Papago lived in two Tohono O'odham villages over the course of the year. The winter village would be at a site in the hills, near some sort of year-round water source. This could be a dripping spring or a natural rock tank that would hold the precious fluid until the next rain. But no matter what its nature, there would always be some kind of reliable water to tide the villagers through the Sonoran Desert's dry season. In the summertime, villagers would move down into the valley flood plains, to the site of their "summer" or "field" village, and start preparing their fields. The rains would find them ready to take advantage of the runoff and its resulting sheet flooding of the valleys—flooding that was carefully managed by check dams and diversions of various kinds.[1]

Today the O'odham participate in a national economy, and very few of them farm in the old, labor-intensive way that made agriculture possible in this desert country for so many generations, but the villages remain—some set down on the flat, some nestled in the hills. Some that are not easily reachable by school busses have been abandoned. Others are occupied by only one or two people for most of the year. All the currently occupied villages are now supplied with deep wells, and the O'odham no longer have to move with the seasons.

No matter what their location, Tohono O'odham villages are decentralized affairs. Houses are often barely within sight of each other. The straight streets and contiguous houses that are one of Mexico's legacies from the Mediterranean world are not the ideal among the O'odham, who prefer to live at a distance from their nearest neighbors. Few villages have commercial buildings of any sort; most trading posts are on the roads, isolated from village life. A very few villages still have the traditional circular brush-covered houses where the annual saguaro wine ceremony takes place. Almost every village, however, does contain at least one building that is not used for domestic purposes. This building is a Catholic church or chapel.

Catholicism first came to the Papaguería in the fall of 1698, when Father Kino and his companion, Captain Diego Carrasco, accompanied by seven Indians, rode through the heart of the desert country, visiting several villages. Among them was the still important settlement of Gu Achi, or Santa Rosa Village, which Kino called Adid, and dedicated to San Francisco, his patron. Kino made several subsequent trips though the western deserts, establishing a pattern of occasional visits that continued for almost two centuries after his death as the standard form of contact on the desert between Tohono O'odham and missionaries.[2]

This was true with one exception. In a letter dated December 27, 1811, Father Fray Juan Bautista Llorenz, then stationed at San Xavier del Bac, reported that he had constructed a small chapel and house at the Papago village of Santa Ana Cuiquiburitac, which he describes as being eighteen or twenty leagues north of San Xavier "by a good road." He also reports having started work on digging a well there. At the time of his writing, the well was twenty-six *varas* (about seventy-two feet) deep and showed promise of producing water soon. The village exists today only as an archaeological site, having apparently been abandoned some time in the early nineteenth century. It is just off the northeast corner of Tohono O'odham Nation, south and west of Picacho Peak.[3]

Later in the nineteenth century, O'odham dug into the well at Cuiquiburitac and removed a copper baptismal font, which later came into the hands of the Reverend I. T. Whittemore, a Presbyterian missionary. He sent it to the Bureau of American Ethnology in Washington, D.C., around 1890. It is now in the collections of the Smithsonian Institution's Museum of American History. Traces of what might have been the chapel foundations mentioned by Father Llorenz were still visible on the ground in 1969. With the exception of this short-lived mission, a formal, sustained Roman Catholic presence among the O'odham had to wait until 1895. In that year, Franciscan missionaries arrived at St. Mary's Church in Phoenix and accepted the care of the Pimas and Papagos of southern Arizona. After first working with Pimas they became aware of the Desert People to the south of the Pima villages.

In 1908 Father Mathias Rechsteiner, O.F.M., visited the Papago village of Chuichu, some nine miles south of Casa Grande. He baptized twenty-five people, including the village chief. Later in the same year, he visited six more villages in a great loop from Casa Grande to Silverbell, baptizing, preaching, and saying Mass in each. In 1909 and 1910 he visited yet more villages, establishing missions and saying Mass. In 1911, while he was preparing to establish a more permanent presence on the desert, he underwent surgery in order to clear up a stomach complaint that had been troubling him. One evening before his scheduled surgery, he was visiting and drinking with fellow Franciscans in the refectory of St. Mary's Church, Phoenix. In the course of the evening, he confided to them his fears of not surviving the ordeal. They tried to "jolly" him out of his depression by planning his funeral in some detail with him. A few days later his companions were shocked to learn that the operation had not been successful and that he had died shortly thereafter. The funeral went exactly as he had planned it.[4]

The next Franciscan visitors to the Papaguería were destined to establish a long-term Catholic missionary presence on the desert. In 1911 Fathers Tiburtius Wand and Bonaventure Oblasser were sent on a reconnaissance trip over the course of which they visited fourteen villages. In 1912 the Papago Missions were formally awarded to the Order of Friars Minor and work began in earnest. The first mission church built on what is now Tohono O'odham Nation was in the village of Little Tucson—Ali Chukson—and dedicated to Our Lady of Lourdes in 1912. It still stands in the village, little changed from the time when it was constructed.

All in all, the Franciscans built thirty-six mission churches on the Papaguería between 1912 and 1976, the date of the dedication of the church at Kaka. Of these, thirty-five were in Arizona and one just across the border in Sonora. Three of the Arizona churches no longer stand, while one—in the former mining town of Ajo—has been converted to secular uses. An impressive body of architecture was thus created over the course of some sixty years, symbolic of deep changes that were then occurring among the Tohono O'odham.

Franciscan Churches and Chapels

Until about 1940, most of the decisions concerning the building of Roman Catholic churches on the Papago Reservation were made by the Franciscan missionaries and by members of the broad national Catholic community with whom they were in contact. Roman Catholicism is an international religion with two thousand years of tradition and its own legal system—Canon Law. Within the church there is a twofold division into ordained clergy and laity. The purpose of the clergy is to administer the seven sacraments to other Catholics. These sacraments are considered by the Church to have been instituted by Christ and to be necessary to a Christian life. Five of the sacraments, including the celebration of the Mass, which is a reenactment of the Last Supper of Jesus Christ and the central, unifying ritual of the Catholic Church, can only be performed by ordained priests. Whenever possible, the sacraments should be administered in a suitable building, erected especially for the purpose. Thus it was that, although Mass could be and often was celebrated in a private house or even in the open air with an automobile running board as an altar, building a church was—and still is—a goal of missionary priests.

Other motivations came into play as well. A church in a village could serve as a daily reminder of the Catholic faith and a focus for other community-strengthening activities. And it could help the missionary, surely engaged in one of the world's most frustrating jobs, feel that he was accomplishing something. But the real reason for the mission churches on the Papaguería, as it is for the existence of Catholic churches anywhere else, is that they are needed as settings for the Mass and the other sacraments.

Once a priest decided to build a church in a specific village, a decision that could be based on any number of factors, a suitable site within the village had to be selected. The older missions seem to have been built on the edges of the scattered villages rather than in a central location. In a few cases, missionaries obtained title to the land from the United States federal government under a law regarding the building of churches, which was on the books until the Indian Reorganization Act of 1934. Prior to that date, reservation Indians were given little say in matters concerning their welfare and destinies. This resulted from an attitude on the part of most influential Anglo Americans that the best course for Indians was to convert them as speedily as possible into productive, progress-oriented versions of idealized, mainstream American working and farming folk.

In other cases, mining companies or private individuals provided the necessary land. I gather that in at least a few instances, some sort of negotiation went on between the missionary and villagers, although such an activity is not outlined in the correspondence and publications concerning mission building.

Once a church was decided on, funds were obtained, usually from Catholic donors in the East or the Midwest. Such Catholic journals as *The Indian Sentinel,* produced quarterly by the Bureau of Catholic Indian Missions in Washington, D.C., ran advertisements soliciting funds for the general task of church building on Indian reservations. Articles written by missionaries and published in the same periodicals recounted successes, provided local color, and presumably whetted the enthusiasm of prospective donors. Every Catholic church is dedicated to a specific saint or member of the Holy Family. If a donor contributed enough money to build a church, it was customary to permit him or her to select the patron of that church. Back in Arizona, plans would be drawn up and a priest or lay brother would supervise construction of the church. Sometimes an outside contractor would be hired for this job. Labor would be supplied by the villagers, who would not be paid, but would be fed while they worked on the project. Building materials would usually be sun-dried adobes made on the spot and lumber, roofing paper, and hardware bought in Tucson or Phoenix and transported to the site by truck or wagon. For such furniture as benches, altar, and a church bell the missionaries relied on the generosity of Catholic congregations elsewhere. Church furnishings that had outlived their usefulness or had become unfashionable in their original sites can still be found gracing the mission churches of the Papaguería.

Like so many processes here on the desert, this missionary reliance on the charity of congregations in more settled areas seems to have its depth in time. The mid-eighteenth-century visita church at Oquitoa, Sonora, is a simple rectangular structure. Until the 1930s, it contained an elaborate, early baroque *retablo* or altarpiece. Made of gilded wood and set with oil paintings, this elaborate piece succumbed to termites and the ravages of time around 1940 and is only known to us through photographs. It appears to date from the mid-seventeenth century, however, and it seems highly improbable that it was made for this specific Sonoran church or village. A more logical scenario is that it was made for a church somewhere in central Mexico. Here it probably remained until the eighteenth century when it was replaced by a more fashionable and up-to-date retablo. At that time it found its way to an Indian mission on the frontier. In much the same way, the mission church of Saint Clare at Anegam (built in 1918 under the direction of Father Tiburtius Wand) possessed until recently an elaborate carved wooden neogothic altarpiece that was undoubtedly a "hand-me-down" from some Eastern church.[5]

So it was that the missionaries, guided by Catholic tradition and Canon Law, funded by pious Catholics in other parts of the country, and fueled by their own zeal, enthusiasm, and resourcefulness, constructed a chain of churches in the Papaguería. Many of these buildings still stand. In appearance they owe much to the Mission Revival style of architecture. This style was developed as a regional California architectural style in the 1880s and 1890s, taking its spirit and some of its details from the Spanish mission churches and outbuildings that dotted that state. Characteristics of the style include scalloped gable ends, often containing round or star-shaped windows, great expanses of plain stucco, tiled roofs, attached bell towers, and long arcades. The Mission Revival style was used for all sorts of public buildings as well as for private homes. It reached Phoenix and Tucson just after the turn of the century, so that by the time the Franciscans started building their churches, it was available as a regional model.

Taking details from this style, as well as from the actual California missions themselves, the Franciscan Fathers built their mission churches. By doing so, they made an architectural statement to the effect that they were following in the footsteps of the Spanish missionaries, Jesuit and Franciscan, who had preceded them in Arizona, Sonora, and California. Even the plainer buildings seem to owe what decorative details they possess to the missions of California.

One group of people seems to have been rather left out of the whole process of decision making—the Papago Indians for whom the churches were built. This situation held true until 1934 and the passage of the Indian Reorganization Act, which changed the rules under which things were done on Indian reservations. After that date, Franciscans acted more and more in response to needs that were felt and expressed by the O'odham villagers themselves, and building churches became a much more cooperative venture.

An Early Franciscan Mission Church

One of the earliest of the Franciscan mission churches, Saint Augustine's Mission, still stands in the village of Chuichu (Many Caves), a few miles south of Casa Grande, on the northern edge of Tohono

O'odham Nation. This Mission Revival church was built under the direction of Father Tiburtius Wand, O.F.M., with the actual work being done by villagers and supervised by two professional Mexican-American builders from Casa Grande. It was dedicated on January 29, 1914, by the Right Reverend Henry Granjon, Bishop of Tucson. I have visited it several times over the past twenty years; the following description is based on notes taken on November 8, 1989.

The church, surrounded by a small, fenced yard, faces east in the middle of a cleared space. The east end of the church has a scalloped gable rising to a rounded peak. A wooden cross stands at the top of the gable, directly above the central door. Attached to the southeast corner of the facade is a narrow bell tower. Recently added buttresses, each pierced by a window, flank the facade. The door is of carved wood; it and the wrought-iron lamp brackets flanking it were probably purchased in Phoenix or Tucson. The entire church is covered with a fresh coat of white paint.

Behind the church and slightly to the north are a kitchen and serving area. Next to these is what appears to be a combination basketball court and dance floor, with a small, one-walled ramada to one side.

The interior of the church looks much like that of any small Roman Catholic church in a relatively poor neighborhood in the Southwest. Rows of benches rest on the tiled floor, with a central aisle leading to the sanctuary, which is raised a few inches above the level of the nave. Two candles sit on the white cloth covering a wrought-iron altar table in the middle of the sanctuary. A sign proclaiming (with a lightbulb as a rebus for the word "light") that "Faith in God Makes You the Light of the World" hangs in front of the altar. Four pots of chrysanthemums stand on the floor in front of the altar.

Behind the altar, ranged along the back and side walls of the sanctuary, are several pedestals bearing representations of saints and members of the Holy Family. From south to north these include: Saint Anthony,[6] the Blessed Kateri Tekakwitha (a Christian Algonquin Indian woman who lived in the seventeenth century and whose cause for sainthood is being put through the formal process in Rome),[7] the Sacred Heart of Jesus,[8] and the Blessed Virgin Mary. Each pedestal is decorated with real or artificial flowers. A bench

74

stands against the head wall directly behind the altar table; above it is a framed mural depicting the Crucifixion. The head wall of a Catholic church is located at the end of the church opposite the doorway. This expression originates in the Medieval concept of a church as representing the body of the crucified Christ, with the altar as the head.

On a table in the north side of the sanctuary are a tabernacle, statues of the Virgin and the Holy Child of Atocha,[9] and a small processional arch covered with paper flowers. Arches such as this, made of branches that have been peeled and bent into shape, covered with white cloth, and decorated with ribbons and paper flowers, are a common sight in the churches and chapels of the Papaguería. Their use and possible meanings will be discussed later.

This church is in my experience typical of the Franciscan-built missions on Tohono O'odham Nation. Similar to most Catholic churches, it nevertheless stands out in several ways. It is unlikely that a non-Indian parish would have a depiction of the Blessed Kateri Tekakwitha, for instance. On the other hand, she is popular among Native American Catholics throughout the United States and Canada, many of whom look forward eagerly to her eventual canonization. This act would result in the addition of a specifically Indian saint to the Catholic calendar.[10]

There are more artificial flowers in the church at Chuichu, especially those that are homemade of paper, than I would expect to see even at a Mexican or Mexican-American church. The processional arch is also a bit uncommon to see in a church belonging to a mainstream congregation. Outside, the presence of the facilities for public cooking, feasting, and dancing also set this mission church off from the run-of-the-mill parish churches. To understand the meaning of many of these distinctive details, one would have to go back in time to the middle of the last century, long before the days when Father Matthias made his first visits to the Papaguería.

O'odham Folk Chapels

Curiously enough, Father Matthias found chapels in place at many of the O'odham villages when he first arrived on the Papaguería.

These were not built by missionaries but rather by the Indians them-selves for use in what some writers have called "Sonoran Catholic-ism" or "Papago folk Catholicism." This religion, which seems to have been developed over time by O'odham in Arizona and Sonora, can perhaps best be described as a form of native Christianity—a complex but unified religious system built from elements taken from both European and Native-American concepts and practices and combined in a unique way. Papago native Christianity is unique to the Tohono O'odham. Like other traditional belief systems, it is a constantly developing and evolving set of ideas and practices. Pa-pago Native Christianity is actually the sum total of the beliefs held by members of the culture, rather than a strictly codified set of "rules" that are followed by everyone.

Within O'odham culture, this system is called "God Way" (*Jios himdag*) or "Saint Way" (*santo himdag*). It seems to have entered Pa-pago culture in the third quarter of the nineteenth century. Mexicans and Christianized O'odham in both Sonora and Arizona were prob-ably the major sources for this creed, which appears for the most part to be based on kinds of observable Catholic ritual behavior that have been integrated into what is basically an O'odham system for preserving balance and health in families and communities. The chapel, often called a "Sonoran" or "folk" chapel by non-O'odham writers, is central to the practice of santo himdag.[11]

Although there is no written account of the process by which santo himdag became a part of Tohono O'odham culture, it appears to have happened during the last century, in Sonora. Tohono O'od-ham had been exposed to Catholic beliefs and practices through missionary visits to the desert, as well as at the missions of Arizona and Sonora. The Desert People were and are highly mobile and dur-ing times of little rain in their own country would visit the settled communities on the edges of the desert in search of food and em-ployment. It seems likely that Catholic practices seen on such visits provided the foundations for what developed into santo himdag.

The easiest way to understand santo himdag as it is reflected in the religious architecture of Tohono O'odham Nation is to visit an O'odham chapel. The chapel I have chosen is in the tiny village of Shopishk, "Place of the Pass," a few miles southeast of Chuichu.

The chapel at Shopishk faces east, inside a fenced yard or atrio.[12] Outside the atrio, to the east of the church, is a low, whitewashed pedestal with a square hole in its top. On feast days, this pedestal supports a wooden cross that at other times is kept inside the church. To the southeast of the church, within the atrio, is an open-air dance floor measuring approximately twenty-five feet on each side. A small, three-sided shelter faces the floor on its west side; the other three sides are lined with wooden benches. In the center of the floor is a tall pole with overhead wires running from it to the tops of shorter poles set around the edge of the floor. On November 8, 1989, these wires were hung with orange and black paper streamers. An ornate wooden cross sits atop the central pole. A stack of mesquite wood and a shallow firepit are outside the atrio to the south, and there are low ridges of ashes under the benches. East of the dance floor are a large bread oven, an outdoor kitchen surrounded by a high wall, and an indoor dining room. All the buildings and many of the posts in the atrium are painted a brilliant, fresh-looking white.

The chapel itself is a small building with transepts and a pitched, gabled roof. It is painted white, with a dark red gable. A white wooden cross decorated with a wreath of many-colored, homemade paper flowers sits at the peak of the gable, over the door on the east end. It is less than half the size of the church at Chuichu.

The first thing I noticed upon entering the Shopishk chapel was an altar table set out from the head wall, bearing a reclining statue of San Francisco. The plaster statue was about three feet long and was dressed in electric blue robes over a white undergarment. Behind this table, the entire head wall of the building was taken up with a three-foot-high altar shelf, covered with a blue cloth. On this shelf were seven smaller reclining San Franciscos dressed in brown robes, and several other statues, including the Sacred Heart of Jesus, Our Lady of Guadalupe,[13] and St. Martin of Porres.[14] Also on the altar were candles and vases of artificial flowers.

The head wall was covered with white wallpaper patterned with red and orange flowers and green leaves. The top and sides of the wall were framed with a row of paper flowers and leaves; vertical rows of similar flowers divided the wall into seven columns. In the center column were two crosses and a head of Christ; the others were symmetrically filled with arrangements of holy pictures. Most of these come from Magdalena and are enclosed in painted glass frames. Thirty-five framed pictures in all hung on the wall, and several more rested on the altar. This profusion of sacred images presented a striking contrast to the relatively few, large statues in the mission church at Chuichu.

A processional arch similar to, but larger than, the one at Chuichu rested against the north wall next to the altar; a portable altar table that can be used for Mass stood against the same wall. The north transept was used for storage; it contained a white wooden cross decorated with a wreath of paper flowers and a similarly adorned carrying litter. The cross is apparently the one which is set on the pedestal to the east of the chapel on feast days; the litter is probably used to carry the reclining San Francisco statue in processions.

Folk chapels like this are not just smaller reproductions of the mission churches. The two sets of buildings have been constructed for use in two related but distinct religious systems: Roman Catholicism and *santo himdag*, or O'odham folk Catholicism. Differences and similarities between these two systems are directly reflected in the buildings we have been examining. [15]

Uses of the Chapels

Many of the features of the man-made landscape that surround the chapel at Shopishk are related to activities that take place on feast days. Religious feasts usually begin with a procession, which leaves the church or chapel door, travels to the cross located to the east of the chapel, and returns to the chapel. In the processions I have witnessed, most of the holy images from the church are brought out and carried by villagers, along with the image of the specific sacred individual in whose honor the feast is being held. Arches covered with paper flowers are also carried in the procession.

These arches are often called "rainbows." The symbolism involved here may be more complex than one would at first imagine.

The rainbow appears in the Old Testament as a sign of God's promise that never again would He send a flood to cover the whole earth. However, rainbows are also potent symbols of rain in a desert country and as such are carried by participants in traditional, non-Catholic O'odham ceremonies. In the *chelkona* dance mentioned in chapter 2, the young men carry images of large white birds, and the young women carry semi-circular or triangular cloud symbols, often embellished with lightning streaks. And in the *wi:gida,* a now-defunct ceremony that used to be held at Santa Rosa Village, "floats" representing landscape features and natural phenomena were carried in a procession. Rain imagery also appears in O'odham sacred song poetry.[16] Like so many images and activities of O'odham Christianity, the rainbow symbol carries with it complex meanings that reflect both the European and the native roots of this religious system. Singing sacred songs in Spanish, the procession moves eastward from the chapel door to the cross, which is frequently decorated for the occasion with a wreath of paper flowers. Here the people pause. This is often a time for each individual to establish a personal relationship with each of the holy objects that has been carried out. From the cross, which is often called in English the "field cross," the procession moves back into the church or chapel.

At some time after the procession takes place, often in the late afternoon, a band will start playing in the small, three-sided shelter next to the dance floor. The dance area will have been decorated for the occasion with paper streamers that are hung from and wrapped around the overhead wires. The typical band that plays at village feasts consists entirely of males. Instruments include a saxophone and an accordion, an electric guitar and electric bass, and a full drum set. The musicians tune up and start playing from a repertoire of polkas, two-steps, and *cumbias*. This latter rhythm is a Caribbean dance rhythm that evolved in Colombia and has been a part of the standard Border Mexican repertoire for the last forty years. It has been played by O'odham musicians for almost that long. Traditionally, there were different tunes assigned to different times in the all-night dance, so that one set of melodies is played before midnight, others after that hour, and still another at dawn. From conversations with older musicians, I get the impression that these conventions are not being followed as strictly as they were a generation or so ago, around World War II.

The generic term in O'odham for this dance music is *waila,* which derives from the Spanish *baile,* or "social dance." Waila can refer to the whole genre of O'odham dance music, or to the specific rhythm of the polka. The English term "Chicken Scratch" has a certain degree of currency, especially among Pima Indians on the Gila and Salt River reservations and among Anglo Americans. Some Tohono O'odham with whom I have discussed the term, however, feel it to be derogatory and prefer to use the native term.[17]

What I have described is the contemporary waila instrumentation, which has been popular since the 1950s. The older traditional Tohono O'odham dance band consists of two violins as melody instruments, with rhythm provided by a guitar, a snare drum played by one man, and a bass drum played by another. Like the modern waila bands, these groups play strictly instrumental music. Although they have been replaced to a great extent by the modern waila bands, the fiddle-based orchestras are still heard occasionally at festivals and dances on and off the reservation.

The dances traditionally last all night, until dawn. In recent years, some musicians have begun to play only until midnight or shortly after. To a large extent this is due to the fact that bootleg beer and liquor are sold and consumed at the dances in great quantities, even though most of the districts of Tohono O'odham Nation have elected to be "dry." Heavy drinking at the all-night dances results all too frequently in sudden death in fights and automobile accidents.

One detail regarding the dance area remains to be explained: The long piles of ashes under the benches. These are to keep the spectators warm while they sit through the sometimes chilly night hours. A fire is kept burning in the firepit near the dance floor, and from time to time a man will bring a shovel full of hot coals and scatter them gently in a row under or just behind the benches. I have visited abandoned O'odham villages where the dance floor was of packed earth and the benches had long since fallen apart or been carted away. The edges of the dance area could still be traced by the slight discoloration produced by the lines of ashes where the benches had been.

Behind the dance floor stands the feast complex. This almost always includes a walled, open-air kitchen with large wood-burning stoves of adobe. These are really raised firepits, built to hold huge stew pots with mesquite coals under them. In or near the kitchen is a large, wood-burning bake oven. The one at Shopishk is made of cement blocks; many that I have seen are of adobe bricks. An indoor dining room attached to the kitchen contains one or more long tables lined with benches. Here all comers will be fed without charge in shifts, beginning in the afternoon and continuing all through the night.

The food that is served at these village feasts is the basic traditional Mexican diet of northern Sonora.[18] Beef stewed in red chile has been a staple in this country since long before Father Ignaz Pfefferkorn, S.J., tasted it in the 1750s and thought that his mouth was full of hell-fire.[19] One or more beeves are slaughtered for a typical feast in order to provide the meat for this most important of fiesta dishes. The bones left over from making the chile stew are cooked up with various vegetables to provide the other basic meat dish prepared for feasts. Menudo, a soup of tripe cooked with hominy, may be served as well. Pinto beans, another loan item from Mexican culture, completes the list of hot dishes. Wheat bread from the wood-burning oven is served, along with wheat flour tortillas. Wheat used to be an important crop in the Papaguería through the first decades of the twentieth century. Coffee rounds out the Mexican portion of the standard feast menu.

Several feast foods have been borrowed from Anglo-American culture. Foremost among these is potato salad. Eaten with very hot chile stew, it is a totally unique taste sensation and a real contribution to the local cuisine. Some sort of prepared, sweetened fruit-based drink like Kool-Aid or Hawaiian Punch is likely to be served. The feast often ends with a fresh or canned fruit salad and a cake, complete with icing.

What is striking about this folk Catholic feast menu is that it usually consists solely of imported foods. Some wild native foods are still found in the Tohono O'odham diet, particularly those derived from various kinds of cactus. These seldom if ever appear at the feasts. Christian occasions are celebrated by serving and consuming "Christian" foods. In addition, anthropologist Donald Bahr has suggested that this menu gives O'odham the feeling of "being out on the town."[20]

Although Mass is often said nowadays in chapels such as the one at Shopishk, the primary use of chapels is for prayer and rosary sessions. These are led by one or more selected individuals, with hymns alternating with the prayers. Traditionally both rosary and songs are in Spanish, although nowadays they can also be heard in English or O'odham, depending on the knowledge and preferences of the people who are leading the ritual. A priest always visits the village to say Mass on the morning of the feast day. However, it is the procession that follows Mass that seems to start things off from an O'odham point of view. Feasting starts as soon as the procession is over, and the priests and any Anglos who may have accompanied them are fed in the first shift. These outsiders usually leave soon after eating; the rosary sessions led by O'odham will continue through much of the afternoon and evening.

The other major use of the chapels is more passive; they are places in which holy images are kept safe. Many, if not all, of the holy images in the Shopishk chapel were obtained in Magdalena. These images are the property of individual families. After being purchased, they have been charged with San Francisco's spiritual power by having been rubbed over his statue in the Magdalena church, or by having been placed next to that statue for a period of time. Once so charged, they are brought back to the village and put through a ceremony designed to align their power with the needs of the village and villagers. This done, they serve to help keep the health of the villagers and their livestock as it should be. Some of these images are kept on home altars, and others are brought to the village chapel. After a number of years they may be taken back to Magdalena and "recharged" with power by being placed next to San Francisco once more.

Many of the accumulations of holy pictures on the walls behind Tohono O'odham folk altars are arranged in vertical rows, separated from each other by rows of artificial flowers. This may be a reflection of the vertical arrangements of statues and paintings often found on Spanish colonial baroque altarpieces, or *retablos*. Such retablos exist at San Xavier and at Tubutama, in the Altar Valley of Sonora. A similar retablo stood at Oquitoa until the 1930s. Both Tubutama and Oquitoa were on the fringes of Papago country until the end of the last century; the San Xavier community has remained as an O'odham village. In each of these retablos, vertical rows of statues or paintings are separated by columns or other vertical units on which flowers are carved. These or similar retablos may well have provided the original inspiration for the arrangement of the head walls of the O'odham folk chapels.

There is one more significant difference between the mission churches and the folk chapels. Until recently, the church at Chuichu remained much as it had been when it was dedicated in 1914. This is by and large true of the other mission churches, which were built in a single campaign of several months' or years' duration. Following their completion and dedication, they were maintained pretty much as they were. Some were enlarged in subsequent building campaigns as the congregation grew through conversion or population increase. Some burned down or had their roofs blown off in high winds and were rebuilt. All were remodeled in the late 1960s to accommodate the changes in the celebration of the Mass as mandated by the Second Vatican Council, known popularly as Vatican II. The change that most affected church buildings was the one decreeing that the priest should say Mass facing the people rather than facing an altar placed against the head wall of the church, as had been previously the case. The altars of the mission churches were entirely removed and replaced by free-standing tables; those in the O'odham folk chapels remain, with an altar table often added so that Mass can be said.

In this way, the appearance of the mission churches changed in response to major stimuli: parish growth, natural disasters, a change in the rules for saying Mass. As a general rule, however, if one wants to see what sort of building the Franciscans were erecting as a Papago mission in the 1920s, one can learn much from a careful examination of standing churches that were erected during that period. In the field of architectural history, one assumes that most buildings erected during a certain period may be treated as documents from that period. In the same way I will use San Xavier del Bac in a later chapter to provide an understanding of the aesthetic principles underlying the eighteenth-century baroque style in New Spain.

The rules are different in the case of the Tohono O'odham chapels. I first realized this in the early 1970s when I paid repeated visits to most of the reservation's sixty-odd churches and chapels over the course of four years. I discovered that, while the mission churches remained the same year after year, many of the O'odham chapels seemed to change on a fairly regular basis. I would find that fresh paint had been applied, a new tower had been built, or that transepts had been added. In several cases the entire building had been replaced. For example, in 1971 I visited Kohatk (Where a hollow has been made), a village northwest of Santa Rosa; its chapel was built on a simple hall plan, with a rounded gable end over the facade. Over the next four years a tower was added, and the gable was made more elaborate. In the late 1970s and early 1980s transepts were added to the chapel building, a small, free-standing nicho was built next to the chapel, an additional field cross was erected about one hundred yards to the south of the building, and the entire complex was given a coat of white paint. And this is not an isolated example. When I visit one of the folk chapels after an absence of several years, I automatically look to see if changes have been made somewhere in the chapel complex.

It appears, therefore, that one of the real differences between Franciscan churches and O'odham chapels involves what happens to them after they are constructed. In conversations with O'odham, I got the impression that one of the ways in which one can prepare a chapel for the annual or biennial village feast is to change it in some way. The change is at times fairly drastic; I know several chapels that were actually replaced in the course of a year or two. In several cases, the new chapel was larger or more elegant; in one case, the new building seemed to be a carbon copy of the old one except that it was made of new materials.

Do any other traditional Tohono O'odham religious structures seem to be treated in this way? The answer seems to be "yes." Every four years, the ocotillo stalks of the Children's Shrine are replaced, and the stones in the central pile are taken out, cleaned, and put back. The great ceremony of the wi:gida, which used to be held every four years near Santa Rosa Village, required the construction of special temporary architectural features. Some shrines are "used" by augmenting or adding to them. A pile of rocks on the road between the village of Sil Nakya and State Highway 86 marks the place where a ceremonial runner dropped dead. Every time I have driven past it with O'odham, we have stopped the car and my companions have gotten out and added a stone to the pile "to make the trip easy."[21] The shrine, like others in the Papaguería, is also a place where gifts and offerings are left. (When I visited the shrine in November 1989, these offerings included cassette tapes, bits of an old saddle, full and empty beer bottles, and even pieces of ritual dance equipment.) It appears that a pattern of using ceremonial structures and places by ritually renewing or in some way adding to them exists in other parts of traditional Tohono O'odham culture.

When one steps back a bit from both bodies of religious architecture and describes them in general terms, this is what one finds. On the one hand are the Roman Catholic churches: buildings associated with an international, highly bureaucratized religion. The internal arrangement reflects the major purpose of these structures, to provide settings in which one or more religious specialists—priests—perform ceremonies in the presence of a more or less passive body of people—the congregation. The space around the altar serves to emphasize it as a place where things happen. The benches facing the altar ensure that the focus of attention remains on the altar and the priest. The buildings were built by outsiders to serve as penetration points in the villages. The decisions concerning their construction were made outside of the village. When repairs were needed, the funds and impetus to make them were provided by the missionaries.

The chapels, on the other hand, seem to be quite different in purpose. They are built and maintained by the villagers themselves specifically for O'odham uses. They exist within elaborate, patterned architectural settings. Chapels always face east, while the missions can—and do—face in all four cardinal directions. The chapels are invariably accompanied by a field cross, a dance floor and orchestra house, and a feasting complex. Although these features are shared by many mission churches, they are later additions to the structures originally built by the Franciscans. Furthermore, while the churches are buildings designed as settings for the performance of complex rituals involving trained, consecrated "foreign" professionals as well as the general public, the chapels serve a different purpose. Prayers are indeed said in them—rosary sessions involving specialists selected from within the community. But beyond that, the chapels function as safe places for storage of holy objects, which are sources of protective power for the village.

One possible description of the O'odham chapels, therefore, goes something like this: They are small buildings designed to contain holy objects that possess considerable spiritual power and which are used to protect and maintain the health of the community. They are also the settings for rituals that involve and are led by members of the community. Around them are a series of architectural features designed to accommodate ritual processions, music making, feasting, and dancing. And one of the ways in which they are used is that they are renewed on a more or less regular calendrical basis.

This certainly sounds Indian rather than European. In fact, it sounds highly reminiscent of the temple structures of pre-Columbian Mesoamerica. Aztec temples, for instance, had relatively small indoor spaces that contained powerful cult statues. Outside the structures, in elaborate architectural settings, priests and populace danced, sang, marched in processions, feasted, and performed public rites, which, in the case of the Aztecs, included human sacrifice.

O'odham are not and never have been Aztecs, of course, but they are culturally related to Central Mexican people and belong with them to the Uto-Aztecan language family. The relationships between this region and Central Mexico suggested by Di Peso and discussed briefly in chapter 1 provide a possible Mesoamerican connection. The peoples whom we call Hohokam, who lived for several hundred years in the regions now occupied by the Desert and River O'odham, apparently had ceremonies that were derived from Central Mexico. These included the use of what appear to be courts for the great Mesoamerican ritual ballgame, and earth platforms, presumably with ceremonial buildings on top of them. The relation-ships, if any, between the archaeological Hohokam and the living O'odham have not been settled to the satisfaction of most archae-ologists. Until they are, we are left with the option of informed speculation. Included among the possible speculations is the pos-sibility that, as they pursue their traditional folk Catholicism, the Tohono O'odham may be keeping faith with a very ancient part of their heritage indeed.

As I said earlier, santo himdag was a part of Tohono O'odham culture when the Franciscan missionaries started visiting the Papa-guería around 1910. Although santo himdag is really quite different from Roman Catholicism in form and intent, there are also strong similarities between the material objects and observable practices employed by the two related systems. These similarities, including the building of chapels, the accumulation of Catholic holy pictures, and the use of the cross as a symbol, led the newly arrived mission-aries to make assumptions which were not altogether warranted.

The missionaries, being accustomed to a system in which the priest was obeyed without question in all matters connected with religion, and under the impression that they were dealing with Ro-man Catholic Indians who operated under the same basic "rules" that they did, were not prepared to meet with indifference and even resistance from the same people who had erected and maintained what appeared to be Catholic chapels. Many of the O'odham were not interested in the discipline and direction brought by the priests. Thus in some villages there developed a tragicomic scenario in which both missionaries and O'odham believed that they were the "real Catholics," and the other group in some way aberrant. In these villages, discomfort and even hostility developed between the Franciscans and some of the more conservative followers of santo himdag.

This situation is commented on in missionary correspondence and publications in the period leading up to 1930—a period in which the Franciscans referred to the more intransigent of the O'od-ham Catholics as "Montezumas"—a term whose precise derivation seems lost in the mists of time, although it may be connected with the Western Papago name for I'itoi mentioned in chapter 2. Apparently, some older O'odham maintained that the Franciscans were not "real Catholics" because they wore robes different from the cassocks worn by Mexican priests, had light-colored hair and eyes, and spoke English. For their part, some of the Franciscans, being accustomed to absolute authority in church matters, behaved in ways that were not easy for the O'odham to understand. The story was still being told by missionaries in the 1970s of a Franciscan priest who decided that one of the folk chapels in which he occasionally said Mass was "too cluttered" and who proceeded to clear out all the saints' images except those he thought were suitable.[22]

Times changed, and by the 1970s most of the Franciscan churches and many of the folk chapels showed signs of adaptation to use by both systems. St. Augustine's Church at Chuichu has a feast complex and a basketball court that can also serve as a dance floor, while the chapel at Shopishk has an altar table that can be moved out into the middle of the building when a priest arrives to say Mass. Most of the mission churches I have visited since 1970 have similar accommodations to folk-Catholic needs. An example of this blending of traditions may be seen at the mission church dedicated to St. Clare at Anegam (Desert Willow), just north of Santa Rosa, in the great central valley of Tohono O'odham Nation.

The church at Anegam was built in 1918, at a total cost of $3,200—a cost which included construction of a day school next to the church building. Church and school have changed little in external appearance since their dedication, except that the steeply pitched roof that was originally on the church has been replaced by a roof with a gentler slope. Franciscan oral tradition has it that these "snow roofs," of which there were several on the Papago Reservation, were the work of a German carpenter from the Upper Midwest who simply built the way he was accustomed to in his home region. A cement dance floor now stands to the east of the atrio, and the old school building has been converted into a feast house.

When I visited the church at Anegam in 1972, the most striking feature of the interior was an elaborate neogothic altarpiece, doubtless given more than fifty years earlier by a parish that wanted to help the Indian missions. It stood directly behind the altar table against the head wall. Flanking it were two small tables, each of which held Magdalena holy pictures. Over the northern table was a poster-sized black-and-white photograph of Father Bonaventure Oblasser. Father Bonaventure was an important presence in Papago country from his arrival in 1911 until his final departure in the 1940s. He learned the language and was instrumental in establishing the districts into which Tohono O'odham Nation is divided. It is fair to say that at one point, he knew and was known by every Tohono O'odham on the reservation. He died in 1967 and is buried at Topawa, on the reservation, at one of the missions he founded. He is remembered among the Tohono O'odham as Father Ventura. It was a moving experience to see his photograph on the wall five years after his death.

I visited Anegam again in November of 1989. The wooden altarpiece was gone, as was Father Ventura's portrait. A picture of Blessed Kateri Tekakwitha hung in the church. Paper flowers and Magdalena holy pictures were still in evidence, and a three-foot-long statue of San Francisco rested on a table. There were other signs of remodeling: the bell tower had been rebuilt since my last visit and the whole church had a new paint job inside and out.

So it seems that in the case of this particular missionary-built church, a lasting compromise had been reached by the early 1970s between O'odham and Roman Catholic needs. Another kind of compromise may be seen in the plan of the chapel that was constructed in 1971 and 1972 at the village of Gu Vo (Big Pond). There had already been a long history of chapels at this village. In 1971 there were two chapels in use, each owned by a specific family. The chapel now in use was built to replace these two and serve the entire village.

While this chapel's Mission Revival exterior was similar in appearance to many others in the Papaguería, its interior plan was innovative in the extreme. Rather than a single head wall at the end of the nave, the building was arranged so as to have a split head wall. To the left was a Roman Catholic altar, complete with crucifix, candles, and statues of the Virgin and the Sacred Heart of Jesus. To the right, in an alcove created by the construction of a sacristy behind the head wall of the Roman Catholic portion of the chapel, was a typical O'odham folk altar complete with a large collection of holy pictures from Magdalena. The ceiling over both altar areas was hung with paper flowers; paper flowers separated the head wall of the folk altar into vertical rows. Thus the O'odham designers and builders of the new chapel at Gu Vo were able to articulate within the space of their building the differences between the two forms of Catholicism then prevalent in their community.

Funds for the construction had been obtained by the villagers from the Save the Children Foundation, a national benevolent organization interested in assisting the development of economically depressed communities. This marked a new stage in O'odham—Franciscan relations regarding chapel buildings. In the early years of the missionaries' presence in the Papaguería, both O'odham and Franciscans constructed their own religious buildings with little or no input from the other group. In the period from 1930 to 1950, the Franciscans seem to have been treated as an important economic resource by the O'odham. A committee would approach the missionary and request help with church construction. Plans would be drawn up by the priest and discussed in community meetings. O'odham would provide the labor, the missionary would attempt to provide most, if not all, of the materials. In the case of the Gu Vo chapel, however, funds came from elsewhere, and a missionary stationed in a nearby village remarked to me that he suspected that the only way in which he would be asked to participate in the project would be when time came for the dedication of the building.[23]

There are more than sixty mission churches and O'odham chapels on the reservation. Each has its own history, its features that set it apart from the rest: the oldest church on the reservation at Ali Chukson, the church at Sil Nakya with its strawberry-red pediment, the strikingly modern church at Kaka, the turquoise, white, and pink chapel at Palo Verde Stands, the chapel at San Luis near Cababi with its three crosses on an interrupted pediment, and the absolutely lovely little chapel at Pioik. Each of these buildings adds in its own way to the beauty and fascination of this particular part of the world.

One day in the early 1980s I took a drive with naturalist Gary Nabhan across the west-central part of the Papago Reservation. We visited Chuichu, Shopishk, Santa Rosa, Kaka, and other villages in

The San Francisco Xavier chapel, Palo Verde Stands, Papago Indian Reservation. This chapel was erected in the 1970s, replacing a tiny building whose twin towers suggested that it might have been modelled after the mission at Caborca or San Xavier. This is one of the most recently built O'odham chapels I am aware of to have a mission revival facade. Photo by James S. Griffith, November 1989.

the course of a beauty-filled July day on the desert. Around midday, we visited a friend of Gary's in a tiny settlement just north of Santa Rosa Village. Upon leaving the friend's house, we walked back to our car, which was parked near his family chapel. This minuscule building measured about ten by fifteen feet. It was made of sun-

Altar of the San Francisco Xavier chapel, Palo Verde Stands,
Papago Indian Reservation. Many of the pictures and statues
on the altar were purchased in Magdalena. The pictures
flanking the central cross have painted glass frames like
the ones discussed in the text. Photo by James S. Griffith,
November 1989.

dried adobe bricks and plastered over with mud. A plain wooden
cross stood atop the brush and dirt roof. A small, circular, cement
dance floor occupied the ground directly in front of the chapel door.
Looking west past the chapel, we could see a summer storm sweep-
ing across the valley toward us. It was so beautiful that we stood
there for several minutes, drinking it in.

The churches and chapels of the Papaguería embody a history of contact between two worlds. Out of the earlier years of this contact has come a new entity—santo himdag, or Tohono O'odham Catholicism. It is a dynamic, living part of a dynamic, living culture. If the Catholicism brought by the missionaries has been modified to suit O'odham needs, so has santo himdag changed in the years since Father Matthias first visited Chuichu. One of the resources for tracing these changes, frictions, and accommodations is the religious architecture of Tohono O'odham Nation.

Yaqui Chapels

Another form of native Christianity is practiced in Arizona's five Yaqui communities: Guadalupe just south of Tempe, Yoem Pueblo in Marana, Pascua Pueblo to the south and west of Tucson, and Old Pascua and the 39th Street community in Tucson itself. The Yaqui homeland isn't in Arizona but rather some three hundred miles south of the International Border along the banks of Sonora's Rio Yaqui. Here the Yaquis, who call themselves *Yoeme,* or "the people," were living at the time of the first Spanish expedition to Sonora, which took place in the year 1533. This was a slave-raiding foray that entered Yaqui lands against the wishes of the Yaquis and got soundly beaten in the ensuing battle. This set the pattern for contacts between Yaquis and Spaniards for almost a century during which time Spanish expeditions would arrive at the borders of Yaqui country and be met and defeated by Yaquis. This state of affairs continued until the early seventeenth century when the Yaquis broke the pattern by requesting that missionary priests be sent them. Accordingly, the Jesuit Fathers Andres Perez de Ribas and Tomás Basilio arrived on the Rio Yaqui in 1617, to an enthusiastic welcome on the part of their Yaqui hosts. Contemporary Yaqui Native Christianity is the end result of the complex cultural processes thus set into motion.[24]

Time passed, the Jesuits were expelled from New Spain, and eventually New Spain became the Republic of Mexico. The late nineteenth century saw a renewal of outside pressures on the Yaqui sacred homeland. The Yaquis responded as they always had, by asserting the integrity of their land by force, if necessary. The Mexican government, viewing the Yaquis as fanatical savages standing in the way of progress, decided upon a policy of Yaqui genocide. Many Yaquis were killed; others were shipped off as slave labor to the henequin plantations of Yucatán. Still others fled to the United States. These last became the founders of today's Arizona Yaqui colonies.

Once settled in Arizona, the Yaquis cautiously began to revive their rich, native Christian ceremonial life, which had been impossible to pursue in Sonora. Over time, small chapels were built, and the ceremonies which the Yaquis reintroduced in their new home began to draw the interest of anthropologists and other non-Yaquis. Some of these ceremonies—notably the ones that take place during Lent and Holy Week—came to be regarded as important contributions to local culture. In 1989 the Lenten and Easter Ceremony was held in four Arizona villages: Pascua Pueblo, 39th Street, Old Pascua, and Guadalupe. Other community and household ceremonies are held at these same villages and at Yoem Pueblo in Marana over the course of each year.

The setting for the community ceremonies, including the Lenten and Holy Week Passion drama and fiestas, is the Yaqui church. Just as the O'odham chapels are tangible statements concerning O'odham himdag, so the Yaqui chapels and their surrounding spaces reflect the ceremonies for which they provide the setting. While each of the four churches in the Tucson area is distinct from the others, all have certain traits in common. Each, for instance, has a wide entrance—in three out of four cases, the entire wall of the building. Given this arrangement, the ritual dancers, called Matachinis, dance right up to the altar, and processions form inside the church and move out into the plaza.

The church faces a large plaza. Also opening onto the plaza is the fiesta ramada, which consists of a three-sided shelter that is divided down the center by a row of posts. An altar table sits against the back wall of the left-hand section, while the right-hand compartment is usually separated from the plaza and the other room by a low wire fence. Somewhere near the ramada is a community kitchen with an attached dining room. During Lent, fourteen white wooden crosses are set in the ground around the plaza's periphery.[25]

Each Friday during Lent, men and women belonging to specific church-related organizations leave the church carrying a number of holy statues and proceed around the edge of the plaza, stopping and praying at each of the wooden crosses. The prayers and the songs that accompany the procession are led by the *maehto* or maestro, a lay prayer leader whose office may be descended from that of mission catechist in the seventeenth and eighteenth centuries.

The procession is accompanied by one or more masked individuals called *chapayekas*. These men, members of a larger organization called *fariseos* (Pharisees), represent alien soldiers who are searching for Christ in order to kill Him. Timid at first, and reacting with fear when holy words are uttered by the church group, they grow in numbers and boldness as the Fridays of Lent wear on. By the time Holy Week arrives, there may be as many as twenty chapayekas.

On Holy Thursday the fariseos capture Christ, represented by a small crucifix hidden in a temporary thicket of green branches—the Garden of Gethsemane. On Good Friday they kill Him by touching the center of a wooden cross in the Way of the Cross with the wooden swords that they carry. On Holy Saturday they arrive in force in the plaza, bringing with them a straw-filled effigy of their leader, Judas. After marching with him in a procession, accompanying themselves with guitar and accordion and burning foul-smelling "incense" in an old tin can, they tie Judas to a post at the end of the plaza to observe their final victory, which seems to them inevitable.

After much marching and counter marching, they charge the church three times to the accompaniment of the ringing of the church bell. Each time they are beaten back by the church group and others who pelt them with confetti and green leaves. These represent flowers, which in Yaqui belief are extremely holy things, symbols of the grace of God and blessings of all sorts. (One Yaqui belief has it that when Christ died on the cross, His blood fell to the ground and became flowers.) After the third defeat, the fariseos and chapayekas, divested of their costumes and masks, rush into church to be reentered into the ranks of the faithful. At the same time, Judas, who has been filled with firecrackers, is set on fire.

By now it is early afternoon on Holy Saturday. A fiesta begins, which lasts until well after dawn the next day. Some time on Easter Sunday morning the head maehto preaches a sermon in which he acknowledges the vast amount of ritual labor that went into the correct observance of Lent and Holy Week. All the participants shake hands with each other and thank each other, and the year's ceremonial high point has passed once more.

The fiesta that begins on Holy Saturday afternoon and lasts all night is similar to other Yaqui fiestas held throughout the year. It begins with a procession in which the appropriate holy images are carried out of the church and over to the three-sided fiesta ramada that faces the plaza. Here they are placed on the altar on the left-hand side of the ramada, an altar which has already been decorated with cloth coverings and paper flowers. While the rest of the fiesta continues around them, the maehto and the women singers pray and sing antiphonally all night in front of the altar.

Meanwhile, fiesta participants are involved in a complex series of activities, including ritual feasting and performances of special religious music and dance. (The musicians and dancers had joined earlier with the church party to challenge and repel the charging fariseos.) Those who perform in the right-hand portion of the fiesta ramada belong to a part of the Yaqui ceremonial world that retains much which appears native in origin. The *pascolas* belong to this world. Ritual hosts of the fiesta, clowns, and solo step-dancers, they preside over the right side of the fiesta ramada. Naked to the waist and with small wooden masks on the back or sides of their heads, they dance to the music of the violin and harp, accentuating the already complex rhythms with the moth cocoon rattles tied around their ankles. When there is a deer dancer present, they also dance to the music of the flute-and-drum player and interact with the deer dancer (when one is present) in various comic ways.

The deer dancer occupies an ancient place in the Yaqui ceremonial world. He imitates the actions of a deer living in the flowery world, while the three singers communicate with the deer and other animals through an ancient and beautiful body of traditional Yaqui poetry—the deer songs.[26] Over the course of the all-night fiesta, the deer moves through various stages of his life and on occasion is finally "killed" by the pascolas, who for this part of the ritual assume the role of hunters. All the activities that take place in the fiesta ramada—the praying in front of the altar, the singing, playing, and dancing—bring blessings with them and create a sacred space in the plaza.

There remains one group of ritual performers to be discussed. The *Matachinis,* a group of men and boys who are dedicated to Our Lady of Guadalupe and who are considered to be "soldiers of the Virgin." Dressed in their best clothes, crowned with colored paper streamers, and carrying wands and rattles, the Matachinis perform intricate contradances to violin and guitar music as an act of prayer and devotion. Unlike pascolas and the deer dancer, the Matachinis do not appear at any sort of secular event—they are extremely sacred dancers, and their dance is an act of faith and prayer rather than a performance in the Western sense of the word. They, too, dance all night at fiestas, including the one held on Holy Saturday. They do not appear during Lent, a time of penance and preparation, except at the joyful fiesta held on the eve of Palm Sunday. But at other times of the year, the Matachinis are a part of large and small religious fiestas. Ground that has been danced over by Matachinis is considered by many Yaquis to be holy ground until the end of time.

On two occasions Matachinis may be seen outside Yaqui communities, the Tumacacori Fiesta on the first Sunday in December and at the San Xavier Fiesta on the first Friday after Easter. While each of these events is organized for secular reasons by non-Yaquis, both take place in church settings, and they apparently have sufficient sacred content to satisfy the Yaqui participants.

Thus there flourish in our region two different ceremonial systems that are the result of contact and interaction between specific Native American religions and the Christianity imported by the Spaniards in the seventeenth and eighteenth centuries. Each is a unique entity, rather than a form of "Indianized" Christianity; that is to say, while in each case the ritual and material objects of the religion are similar to those of mainstream Catholicism, a closer examination reveals a complex religious and philosophical system whose concepts owe as much to native America as they do to Christian Europe.

In each case special architecture, European in form but at least partly Native American in concept and use, has been created to provide a setting for ceremonies that include ritual music, dance, oratory, processions, prayer, and feasting. This architecture, and the ceremonies that take place in and around it, form lasting, visible reminders of the complex processes of change and persistence that were set into motion by the arrival of Father Kino and his missionary colleagues more than three hundred years ago. These processes continue, as each generation of O'odham and Yaquis provides its own synthesis and understanding of its traditional culture; yet the two systems differ from each other in many ways. Santo himdag came into being as a result of Papagos observing and absorbing Catholic behavior over a space of two hundred years. Father Kino entered the Pimería Alta in 1686. By 1900 most Sonora O'odham had moved to Arizona, bringing with them the ideas and practices of santo himdag. These they seem to have learned by observing religious activity among their Catholic neighbors and fitting the activities into a basically O'odham worldview. Santo himdag does not seem to be organized around a single, world-altering event—the death and resurrection of Christ—as is Roman Catholicism. Rather, it appears to be a borrowing of Catholic practices and supernatural beings that are then applied to the traditional O'odham needs for maintaining physical and spiritual health. Other vital O'odham needs—assuring that the rains arrive, for instance—are met through the philosophical system called O'odham himdag, or Papago way. To this system belong the annual saguaro wine feasts still held in some villages, as well as the ceremonies surrounding the maintenance of the Children's Shrine. (Many places associated with O'odham himdag were discussed in chapter 2 of this book.)

Yaqui Christianity is the result of more than a century of intense missionary activity in the eight Sonoran Yaqui villages, followed by an even longer period without resident missionaries. Unlike the Papagos, Yaquis integrated the new religion into their old system, finding such equivalences as that between the Christian God and the sun, whom Yaquis believe they worshipped before the arrival of the missionaries. Many religious symbols have a dual meaning for Yaquis. I once spoke with an older Yaqui man about the Cristo Rey

Chapel in New Pascua Village, a chapel that was built with Yaqui labor as well as financial assistance from the Knights of Columbus. I commented on its unusual floor plan in the shape of a Greek Cross, with all four arms of equal length. "Yes," he replied, "it represents the four sacred directions." It may well have represented something else in the minds of the Catholic clergy who approved the plan.

While some O'odham symbols, such as the rainbow, may be interpreted in both native and Christian ways, most of the details of Yaqui Christianity seem to be susceptible to this sort of dual interpretation. There is no unified Yaqui Way that survives as a separate reminder of how things were before the missionaries came, as there is in O'odham himdag.

There are other differences as well. The O'odham have always lived in small villages. Therefore, the ceremonies of santo himdag do not require large numbers of participants divided into different ceremonial groups as do those of the Yaqui, whose riverbank homeland supported a larger population than the Sonoran desert ever did. Only on the occasion of the now-defunct wi:gida at Santa Rosa Village did the O'odham divide their ceremonial participants into groups of performers with differing roles, and that ceremony was a cooperative venture on the part of several villages.

There are other distinctions between the two native Christian systems of today's Pimería Alta. Each, however, fits imported ideas into a framework informed by traditional native philosophy. Each functions less for individual salvation than for the maintenance of the health of the community, and by extension, of the whole world. Each depends heavily on the ritual sharing of food and labor in a basically egalitarian community. And each has left its mark upon the physical appearance of this region through the construction of specialized religious architecture and landscaping that reflect in many ways the needs and nature of the religions they serve.

5. The Presence of the Dead

First-time travelers in southern Arizona frequently ask about all the wooden crosses along the roads. There are approximately fifty-five such markers, for example, on the ninety-seven miles of State Highway 86 between Three Points and Why, Arizona. They are usually painted white, and many are decorated with wreaths of artificial flowers. The roadside crosses aren't limited to the Tohono O'odham Nation; they are common roadside sights on many of southern Arizona's back roads, as well as on virtually every road and highway in northern Sonora. Each cross marks the spot where someone has been killed, usually in an automobile accident.

The custom of erecting a cross to mark the location of a sudden death is an old one in the Hispanic world. The theological purpose for erecting such a cross, as I understand it, is to signal for passersby that at this spot a soul suddenly left its body without the benefit of the last rites of the Roman Catholic Church. According to Catholic belief, most souls spend time after death in purgatory, a place of cleansing and purification. There they may be helped by the prayers of the living. The appropriate response to seeing such a cross, therefore, is to pause and say a prayer for the person who died there.

The crosses serve the living as well as the dead. Sudden death of a loved one is horribly disruptive for most survivors. At one moment the person is alive; the next instant, often as the result of a violent accident, he or she is dead. There has been no period of sickness during which the survivors can prepare themselves for the coming loss, no formalized ritual such as the last rites of the church to mark the transition. Erection of a roadside cross can ritualize the fact of a loss, and provide the survivors with some meaningful action by which they can begin to loose the ties that bound them to their loved one. This may be a powerful reason behind the fact that death markers are apparently being erected in southern Arizona by non-Catholics and even by non-Christians.[1]

Sometimes more than prayers are left for the dead person. In his book, *Tongues of the Monte,* J. Frank Dobie tells of one cross in the Sierra Madre that marks the spot where "a good man had been murdered by a drunken devil." Travelers left small coins in front of the cross, coins that were eventually collected and spent on candles. These candles were brought back to the site and burned for the good man's soul.[2] Candles are a symbol of prayer and in many communities have become prayers—offerings—in and of themselves. Other crosses sit atop piles of stones, piles that are added to by each traveler who goes by. Such a pile of stones, lacking a cross, was described in chapter 4 as being near the village of Sil Nakya on the Tohono O'odham Nation. Other stone piles may be seen beside ancient trails in various parts of our desert region, giving rise to the speculation that they, too, may be death markers.

Whether or not the custom goes back to pre-Spanish days, there have certainly been death markers in the Pimería Alta for a long time. Father Kieran McCarty, a Franciscan historian, recently translated a 1783 letter concerning them.[3] It was from Felipe de Neve, commandant-general of the Interior Provinces of New Spain, to Pedro Corbalán, intendant-governor of Sonora. In it de Neve describes a meeting with Fray Antonio de los Reyes, the first Bishop of Sonora. Bishop Reyes was concerned about the custom of erecting crosses where travelers had been killed by Apaches. It cheapened the holy symbol of the cross, he said, and even exposed it to acts of irreverence. Not only that, but the sight of the crosses served to frighten passers-by and might well render them so terrified that they would

These crosses beside Mexican Highway 2 east of Imuris mark the site where Father Ignacio de la Torre, Nogales, Sonora's much loved parish priest, was murdered in 1980. Photo by James S. Griffith, March 1991.

be unable to defend themselves in case of a real attack. Finally, the custom would only add to the boldness of the enemy Apaches, "for they too know the meaning of the crosses."

The letter goes on to order Corbalán to see to it that existing crosses are taken down and that no new crosses are erected. This was to be accomplished by having copies of the letter made and circulated among Sonoran officials and missionaries. This exercise in colonial bureaucracy had no lasting effect, for many of the roads of the Pimería Alta are still adorned with crosses. The internal combustion engine, in combination with alcohol, has replaced the Apaches as the prime source of sudden death, but the crosses are still with us.

For a time, at least, crosses were erected by the Arizona Highway Department at the sites of fatal highway accidents. I remember them best along the old Nogales Highway in the mid-1950s. In those days, this could be a pretty deadly stretch of road. Young men would party in Tucson, decide to go to Nogales for further partying, and find themselves driving back under a heavy load of alcohol. I remember one bridge in particular that was fairly narrow and set on a curve. There were so many foot-high wooden crosses attached to it that it showed up in the headlights like an albino porcupine. The practice was apparently discontinued by around 1960, possibly due to some of the same sentiments as those expressed by Bishop Reyes. Interestingly enough, it has been revived in recent years along U.S. Highway 93 north of Wickenburg. A standard green metal highway information sign explaining the markers is located at the beginning and the end of the stretch of highway where they have been placed.

Each of the death crosses on our roads and highways in Arizona and Sonora has its tragic story for those who know. They are erected and tended by family members or friends. And they add a touch of beauty, sadness, and human interest to many of our roads and highways. As I drove along the dirt road connecting Nogales, Sonora, with Saric and the Altar Valley in November 1989, a flash of color caught my eye. A plaster crucifix, crudely sprayed with glowing orange paint, was attached to an oak tree beside the road. Be-

103

neath it was a double cross of black metal, formed of one crosspiece and two uprights. Two names and a date in May 1988 were inscribed on the cross. Behind the crosses a small heap of car fragments was arranged on the assembled pieces of a shattered windshield. The entire assemblage was a truly poignant reminder of the dangers we all face every day.

Occasionally, the marker is more than a simple cross. On the road connecting the old Kinsley's Ranch on Interstate 19 with Arivaca, at Rancho el Sopori, stands a large nicho six feet high. It is made of local stones and is whitewashed. Although it is dedicated to Santa Teresa, several statues of other saints and members of the Holy Family share her space. It was erected in memory of Arthur Lee, a former owner of the Sopori Ranch, who fell off his horse in 1934 and was dragged to death. The shrine is traditionally cared for by some child at the ranch. The last time I visited it, the space in front of the tiny altar was crowded with candles and artificial flowers.

There is another connection between death and highways in our region's traditional life. In the Arizona Folklore Archives of the Southwest Folklore Center in Tucson are several accounts of ghosts seen along our state's roads. Many of these are variations of the familiar "Vanishing Hitchhiker" story, one of America's most common urban legends.

Most follow the usual pattern of the protagonist offering a person a ride (or, in one case, lending him a horse) and discovering later on that the person has been dead for several years. However, one stands out and bears repetition. Here it is as it appears in the archives:

A man driving along the Nogales Highway picked up three nuns. The nuns were appreciative and they told the man where there was some buried treasure. Before the man could drop the nuns off he turned around and looked at them and saw the nuns cloaks and robes but inside there was only a skeleton. The man got hysterical and crashed. He is supposedly still in the hospital, but in a coma or something so that all he does is utter nonsense phrases.[4]

Victim Intercessors—Los Tiraditos

A few death sites have transcended their individual or family significance. The best known of these is Tucson's El Tiradito, called by
some the Wishing Shrine. It is located downtown on the west side
of Main Street, just south of the corner of Main and Cushing. Immediately to the north is the parking lot of the popular El Minuto
Restaurant; a few blocks away are the high-rise office buildings of
modern Tucson. A narrow lot is backed by a brick-topped adobe
wall, scalloped upward into a raised central portion. A small niche
in the back wall occasionally holds a statue. On the ground in front
of this niche, in metal candle racks, burn any number of candles.
The ground for several feet out from the wall is discolored with
melted candle wax. A metal sign near the northeast corner of the lot
announces in English and Spanish that this is El Tiradito, a National
Historic Landmark, and "the only shrine in the United States dedicated to the soul of a sinner buried in unconsecrated ground."

This isn't the original site of El Tiradito, said to have been a short
distance away, and to have been destroyed in a street alignment and
widening project in the 1920s.[5] The lot on which the present shrine
stands was donated to the City of Tucson in 1927, and the wall
erected in 1940 under the auspices of the National Youth Adminis-
tration.[6] Moved or not, El Tiradito is still a place of power—a place
resorted to by people in need.

In the Arizona Folklore Archives are well over twenty different
stories of the origin of El Tiradito. (The name means "the little cast-
away one" in Spanish and can refer to the site as well as to the
person or persons who were killed and buried there.) Many of the
tales describe action that seems to have taken place in the 1870s or
1880s. Here is a condensed version of the "official legend and story"
adopted in 1927 by the Tucson City Council.[7] Dr. F. H. Goodwin
employed a young sheepherder named Juan Oliveros, who lived
with his wife and his father-in-law on Goodwin's ranch. Oliveros
had become infatuated with his mother-in-law, who lived in Tucson, and would visit her when he was able. One day he was with
her when her husband, who had come to town completely unsus-

El Tiradito, Tucson's Wishing Shrine. The iron candle racks are permanent fixtures; their arrangement and the arrangement of the candles, stones, and religious statues and candles changes over time. Photo by James S. Griffith, May 1986.

pecting that anything might be going on, surprised the couple in their adulterous love. The older man evicted Juan violently from the house and, in the ensuing struggle, seized an axe from the woodpile and killed him. The father-in-law fled to Mexico, and Juan was buried where he had fallen.

I have recently heard a more elaborate version of this narrative, in which Goodwin became the father-in-law. Oliveros fell in love with Goodwin's wife while in his employ and was leaving the ranch in desperation when he saw a lovely young woman—Goodwin's daughter—catching birds along the Santa Cruz River. Oliveros decided to marry the daughter as a way out of his dilemma. One day, however, Goodwin sent him to his home to fetch some piece of equipment, and he literally fell into the arms of his employer's wife. The husband surprised them later, killed them both, and, while leaving the site of the murder, removed a silver comb from his dead wife's hair.

When I first arrived in Tucson in the 1950s I was told a different story. An elderly woodcutter who lived just outside what was then the walled town of Tucson married a lovely young woman from Sonora. He knew nothing of her family. One day he came back from his work leading his burros loaded with firewood and carrying his axe; he found her sitting in front of the house talking with a young man he had never seen before. In a fit of jealous rage he seized his axe and killed them both. Later, he was standing in a dazed condition when an old woman came up and asked him if he had met his wife's brother, who had come all the way from Sonora to visit his sister. In his grief, he either killed himself or fled to Mexico.

Several of the other stories involve fatal love triangles as well. One elaboration was related to me around 1980 by a Franciscan priest at San Xavier Mission. He had been told of a lover surprised and murdered by a jealous husband. The wife fled in terror, clutching to her breast a metal crucifix from her home altar. She fell and died with the image's crown of thorns piercing her heart.[8]

One message is clear in all this proliferation of stories and details. The site and its narrative really belong not to some official body like the City of Tucson but to a large number of people. They have expressed their ownership of the shrine by creating and embellishing an ever-growing number of legends to explain its history and significance. This lore, like so many of the legends and stories retold in this book, is alive and constantly changing to meet the needs of its tellers.

Some versions of the legend are much simpler. Lalo Guerrero, a famous singer and composer who grew up near El Tiradito in the 1920s and 1930s, heard when he was a boy that El Tiradito was an innocent man who accidentally stopped a bullet while walking past a barroom door one day when a fight was going on. Some accounts tell that he was a kindly old man who was mugged, murdered, and buried on the spot. A statement I collected in the early 1980s from an elderly Mexican American has it that "El tiradito fué un pobrecito que le mataron y le tiraron del tren. Y por eso le nombraron el tiradito." ("El Tiradito was a poor fellow who was killed and thrown off the train. And that's why they called him 'el Tiradito.'" The nearest railroad was—and is—about a quarter of a mile away, downhill from the site.)

Another account, this one collected from a boy who lived in the neighborhood, explains the importance of the site, even if it is a bit vague on the narrative: "There's this wishing shrine down by the community center. This old man was killed, and if you want anything real bad, like if you want a new car or if you're in the third grade and want to pass into the fourth, you go there and tell the old man that if you get it you'll go and light a candle for him."[9] This, of course, is the whole point of El Tiradito. It is a place of petitions, a place where miracles can be requested and where it is believed they can be granted.

Granted by whom? Apparently, by whoever lies buried in the original El Tiradito site. As one friend explained it to me many years ago, what probably happened over the years after the sudden death and burial was as follows: As is customary among Catholics, people may well have come to the death and burial site to pray for the soul of the person or persons who lay there, unprepared for death and buried in unsanctified ground. After a while, some may have noticed that any worthy needs they might have had were being unexpectedly met. And so the site developed a reputation that continues to the present. In the words of the neighborhood boy, "if you want something real bad" you can go there and ask for it. The older belief seems to have been that one must keep vigil there all night; recent accounts have modified that to having one's candle burn all night. If this happens, it is said to be a sign that one's wish will be granted.

In my visits to the site, I have always found one or more candles burning but have never seen anyone actually praying there. I have been told by a man who passed by the Wishing Shrine every day on his paper route in the mid-1920s that things were the same back then: he never saw anyone praying there, although there were always candles burning. One Anglo acquaintance goes javelina hunting each year with an older hunting partner, also an Anglo, who introduced him to the sport. Before each hunt they stop and leave lighted candles at El Tiradito, a practice his partner learned from *his* older hunting partner, a Mexican American. An Anglo dog breeder lights a candle at the shrine before each major dog show she enters. In her opinion, the effort pays off.

As I write this, a well-known and much-loved local Chicano artist lies in a coma following a serious accident. A mutual acquaintance just told me that several of the artist's friends, many of whom were neither Mexican American nor Catholic, met to light candles (and presumably to pray) at El Tiradito. And so the site is not only used but is used in ways that may be changing and adapting with time.

This change is illustrated by the story of how El Tiradito became a national historic landmark. In 1971 the proposed Butterfield Freeway was planned to cut through several of the barrios on Tucson's west side, destroying El Tiradito. It must be remembered that by this time a good deal of historic residential Tucson had already been swallowed up by the urban renewal project that resulted in the construction of the Tucson Community Center, now the Tucson Convention Center. Long-term Mexican American residents of the area banded together in what appeared to many to be a futile attempt at opposing the freeway. According to many, a key event in the eventual halting of the project was the successful petition for Historic Landmark status for El Tiradito. Subsequent debates in the State Legislature eventually led to a moratorium on urban freeway construction in Arizona. Thus El Tiradito took on a new status—symbol of and rallying point for community and ethnic identity.[10]

As a footnote to this incident, I should add that this strategy did not go unnoticed by later neighborhood activists. In 1989 a proposed realignment of Mission Road threatened to obliterate totally the already badly damaged site of the original San Agustín de Tucson Mission church and compound on the west bank of the Santa Cruz River, by the foot of "A" Mountain. One strategy employed to oppose this move was the erection of a small shrine directly in the path of the proposed roadway. The activists involved obtained the services of a Jesuit priest and a Tohono O'odham medicine woman, each of whom blessed the shrine and the surrounding land. They then sat back and waited for the city's response. Six months later, the shrine had not been disturbed and plans for the roadwork were on hold.

The shift of El Tiradito from a private place of petitions to a symbol of ethnic and neighborhood identity has had a curious effect on official Catholic participation. Although el Tiradito, the individual, seems to behave like a saint, interceding with God on behalf of petitioners, he is certainly not a saint in the official sense of the Roman Catholic Church. Saints must be historically identifiable individuals of known Christian virtues, with attested miracles to their credit, who have gone through a complicated process of beatification and canonization by the authorities in Rome. El Tiradito, whoever he or she may be, certainly does not fit into that category. He is merely a spirit of some sort who is believed by humble people to work miracles through his intercession with God. In fact, several friends have pointedly told me that they were good Catholics and therefore prayed in church rather than to an unofficial spirit such as El Tiradito.

This has been slightly changed, however, by the Butterfield Freeway incident. While local clergy can and do discourage such unsanctioned popular devotions as El Tiradito, it is much harder for them to deny powerful symbols of unity among a predominantly Catholic ethnic population. And so the rules of the game seem to have changed slightly. The fascinating aspect of it all is that in its new guise El Tiradito is still a place of power. It seems to have been secularized to at least some extent, and the understandings of that power and its sources and uses may be very different from what they were three generations ago, but some sort of power still appears to reside in that place and to be tapped when needed by those in our society who normally are lacking in power.[11]

There are other tiraditos in southern Arizona. Three Mexicans were hanged in Benson for a crime they did not commit and buried just outside the cemetery. For years their graves were visited by petitioners who burned candles and tied ribbons to the branches of an adjacent mesquite tree. Knowledge of this site and its stories survives only in memory, however, and I have not been able to locate the tree.

A young soldier remembered as Pedro Blanco was a heavy winner in a Nogales, Sonora, gambling game one evening, probably in the 1920s. As he walked home alone, he was set upon, robbed, and killed. He, too, was buried where he fell, where the street had crossed an arroyo. A small chapel was erected over his grave. As with the other tiraditos, people began to believe that Blanco answered prayers and granted miracles. Later on, when the street was paved and the arroyo was enclosed in a storm drain, Pedro Blanco's body was moved to the Panteón Rosario, Nogales's oldest cemetery. Here his grave may still be seen. It is marked by a cross and a brick monument and surrounded by a white wrought-iron fence. Although Pedro Blanco's grave is identified with his name, it tends not to be kept very clean, and the feeling is that the man's reputation as a miracle worker no longer attracts many people. When I visited his grave just after All Souls' Day in 1989, it did not appear to have been cleaned or decorated.

Also in Nogales, but perhaps a few years after Blanco's murder, a young woman named Tita Gomez went one afternoon with her boyfriend to a hill south of town to pick wild onions. Here she was murdered with a tire iron by the boyfriend and his wife, and buried where she fell. Her grave also became a place of petitions and seems to have remained so to some extent after she was reburied in the Panteón Nacional, the huge public cemetery located just south of the International Border between downtown Nogales and the Mariposa Road truck crossing.

Such stories and beliefs are not unique to this region. A bandit named Jesús Malverde is said to have lived in Sinaloa in northwest Mexico. He was hanged in 1909 at Culiacán, Sinaloa, and has been described as a "patron saint to contemporary thieves and smugglers." [12] I have seen a printed prayer to him, purchased in a religious articles store in Tucson. It shows a young man dressed in a light-colored shirt with dark pocket flaps, standing with his hands bound and a noose around his neck. A woman in Magdalena who makes plaster statues of Juan Soldado, a figure who will be discussed at

111

length below, told me that Malverde was another "inocente" like Juan but knew nothing more about him. Moving farther from home, Antonio Gil of northeastern Argentina seems to be another such figure. Gil deserted from the Argentine army in the late nineteenth century, refusing to "spill the blood of his fellow Argentines," and was shot. Miracles are still sought and obtained at his grave and death site.[13] There are many other such figures all through Latin America, each with his or her story, most of them existing outside of, or in spite of, the official church.

Juan Soldado

Richard Morales and I were driving from Santa Ana to Magdalena on December 10, 1982, when we noticed a small, white chapel on the east side of the highway. Over the door was a wooden sign that read "El Anima de Juan Soldado." Neither Richard nor I had ever heard of Juan Soldado, much less his spirit, so we stopped the car and looked in. On an altar against the far wall of the chapel was a three-foot-high statue of a young man in the olive drab uniform of a Mexican common soldier. He was standing casually, with one hand on a table or tree stump. He shared the chapel with smaller representations of the Sacred Heart of Jesus, the Head of the Suffering Christ, and Saint Martin of Porres. (His devotion is strong all through the borderlands, especially among the poor.) Even though the chapel was only a few miles from Magdalena, there was no statue of San Francisco. Flowers and candles were on and in front of the altar, along with a few plaques thanking Juan Soldado for unspecified miracles.[14]

With our curiosity piqued, we walked back on a dirt road to a small ranchhouse about a quarter of a mile from the highway. Here was an outdoor shrine to the same figure and an older lady who was more than willing to explain who he was. Juan Soldado is an *alma*—a soul—rather than a saint. He was a *soldado raso*, or army private, in Tijuana; his *capitán* raped and murdered a little girl who came to the garrison with food or laundry or something. The captain accused Juan of the crime and then had him "shot while attempting to escape" in order to keep him from being a witness in

112

his own defense. (This form of summary execution, a common tactic of rural police before the Mexican Revolution, is called *la ley fuga*—"the law of flight" in Spanish.) However, this did not keep Juan from appearing after death to the captain and also to the captain's sweetheart. The captain confessed and died, and it was discovered that Juan Soldado could work miracles. The woman who told us his story had first heard about him in Hermosillo and had asked for help with her sick daughter. After the daughter was cured the mother had built the chapel by the highway. She further told us that most of the local clergy approved of Juan (whom she referred to as *mi Juanito*). One priest did not, however, and said that it was all the Devil's work. That priest was dying, she told us, even as we spoke.

Later I visited Juan Soldado's grave in Tijuana, Baja California, and filled in the following details of his story. His real name is said to have been Juan Castillo Morales. ("Juan Soldado" means literally "John Soldier." "G. I. Joe" would be a more culturally accurate English equivalent.) A photograph purported to be of him shows a very young man—a boy, really—dressed in army uniform. He is standing with his right hand resting on a table that supports a crucifix. I have been told that this is a standard pose for photographs taken of young men when they join the army and does not necessarily imply any special religiosity on Juan's part. His date of death is believed to have been February 17, 1938.

The stories I heard in Tijuana were essentially the same as the one I had been told in Sonora. Juan was a young recruit, whose commanding officer (the rank shifted from captain to major to general depending on the narrator) accused him of a horrible crime that the officer himself had in fact committed. Juan was speedily executed without trial. He immediately started appearing, however, first to his mother and other women keeping vigil at the site of his death, later on to others, including the officer himself, who finally confessed and died.

I was also told that Juan derived his powers from God. Like Jesus, he had been falsely accused and killed by those in authority. He has now been judged by God and found innocent. The theme of opposition on the part of the clergy was repeated here as well, for I was told that there would have been a regular church at Juan's grave, except that the priests would not permit one to be built. The chapel at his grave was a rough affair made of bits of scrap lumber. Evidences of strong devotion were everywhere, however, and both the chapel and the shrine at his execution site had quantities of testimonial plaques thanking Juan for miracles performed. Most of the miracles were unspecified. Occasionally, something more specific is mentioned: one man gave thanks because his son was rid of mental illness, and one cement plaque at Juan's supposed place of execution thanks him for having gotten the individual concerned out of prison.

What sort of religious figures are el Tiradito, Pedro Blanco, Juan Soldado, and the rest? As I have said before, they are popularly believed to behave like saints but are not recognized as saints by the Catholic Church. In most cases, the only stories told of them concern their sudden death by murder. They seem to belong to a class of murdered, miracle-working individuals called *almas* (souls) or *inocentes* (innocent ones). No narratives of decent lives or Christian belief or virtues attach to them; what they have in common is that they were victims. My term for them is "victim-intercessors." As I said, they are definitely not official saints, nor can they ever become such unless a good deal more is learned about their lives. The Catholic Church makes it very clear that martyrdom, even in a Christian cause, cannot alone be considered evidence of sainthood. And so these victim-intercessors of the Arizona-Sonora borderlands remain outside the formal church structure, acting like saints and interceding in favor of many who are also, in one way or another, powerless outsiders.

Why are these victim intercessors, these "inocentes," so important? I suspect it is because they were *victims,* like so many of the people who ask them for help. If you are on the bottom of the social and economic heap in a modern, impersonal society, it must be easy to identify with a figure like Juan Soldado, who was persecuted and killed but who was judged by God and found innocent. The Catholic Church needs proof of a life lived on Christian religious principles in order to presume the individual's existence in the presence of God, or sainthood. For poor Mexicans and Mexican Americans it is apparently sufficient to hear of suffering and victimization, leading to that most powerful mystery of all, death. Ratification by the Church bureaucracy may not be important to people whose experiences of bureaucracies have not been positive ones. So victim intercessors appear, do their essential work of providing power to the powerless, and eventually disappear or change, only to be replaced by others.

Cemeteries

Most Catholics who die in the Pimería Alta, whether or not they are memorialized with a death-site marker, are buried in a cemetery. Cemeteries are traditionally looked on somewhat ambivalently. They are the resting places of beloved friends and family members, to be visited and cared for in specified ways at certain times of the year. They are sanctified by ties of family and friendship and blessed by Catholic priests. But they are also places that belong to the dead rather than the living. The following story, collected in the Patagonia area in the 1940s, eloquently expresses some traditional Mexican attitudes toward cemeteries.

A woman was visiting her sister, who lived just across the street from the Panteón Rosario, the oldest functioning cemetery in Nogales, Sonora. Her month-old baby cried out and awoke her about midnight, and she stood in the front door, trying to comfort it. As she stood there, she saw a candle-lit procession led by a priest leave the cemetery and pass by her sister's door. As they passed by, the priest looked at her but said nothing. Next morning the woman was sure she had been dreaming but determined to get up at the same hour the next night and see if anything happened. She did so, waking her baby, who started to cry. As she stood in the doorway with the infant in her arms, she saw the same procession, led by the same priest. "This time the priest stood before her and told her she had no business looking at them. He told her that the only thing that saved her was the baby that she had in her arms, but the next time not even the baby would save her. This was the last time the woman got up."[15]

The message is clear: cemeteries belong to the dead, not to the living, especially during the hours of darkness. And the dead can be dangerous. Another story in the same collection tells of a young man who made a laughing remark to a skull he found in a garden, inviting it to his wedding the next day. At or after the wedding, the skull appeared to the boy and invited him to *its* wedding. When the boy confessed to the priest at church, the priest told him to go to the cemetery the next night. The priest accompanied the now terrified boy to the gates of the cemetery, telling him to go in alone but not to shake hands with or turn his back on anyone he met there, on penalty of his life.

On entering the cemetery, the boy found a wedding in process, just like his own wedding. He was offered food and drink but refused. When he was ready to leave, the groom accompanied him to the gate and offered to shake hands with the boy. The boy, who had been walking backwards out of the cemetery, refused to do this. At the gate, the groom "slapped him because he did not want to turn. Then the priest appeared and said a prayer and as soon as he had finished his prayer this man [the groom] disappeared." When they returned home, the priest told the boy that the incident was "a lesson that he should not laugh at others."[16] And be respectful to the dead, I might add.

Sometimes the dead in a cemetery need to communicate with the living. I was told of some older women who were visiting the little cemetery near the old mining town of Sasco, north of Marana. There are a lot of plain crosses without names in that cemetery, and it is locally believed that they mark the graves of people who were buried in haste during the flu epidemic of the early 1920s. While the ladies were in the cemetery, they heard a voice issuing from one of the unnamed graves. "Rezame un par de Padre Nuestros," it said; "Pray a couple of 'Our Fathers' for me." The women were startled, of course, and the voice repeated its request: "Rezame un par de Padre Nuestros." At this point they did what they were asked to do, falling to their knees at the graveside and praying the "Our Father" for the unknown occupant of the grave. The voice was never heard again. The friend who told me this story explained that the episode took place because the person buried in that grave probably had not had the proper prayers said for him or her and needed them in order to continue on to wherever he or she needed to go.

What are these traditional cemeteries like, these places that belong to the dead but are also visited and used by the living? The tiny

Rincon Memorial Cemetery is on Old Spanish Trail Road east of
Tucson, about one mile north of the Rincon Valley Fire Department. It has been used for more than a century by both Anglo and
Mexican-American ranching people from this part of the valley. In
many ways it is typical of southern Arizona's smaller, traditional
cemeteries.

Rincon Cemetery occupies a low ridge on the west side of the
roughly north-south road. It measures perhaps 240 by 110 feet and
is surrounded by a three-foot-high cinder block wall. The wall is
painted white on the south side, where the entrance is; otherwise it
has been left its natural gray color. There are two entrances side by
side: a narrow footpath protected by an L-shaped wall so that large
livestock can't enter and an elaborate double gate of wrought- and
cast-iron. This gate is flanked by two block pillars painted white. On
the inside of the west pillar is a hand-painted, ceramic tile picture of
Our Lady of Guadalupe.

Just north of the gate is a cement slab measuring perhaps 40 by
25 feet. A pitched, wooden roof covered with asphalt shingles is
held up over the slab by six sections of power pole. Benches flank
the slab on the east and west sides. Here mourners and other visitors
to the cemetery may rest in the shade. A flagpole stands just north
of the gate on the crest of the ridge.

Within the cemetery walls is the only area that has been cleared
of native vegetation; it is along the ridge, where the burials are. Elsewhere cholla, prickly pear and barrel cactuses, mesquite, catclaw
and whitethorn, saltbush, burroweed, and Mormon tea all grow
wild. The view from the cemetery is lovely, with a low, saguaro-
covered ridge shutting in the west and the Catalina and Rincon
mountains to the north and east.

There are about sixty graves still visible in the cemetery. The
oldest one with a readable inscription dates to 1882, while the most
recent one was dug in 1989. Most face roughly east-west, with the
heads toward the west. A number of the graves are covered with
something in addition to dirt: piles of stones or cement slabs. This
custom seems to have its origin in a highly practical concern; graves
covered with rocks or cement won't get dug up by predators. Other
graves have cement or brick or rock borders around them. Approxi-

117

mately thirty of the graves have some sort of headstone. Typically, these give the name and dates of the deceased. Sometimes the relationship of the deceased to those setting up the marker is noted. Some of the markers give places of birth; there are people in the cemetery who were born in New Jersey, Massachusetts, and Guatemala. Occupation is sometimes described or symbolized; one hand-carved headstone has a low-relief portrait of a man, probably the deceased, holding a camera. Several stones are marked with their owner's brands; one has a silhouette of the horse on it. These, along with several crosses made of horseshoes, seem to indicate the presence of ranch folk. Hobbies are also suggested: one headstone has the picture of a guitar sandblasted on it. On the back of a headstone of a three-day-old infant is carved a poem, which is signed by an older sister.

There are crosses as well in the Rincon Cemetery. These are made of wood, hollow iron bars, horseshoes, plumbers' pipe, cement, and commercially cast composition marble. Many are decorated in some way; the pipe cross has silver telephone line insulators as finials.

The cemetery contains deliberately introduced plants as well as wild, native ones. Many of the graves have iris growing on them, often around the tombstones. I also saw Queen's wreath growing by one headstone, an imported mesquite tree near another, and a Christmas tree by the head of a child's grave.

Visiting the cemetery on November 6, 1989, I noticed that all but two of the graves seemed to have been freshly decorated. Floral offerings were left on most. These were arranged in bunches and in wreaths and included chrysanthemums and roses (but none of the ubiquitous marigolds so common elsewhere on Mexican and Mexican-American graves), as well as silk and plastic flowers. An artificial Christmas wreath was hung around one cross. Natural and artificial flowers alike were placed in containers. Some containers were built into the covering of the grave; for the rest flower vases, coffee cups, ceramic bowls, and tin cans were used. Two children's graves had toys left on them; on one grave of an adult was an unopened bottle of Champagne.

The Broader Picture

A cemetery like this one is very different from the grassy, uniformly kept memorial parks of mainstream America. However, it is typical of the traditional Mexican Catholic cemeteries of this border country. Many are on high ground, out of reach of floods. Few are smoothed and planted in lawns; most have at least some native vegetation remaining, especially in those areas that have not yet been used for burial. Most have some sort of an ornamental main gate. Over the gate at the Tubac Cemetery are wrought-iron letters spelling "CEMENTERY"—a compromise between the English "cemetery" and the Spanish *cementerio*, and the actual pronunciation of the word in the local dialect used by many English speakers of Mexican descent.[17]

Many of the traditional cemeteries in southern Arizona have the graves arranged with the heads to the west, enough so that when visiting a new cemetery with photography in mind, I deliberately try to get there in the morning so as to be able to have direct sunlight on whatever inscriptions there may be. This orientation doesn't always hold true, however; the graves at Tubac, for example, lie on a north-south axis. Covering the graves with heaps of stones or cement slabs is also commonplace; this is often accomplished in highly decorative ways.

The headstones at Rincon Cemetery and the sorts of information conveyed on them seem typical of the region's traditional graveyards. Details vary, of course, from site to site. For instance, Rincon cemetery has fewer images of Catholic holy figures on its headstones than do some other cemeteries. But the general kinds of information—family ties, religion, occupation—appear over and over again.

The variety of ornamented crosses in many different materials is also a common sight. Southern Arizona's folk cemeteries have crosses cut into boulders and crosses carved from stone; crosses cast from cement and crosses made of wood; crosses cut from strap metal and assembled from bits of pipe and other available materials. Most typical, perhaps, are the metal crosses with decorative filigree ironwork, which have been a tradition in what is now southern Arizona at least since the 1790s, when ornate wrought-iron crosses were placed atop the dome and the west tower at San Xavier del Bac.[18]

One extremely common kind of permanent grave decoration is totally lacking at Rincon Cemetery: the nicho or small, free-standing niche. Holding one or more statues of favorite saints or members of the Holy Family, these nichos are a common sight in traditional cemeteries all over the borderlands. Sometimes the statues they contain are actually a treasured feature of the deceased person's home altar; there is always some strong personal connection between the subject of the statue and the person buried beneath it.

These nichos can be large or small. Like the crosses, they may be homemade or purchased from commercial workshops. The homemade ones are of a variety of materials; the workshops specialize in *mármol*, a kind of composition marble. In a town like Nogales, Sonora, there is almost always a blacksmith shop and a *marmoleria* near each cemetery. Smaller towns have their metalworkers, but the cast monuments must be ordered from such larger communities as Nogales or Magdalena.

In the tiny cemetery across the river from Tumacacori there is a six-foot high nicho made of smooth river cobbles cemented together. The keystone is an old metate. Inside is a white plaster statue of the Pietà. A few miles downriver, in the Tubac Cemetery, nichos are made of wood, of brick, of cement. One of the most startling to the casual visitor contains a life-sized representation of the head of the Suffering Christ, complete with downcast eyes and crown of thorns. Across the border in Nogales, Sonora, the huge Panteón Nacional (National Cemetery) has several nichos cast in the form of entire church facades, complete with towers well over six feet high.

Typical as well is the pattern by which the graves are cleaned, renewed, and decorated in early November. November 2 is All Souls' Day in the Roman Catholic Church, the day of the year on which the Catholic community remembers and prays for all its dead. In Mexico it is also called *el día de los muertos*—the Day of the Dead. In central and southern Mexico this is a time for almost affectionately embracing the concept of death—for making and purchasing tiny candy skulls, for instance, or little statues of skeletons doing all the things that people do in real life. It is also a time for erecting altars to one's family dead, for decorating their graves, for remembering them.

El día de los muertos in the Pimería Alta is a bit different. Many of the artifacts which are a commonplace farther south—the skeletons, the candy skulls, even the elaborate loaves of *pan de muerto* or Day of the Dead bread, are hard to find here in the far Northwest. What does happen here is that people visit the cemeteries and clean and redecorate their family graves. This takes place on and just before All Souls' Day. Although this happens in all the cemeteries where there are people of Mexican descent, my experience is that the activity is at its most intense in the Panteón Nacional, the largest cemetery in Nogales, Sonora. Here is what that cemetery looked like on the afternoon of November 1, 1984:

Hundreds of people were inside the cemetery, cleaning, repainting, mounding earth, scrubbing slabs, applying flowers. One man was chiseling something off a tombstone, another was lettering a new nameplate that had recently been painted black over light blue. "Ricardo" was as far as he had gotten when I watched him. He was seated on a grave slab, holding the twelve-by-sixteen-inch metal plate in one hand while with the other he painted blue block letters.

The central pathway was the scene of a steady procession toward and away from the gate; men and women carrying shovels, brooms, hoes, *coronas* (wreaths) and crosses, flowers both potted and in bunches, paint buckets and brushes, pails and tin cans, and plastic milk jugs of water. Small boys chased each other, carried pails of water, and offered their services cleaning graves. A balloon vendor strolled through the cemetery. People visited, worked, and ate. There was little noise—no radios, no musicians—except for the loudspeaker of a car in the street advertising the headlines of a local newspaper, which involved a drug-related killing in Calle Buenos Aires. Outside the gates vendors sold sodas, carne asada, corn on the cob, churros, sugarcane, yellow and white flowers, and homemade paper wreaths. Small groups of people walked up the road from town, some carrying wreaths and flowers, past the blacksmith shop where men were welding in the yard and newly painted, wrought-iron crosses shone black in the afternoon sun, past the dusty *marmolerias* where grave markers were being made, past the rows of trucks from Imuris and La Mesa, each bearing its owner's name and hometown painted in elegant, shaded letters on the door, each backed to the street to display white margaritas, yellow *cempazúchiles* [marigolds], and coronas of homemade paper flowers. And this, I was told, was nothing compared to the crowds that would be there the next day, on November 2, *¡el mero día de los muertos!*

The results of all this activity must be seen to be believed. A day or so after el día de los muertos the cemeteries are clean and shining with a dazzling variety of colors. Graves have been weeded, earth and rock mounds restored. Old, damaged markers have been repaired or replaced; many have been repainted in brilliant colors. Flowers have been lavished on the graves: wreaths of plastic and silk artificial flowers; wreaths of homemade flowers of paper, sections of soda straw or bits of egg-carton; natural flowers of all varieties. Most common among these latter are *cempazúchiles,* or marigolds, the flower of the dead all over Mexico. Beginning in the spring, fields of marigolds are planted and grown in the fertile valleys near Imuris, Magdalena, and Santa Ana. By October 31 they have been harvested and are sold out of trucks all over northcentral Sonora. They are then placed on graves: singly, in bunches, in mounds. A single marigold may be pushed into each of the three ends of a pipe cross; marigolds may spell out the initials of the deceased on a mound of raked earth; a cross of light yellow marigolds may stand out against a heap of orange ones completely covering a grave. They are used in a hundred different ways, each creative, each lovely.

More is left on some graves than flowers. Often one can see a rosary draped over a cross or hung around a saint's statue in a nicho. Toys may be left on the graves of children. And the champagne bottle at the Rincon Cemetery was not an isolated instance. I know of one grave in Santa Cruz County where the widow regularly leaves a can of beer for her husband in the summer months.

O'Odham Cemeteries

A few years ago I heard a joke from a woman who lived in Caborca, site of one of Father Kino's early missions, contemporary agricultural boomtown, and home to some of Sonora's few remaining Tohono O'odham. A Mexican man and an O'odham were walking along the road, around November 2. The Mexican was ribbing the Indian mercilessly about the O'odham custom of leaving food offerings for their dead. "Come on," he would say, "you don't really believe that your dead people come and eat that food! You've got to know it's the dogs or the coyotes. You don't really believe that your dead people can come back and eat that stuff?"

The O'odham paid little attention to the teasing he was getting but simply walked along quietly. After a while the Mexican stopped talking, and they walked together in silence. Finally the Indian spoke up: "Well," he said, "the way I look at it is this. About the time your dead people come back and smell those flowers, our dead people come and eat the food."

It should surprise nobody who has read this far that cemeteries are slightly different places for Tohono O'odham Catholics than for Mexicans. In the first place, they *look* different. Most of the graves are covered with high earth mounds, and most of the monuments are crosses, often painted in brilliant colors. I have so far been unable to discover any meaning underlying the choice of colors, but the fact remains that many O'odham crosses are blue, pink, or green. And many of the crosses are not identified by any sort of painted name. This probably relates to the O'odham tradition, honored less today than it was a generation ago, of not mentioning a person by name after he or she was dead and buried.

I get the impression that O'odham cemeteries are not comfortable places. Most are located outside the villages, with at least a potential source of running water separating them from human habitations. Even more than in the case of Mexican cemeteries, the dead are *there,* a real presence. And on All Souls' Day, they come back to the places where they lived to find their favorite foods set out for them to enjoy. Meanwhile, their families are keeping vigil in the cemeteries. The graves have been cleaned and decorated with artificial flowers. At the San Xavier cemetery, hundreds of candles are lit and burn all night. At midnight, when the dead are believed to have gone back to where they came from and it is safe for the living to return to the houses, the families collect the food and take it back to the village, where it is consumed by the living.[19]

Ghosts

Some of this region's dead are believed to haunt the places where they used to be active. Sometimes the return seems to have no purpose, as when a man stayed overnight in the house belonging to his brother—the same house where his uncle had died some time before. In the middle of the night he felt a man get into bed with him, shoving him over to make room. He thought nothing of this because he was expecting another brother that evening. When he woke up he found himself alone in the bed. Later on he discovered that his brother hadn't come to the house at all but had stayed somewhere else. The implication is that it was the deceased uncle who had climbed in bed with the man, but no reason was given for the ghost's behavior.[20] A similar mystery surrounds the occasional appearances of an eleven- or twelve-year-old girl who used to run from the door to the window of a deserted house on the old Tucson-Nogales road. Several people saw her in the 1940s, apparently in broad daylight. She always did the same thing, and nobody seemed to have any explanation for her actions. They didn't find her scary; she was just there at that place, doing the same thing whenever people saw her.[21]

I remember sitting one Easter several years ago at the picnic of a Mexican-American family, listening to two older men telling stories about ghostly experiences they had had. One of the men recounted how he had gone to visit a friend who lived in an old two-room adobe house up north of Marana. Each room apparently had an outside door, as is often the case in traditional adobes in this region. They were sitting and talking when the guest heard the kitchen door open and the sound of footsteps moving toward the wood stove. Noises followed of a fire being lit and then the soft slap-slap of tortillas being patted out. He looked at his host, who said something on the order of "Don't pay any attention—that's just my cook." After a while the footsteps went back out and the door closed. The host told him to walk into the kitchen and feel the ashes in the stove. He did and they were cold to the touch. The host then explained that it was a fairly common occurrence. The ghost didn't do any harm and in fact never did anything but come in, light a ghostly fire, make her tortillas, and leave.

Many stories do give a reason behind the appearance of a ghost. Sometimes there is malevolence involved. La Llorona, the famous Wailing Woman who haunts water courses all over Mexico, is a case in point. She collects children for her own purposes. Many of the stories concerning her origin explain this: one widespread account describes her as being a beautiful young woman who drowned her babies in order to free herself to run off with a man with whom she was infatuated. She was doomed to wander for eternity in search of her murdered children.[22]

A southern Arizona account describes her as a local woman who had one child, whom she warned not to play in dry arroyos. This is flash-flood country, and water can come very suddenly. There are eyewitness accounts of walls of water several feet high, complete with tree trunks and large boulders, rushing down hitherto dry streambeds following a storm in some far distant mountains. The child disobeyed and was washed away in a flash flood. Insane with grief, the mother still looks for him. If she finds a child alone, she tries to take it with her.

La Llorona is known in purely local versions of her legend, but she is far from a local phenomenon. Her stories are told, and she has been heard and seen, all over Mexico and most of Central America, and in fact, in most places where Mexicans and Mexican Americans live. Here in the United States, she is not confined to the Southwest. She has been heard along the lake front in Chicago, as well as on the banks of the Mississippi River where it flows through Minneapolis. She is a truly ubiquitous ghost, a "killer mama" who collects Mexican children.

Ghostly appearances frequently happen where there is buried treasure. Sometimes the motive is to tell passers-by about the existence of the treasure. Mysterious lights are said to hover over some treasures. A column of flames near the old Santa Cruz County townsite of Alto, for instance, is believed to mark the spot where local Indians buried treasure just before an expected Apache raid. The flames "are an invitation for someone to get the treasure." And there is a place in the San Rafael Valley where a passing cowboy heard the clanking of chains.[23] This is considered locally to be a buried treasure site. By far the best known local guardian of buried treasure is a former stage robber named *el Tejano*—the Texan.[24]

El Tejano has no other names in any account of him that I have heard or read. He is simply "the Texan" in a region where people are still known by their nicknames, sometimes to the exclusion of their more formal names. Neither does there seem to be any sure connection between this legendary stage robber and any of the badmen known in historical literature, although a case has been made for identifying him with one William Brazelton, a stage robber from Missouri who was killed in Tucson in 1878. Stories concerning el Tejano are known and told by older Mexicans and Mexican Americans in the lower Santa Cruz Valley between Tucson and Marana, as well as in the Altar Valley to the west of Tucson. The time of the story takes us back into the 1870s and 1880s, around the time the railway arrived in Tucson. The community was very much a Mexican one in those days, with what were called "Americanos" constantly arriving, leaving, or settling in. One of those relative newcomers was a Texan who robbed stages.

El Tejano was an extremely successful stage robber. Many speculated that this must be due to some sort of inside contact with the stage company. Pete Castillo of Marana told me he had asked a lot of old-timers about him, and this is the story that he had pieced together. El Tejano was so successful because he was, in fact, an employee of the stage company. Nobody could prove anything on him, however, until a very sharp—*muy vivo*—detective was hired to come from California. He arrived at the stage stop at El Picacho while el Tejano's wife was working and asked to see her husband. She replied that he wasn't there but would return eventually. This reminded the detective that he had just seen him in Phoenix. He was having a wonderful time, the detective said, drinking and carrying on with the ladies. This was too much for the wife, who exclaimed in a jealous rage, "He told *me* he was going to rob a stage!"

126

They never captured el Tejano, however. All accounts that mention his demise have him shot, frequently with a shotgun, and almost always somewhere on *el Cerro del Gato*. This is Cat Mountain, or Catback Mountain, the peak in the Tucson Mountains just north of where present-day Ajo Way cuts through the chain. According to some accounts, his body was displayed on the steps of the courthouse where all Tucson filed past to see him. But that didn't stop el Tejano.

His ghost has been seen and heard by many people in the years since his death. Some have heard his spurs jingling as he creeps down at night to water his horse in the Santa Cruz River—a stream that had surface water in his day but which is now a deep, wide ditch, bone dry except after heavy rains in the Santa Rita Mountains. He has been seen near Sasabe, Sonora, dressed in black and riding a black horse. Up by Picacho Peak he is dressed as a *charro*, and those who see him can sometimes notice that no dust spurts from beneath his horse's hoofs as he gallops along. But the most important thing about him is the treasure he left and still guards.

When el Tejano died, the secret of his treasure died with him. He stole a lot of money, and it is felt that it still lies buried somewhere to the west of Tucson. For many the Tucson Mountains, scene of his violent death, are the most logical site. But wherever the treasure may be, it is felt that el Tejano is there as well, guarding it against all comers. A Tucson school administrator recently remembered that when he was a young boy his grandmother told him about the treasure. It was in a cave somewhere in the Tucson Mountains, she said, and he and his friends would go looking for it. She also told them about el Tejano and how he would guard the treasure. You could tell when he was near, she said, because you could hear him cracking his long whip.[25] Some people add another detail: if you see el Tejano, you die.

That is frequently what happens to people who get too close to the treasure and its Texas guardian. One close encounter with el Tejano is likely to be the last thing one experiences on this earth. Those who come upon his treasure, however, find themselves with another problem. For at the instant one discovers the gold, a voice—presumably that of el Tejano—is heard saying, "Todo o nada," "all or nothing." Some interpret this to mean that if you don't take all the treasure at once, you won't be able to carry any of it away. Perhaps you won't find your way out of the cave, or something else will keep you from carting anything less than the entire treasure off with you. And, of course, you'll never find the cave for a second try.

Another interpretation, however, is more ominous. The same friend who told me of el Tejano's being seen near Sasabe, dressed *como un tejano*—"like a Texan," but all in black—told me a long tale of a man who was working cattle somewhere west of the Santa Cruz Valley. He was gone all day, and when he came back he complained that he had seen someone following him on horseback at a good distance. He was very excited, and told his grown son that the next day they would hitch up the wagon and when they came back they would be rich men. Next morning, however, he was very sick with a high fever. He kept telling his son to hitch the horses to the wagon, and his son would answer that they would, just as soon as the father recovered. But the father didn't recover. In a very few days he was dead. Later on, when the son was cleaning his father's saddle, he found an old gold coin thrust up under the skirts. Then he understood what had happened. His father had found el Tejano's gold. Ignoring the warning, he had taken a coin away with him. The man following him had been el Tejano. And now the father was dead and el Tejano's secret was still safe.

These are some of the ways in which the dead tie the living to the Pimería Alta. They are not the only ones; the dead have been present through much of the book so far. I'itoi was killed by Siwani and came back to life. The San Francisco statues in Magdalena, San Xavier, and elsewhere represent the saint's corpse. Father Kino lies, surrounded by milagros, in his open grave in Magdalena. The saints whose representations appear in churches and on the holy pictures and printed prayers sold in Magdalena are also dead. Once dead and in the presence of God, they can help the living. In a sense, this book is dominated by the dead, and their presence lies strong on the desert land.

The processes by which the dead bind the living to the land have been going on in the Pimería for centuries. By now the ties are many and strong, but they aren't necessarily permanent. El Tiradito seems to be changing, and most of the lesser tiraditos have been forgotten. Modern cemeteries aren't like the old ones, and many of the old ones are either filling up or falling into disuse for other reasons. Some Mexican-American friends tell me that it takes about three generations before a family's bonds with its dead are broken and the grave is left untended. People are constantly moving in and out of this region, and the newcomers will, for the most part, form different sorts of ties. Stories are forgotten, and watching television has to a great extent replaced telling and listening to tales of buried treasure and el Tiradito as family entertainment. But for now the ties are still there, and some are very strong indeed.

6. Places of Thanks and Petition

In March 1977 I was driving with three companions along the far northwest corner of the Papago Reservation. We were following a pipeline road that stretches from near Chuichu south and west toward Ajo. As we drove along, it became apparent that we were also following a much older footpath. According to anthropologist Bernard Fontana, who was one of our party, this trail was a part of a much larger network, one that stretched from the Little Colorado River down to the Gulf of California. The trails spread out between water holes and came together again near permanent sources of that life-giving fluid. The trail system had apparently been in use for a long time, for stone tools of a type made several thousand years ago had been found along it.

We were visiting historic O'odham villages that morning, so at one point we turned east off our pipeline road and went over a low pass to the now abandoned village of Sif Vaya (Bitter Well). Sif Vaya (pronounced Sif Wahia) had been occupied until some time after 1922 and occasionally visited by Franciscan missionaries. It was noted in 1911 as having a chapel.[1] It had been abandoned for a number of years at the time of our visit. Our very rough dirt road followed the path of a discernible foot trail over the pass toward the village. As we crested the pass, one of the passengers noticed an unusual grouping of rocks by the trailside. We stopped and got out to look.

A ring of about thirteen stones, ranging in size from two to four inches across, surrounded a larger, central stone of black volcanic rock, perhaps one foot by six inches. That the rocks had been deliberately placed there by humans was self-evident. When they were put there was impossible to tell. It could have been an hour before our visit, or two thousand years. Such rock piles and arrangements are common sights in our region. They can be found by river crossings, in passes, and at other points of potential risk to travelers. At least some must date back to pre-Spanish times.[2]

If the rock piles were indeed placed as protective petitions at potentially dangerous parts of the trail, they have a parallel on today's Papago Reservation. Among the crosses and nichos marking death sites are occasional larger shrines—nichos containing statues of the Virgin Mary. One on the road from Chuichu to Shopishk is partway up the side of a low hill. The path to it is outlined by rocks that have been painted white. Another defined area next to the road was used for the feast activities that accompanied the shrine's dedication. Like other reservation roadside shrines, it was erected by a concerned individual in an attempt to make that stretch of road a safer place on which to drive.[3]

Many of the roadside shrines away from the reservation were erected by Mexican-American families for very specific purposes. On State Highway 82, just south of Patagonia, a set of cement steps leads up to a small niche cut into a cliff on the east side of the road. This shrine was established by Juan and Juanita Telles in 1943, in petition for the safe return from World War II of their sons Ralph and Richard. Both boys made it back home, and the family still tends the shrine. In 1988 the shrine was restored in a cooperative effort involving the Telles family, the Pimería Alta Historical Society, and the Arizona Department of Transportation.[4]

When I visited the shrine in early November 1989, it contained statues and pictures of seven different saints and members of the Holy Family. Between twenty and thirty candles were placed in front of the images, as were several photographs (including one of a

131

Shrine to the Virgin on the road between Chuichu and
Shopishk. This and other shrines to the Virgin have been erected
by O'odham in an effort to protect the potentially dangerous
highways. Photo by John P. Schaefer.

newborn baby). Flowers, a rosary, some simple crosses made of
twigs, and a hospital bracelet were also in evidence. Apparently, the
shrine is more than a place where one family made one specific petition; it has become a general place of petitions for many people.

Travelers along U.S. 80 between Tombstone and Bisbee pass by
a tiny chapel partway up Mule Mountain. It is painted white and is
just large enough to hold one or two people in front of its altar. It
was built in 1951 by Edward Madrid and his late brother, Arnold, in
petition for a safe return from the Korean War, to which they were
about to be sent.[5] It contains a statue of the Virgin Mary and has

132

become an important local place of petitions. Travelers leave candles, photographs of loved ones, and thank offerings of all kinds. A few years ago, I remember seeing a particularly touching request—a poster of a Tucson woman who had disappeared several months before while cycling on the west side of town. The poster was placed on the wall without further written comment, but it seemed apparent that what was then a tragic mystery was being left in the care of the Virgin.

In Sonora, one figure dominates the roadside religious art: that of Our Lady of Guadalupe. A dark-complexioned young woman with head bowed and hands folded in prayer, she wears a gold crown and is clad in a starry robe. She stands on a crescent moon upheld by an angel and is surrounded by rays of light. Roses are often depicted in clusters around her image. She is the most popular religious figure of the entire Mexican and Mexican-American world. She is the Protectress of the Mexicans, Queen of the Americas—the Virgin Mary as she appeared just outside Mexico City to an Indian named Juan Diego.

It was 1531, little more than a decade after the bloody and traumatic Conquest of Mexico. Juan Diego was on his way into Mexico City, past the hill of Tepeyac, which in Aztec times had been sacred to the Goddess Tonantzin, "Our Mother." There by the hill he saw a beautiful woman who commanded him to go to Mexico City. There Juan was to see the bishop and ask him to build a church in honor of the Lady on the very spot where she had appeared. This Juan did, only to meet with a rebuff from the bishop. After a second request had also been denied, the Lady told Juan to gather the roses he found growing on the hill into his *tilma,* or cloak, and carry them to the bishop as proof of the truth of his story. He did as she commanded, spilling the roses at the bishop's feet. When he did so, he revealed on his tilma the image of the Lady with whom he had spoken.[6]

It is this tilma, believed by many to have been miraculously imprinted by the Virgin Mary with her own image, that is still on display in the Basilica of Our Lady of Guadalupe, the most recent successor to the church which Bishop Zumarragá built on the site of Juan Diego's vision. And it is this image that is reproduced in millions of Mexican homes and in public places wherever Mexicans live. Often Juan Diego, kneeling to gather the December roses into his tilma, is a part of the scene. I have seen *la Guadalupana,* as she is called, embroidered and crocheted on altar cloths, etched on the windows of Low Rider cars, and spray-painted on a boarded-up window in Tucson. She appears almost everywhere, in every context. And she is a constant sight along the roads and highways of Sonora.[7]

There is a tiny white chapel to her atop a low hill just north of the old Sonoran mission town of Pitiquito, for instance. A wide, smooth footpath leads directly from International Highway 2 to her front door, an easy walk for pilgrims. Within, her carved image stands in front of red, white, and green cloth hangings, asserting through the national colors her essential Mexicanness. Just south of Magdalena on International Highway 15, a painting of her used to be visible on a cliff near a roadside fruit and vegetable stand. A few years ago, the cliff face was covered with rubble from a major highway construction project, all except the Virgin's head. Now that the construction is over and the cliff has become part of an overpass system, the Virgin has been uncovered and is once more presented with candles and other small offerings.

A few miles north, in the town of Imuris, a large roadside Guadalupe is painted on a vertical cement slab on the north side of the road. Juan Diego kneels in mute wonder, gathering December roses from the hillside in front of her. Some sort of glitter or reflecting material has been mixed into the paint used for the Virgin's clothes so that she sparkles in the sunshine. A quarter of a mile farther north is another image of her, this time painted on a tiled panel on the crest of a hill. And farther east, there is a gigantic painting of her on a cement slab set against a road-cut cliff on the highway between Imuris and Cananea. Perhaps a hundred feet tall and twenty feet wide, this image is rumored to have been installed on the orders of one of Mexico's top mafiosos.

This fits with information I was given when I was asking about the printed prayers addressed to manifestations of the Devil, mentioned in chapter 3. People in the drug trade, I was told, pray to the Devil if they need the sort of help that only the Devil will provide. But once their rivals have been rubbed out or the big shipment of dope has gone through, they will repay, not the Devil, but God, the Virgin, and the saints. This seems to be on the principle of trying to keep square with all sides, but it explains perfectly the huge Guadalupe painting on the highway.[8]

These are only a few of the roadside Guadalupes that have caught my personal fancy. There are dozens more in our region, as there are all over Mexico. And every public Guadalupe image may have its candles, its tiny bunches of flowers left for the only person who really understands, who can and will help anyone, no matter how humble.

Just as it did in the case of the death crosses, the State of Arizona in the 1930s appropriated the form of the roadside shrine for its own secular purposes. A small rock nicho stands along the frontage road to Interstate 19, just north of the entrance to Tubac. It is dedicated to the memory of Father Juan de San Martín, first pastor of Tumacacori Mission and a contemporary of Father Kino. Erected in 1939 by the Santa Cruz County Chamber of Commerce, it was one of several historic shrines placed along what was then designated the "Camino de los Padres." A shrine commemorating Father Kino farther upstream was apparently washed away in the floods of 1967; another one in memory of Fray Marcos de Niza, possibly the first European to enter what is now Arizona, still stands near the tiny border town of Lochiel. These shrines are neither death markers nor places of petition, but instead, memorials to historic figures.[9]

Yard Shrines

The urban equivalent of the roadside shrine is the front-yard shrine. Many homes in southern Arizona have them. Small or large, they always seem to be visible from the street, even when they are behind fences. They usually take the form of nichos, anywhere from two to six feet in height. Inside the nicho is a holy image and perhaps a candle or two. These shrines usually represent petitions on the part of the family occupying the house. A family member may be ill or in need of help, and a favorite sacred figure will be promised a shrine. Sometimes the shrine is erected as a request for help, sometimes in payment for assistance received.[10]

Most of the family yard shrines remain family affairs. They are built or commissioned by family members, cared for by family members, and remain as visual statements of faith and of a solution sought (and often found) to a crisis within the family. A few have grown into something more, however—focal points for devotion and petitions on the part of a broader community. Here are the stories of two such locations in the Tucson area.

In the side yard of a house just inside the South Tucson city limits is a stone grotto dedicated to St. Jude, helper of impossible causes. It is about five feet tall and surmounted by a wooden cross, and stands under a plastic and metal ramada. Kneelers are arranged on the cement slab in front of it. A green metal sign with white letters identifies the occupant as ST. JUDE/ST. JUDAS. Inside the nicho is a large, three-foot high statue of St. Jude, along with smaller busts of the Sorrowing Virgin, Christ, and St. Jude. Several strings of colored lights illuminate the interior. Offerings left at the shrine include hospital bracelets, small metal milagros, photographs of children, adults, and families, a palm-leaf cross, a crucifix, candles, and artificial flowers. A smaller shrine to the same saint is built onto a corner of the house.

The shrine and its surrounding area are the responsibility of Mrs. Edith Clark Espino, the woman who lives in the house. In the early 1950s, Mrs. Espino lived in a different house on the same street. She had always wanted to move into the house she currently occupies. When it went on the market, however, she had no money even for a down payment. She asked St. Jude to help her purchase the house, promising that if she was able to do so, she would build him a shrine and celebrate his feast day each year with a Mass. By a remarkable turn of circumstances, she was able to purchase the house. The shrine stands as testimony to her gratitude and as a resource for many others who also need help with problems that seem impossible. Each year, in late October, St. Jude is honored with a Mass at his shrine.[11]

Another family shrine that has "gone public" is located at a street corner on the west side of the Santa Cruz River. Beside an ordinary, one-story house, a ramada shelters a small nicho which in turn contains a foot-high wooden crucifix. Tiny metal milagros representing parts of the body are pinned to velvet-covered boards on each side of the crucifix, and candles and floral offerings sit in front of the nicho. The chain-link fence behind the nicho is usually covered with artificial flowers. An elaborate wrought- and cast-iron fence with an openwork cross in it stands in front of the nicho. A sign proclaims that this is the site of *el Señor de los Milagros*—"the Lord of the Miracles." Two kneelers are in front of the fence, and a drinking fountain waits invitingly under the shade of a large tree nearby for the benefit of those who may have arrived in the heat of the Tucson summer.

The crucifix within the nicho is believed by its owners to be about four hundred years old. A similarly named statue is in Uruapan, Michoacán, Mexico, while a third is in Spain. The statue in Tucson is said to have been in the possession of the same family for fifteen generations. According to family tradition, it was instrumental in saving the family from a number of disasters, most notably an attack by Indians on a train in Sinaloa, Mexico, early in this century. Its current owner (it passes to the eldest daughter in each generation) decided in 1963 to share it with the general public. The shrine is a dynamic place, constantly changing as improvements and new furnishings are donated by grateful people who have been helped by el Señor. The years and the temperature changes involved in sitting out of doors year-round in Tucson have not been kind to the statue. Its paint is peeling up in thick squares. But this is less important to the image's owner than the fact that many people have come, some from as far off as California and Colorado, to ask for and receive miracles.[12]

As is the case at the shrine to St. Jude, Mass is said here on an annual basis. September 14, the Feast of the Triumph of the Holy Cross, sees perhaps four hundred people gathered in the yard in the early evening. Mass is celebrated, and there are usually local musicians in attendance. After Mass, the musicians will play a few secular favorites of the older generation, and coffee and cookies are served to all.

What do these yard shrines look like? Most are simply half-domed nichos, made of bricks, stones, or plaster. The plaster ones can be purchased ready-made from many of the stores specializing in cast lawn ornaments, or they can be made by a skilled family member or neighbor. A few get more complicated. There is one in South Tucson with twisted columns flanking the opening. Another in the same city is built in the shape of a miniature baroque church with a six-foot tower on either side of the body of the shrine. Towers and facade are painted white with orange trim. Strings of colored lights, plastic holly, and tiny bells hang across the facade, between the towers.

Sometimes a nicho is made of recycled materials. One occasionally finds a bathtub sunk vertically for half its length in the ground and used as a nicho. There is one such in Safford, on the Gila River, and another in the cemetery at Tombstone. The nicho mentioned in chapter 4 as having been erected on the proposed route of the Mission Road extension on the west bank of the Santa Cruz was cast in plaster, using an old bathtub as a mold. But my favorite piece of recycling is just north and west of Tucson's old downtown district. In a front yard sits a small, bar-sized Regal refrigerator. An extension cord connects it with the house, so that the light within can be lit. A saint's statue occupies the refrigerator's main compartment, while the small upper freezing compartment contains a reclining statue of San Francisco.

Very occasionally a yard shrine moves beyond the standard nicho format. One I know in South Tucson consists of a circular cement pond with a rim about two feet high. In the center of the pond rises a conical hill some five feet high, faced with black lava rocks. Set into the front of this hill is a miniature ceramic church of the sort that one can buy in crafts stores in Nogales, Sonora. It is about a foot high and has been painted white. Atop the conical hill stands a statue of the Virgin Mary. The entire ensemble strikes me as a stylistic compromise between the standard Mexican-American nicho and the lawn statues of saints, most particularly St. Francis of Assisi, which are found in many Anglo-American gardens.

Saints appear on the walls of houses as well. Perhaps a tile or mosaic picture of Our Lady of Guadalupe may be mounted on a front wall. Or there may be a niche actually built into the wall, with its statue or picture, usually equipped with a small light. Several years ago, I heard a story concerning such a nicho. A friend told me that her grandfather, who lived in one of the barrios just north of downtown Tucson, had been a bootlegger. Many neighborhoods have such individuals who are willing to resell beer or liquor to their neighbors after legal hours. This man had a nicho on the wall of his house containing an image of San Pedro. If the light was on over San Pedro, that was a signal that one could knock on the back door and buy some party supplies. This story intrigued me, and one day I was retelling it to another friend, a Mexican-American man then in his late sixties. He knew the house but stoutly maintained that it was in a different barrio. In addition, the saint involved wasn't San Pedro at all, but San Francisco. I went to the location he described—just south of downtown this time—and sure enough, there was a house with a reclining statue of San Francisco occupying a small, rectangular nicho over the front door.

A while later, I was again retelling the story, this time to an Anglo American. The story I got in exchange was a bit different but still very much to the point. A friend of my acquaintance had purchased an old house in one of the barrios near downtown Tucson. When he took over the house, there had been a small shrine in one of its windows. The shrine contained a crucifix and some colored lights. He had rather liked the idea of the shrine and had left it there, even turning on the lights on occasion. But he had noticed that every so often, men would knock on his back door in the small hours, asking if he had beer for sale. I have no doubt that there are other stories about bootleggers in other houses using saints' shrines in this way. I am also quite willing to believe that at least some of the stories are true and that Tucsonans and others have long been in the habit of using the saints for some pretty unsaintly purposes.

The Garden of Gethsemane

A more public shrine yet is the Garden of Gethsemane, also called Felix Lucero Park, on Congress Street just west of the Santa Cruz River bridge. This park, now administered by the City of Tucson and enclosed by a brick and iron fence, contains several life-sized cement statues illustrating episodes in the life of Christ. A huge crucifix dominates the north end, while just below it a low, white sepulcher

139

holds the Entombed Christ. Then comes a Last Supper, with each apostle clearly a different person, gathered around the table. Christ sits in the center, while Judas stands at the right front corner with tension in every line of his face and body and a bag of coins clutched in his left hand. At the far southwest corner of the space is the Holy Family: Joseph and Mary bending over the Infant Christ. Finally, a small shrine in the shape of a two-towered castle contains a miniature scene of Pontius Pilate judging Jesus. The larger statues are painted a glaring white, except for a few drops of red blood on the wounds of the crucified Christ.

These statues, many of which have a wonderful raw power and intensity, are the work of the late Felix Lucero. Lucero is said to have been born in southern Colorado of Mayo Indian ancestry. He was serving as a soldier in France in World War I when he found himself in No Man's Land, wounded and surrounded by German soldiers. He made a promise to God that if he made it out alive with the soldiers who were with him, he would devote himself to religious works. He did survive the ordeal and spent the remainder of his life (he died in 1951) serving God in a number of ways. Two sets of sculpture by him survive in Arizona: the other is at the Shrine of St. Joseph in Yarnell, in the mountains to the north and west of Phoenix.[13]

Some older people who live near Lucero's shrine in the barrios on the West bank of the Santa Cruz still tell stories about him and his work. One story tells how he camped in a makeshift shelter under the old Congress Street bridge while he worked on the project. He apparently cast his statues in the sands of the riverbed. One person remembered that his first statues were "made of sand" and that it was only later that he was persuaded to cast them in more permanent cement. One story I have been told relates how he was working one day on the large statue of the Crucifed Christ when a drunk came along on horseback. The drunk mocked Lucero and his work and caused his horse to "tromple on" the partly completed statue. According to the story, he then departed and had not gone beyond the first bend in the riverbed when a snake startled his horse. The horse reared and threw its rider, who died instantly of a broken neck.

This story illustrates an ancient theme: it is unwise to mock that which is sacred. Other times and places have their own tales of swift retribution visited on the impious. That such a legend is attached to the Garden of Gethsemane, and that it is told as fact in the neighborhood of the shrine is a good sign that this site belongs to its Westside Mexican-American Catholic community in a real way. Note the very Old World role played by the serpent; it is a far cry from *la corúa,* the passive guardian of precious water.

Other signs of community "ownership" of the Garden of Gethsemane await the visitor to the site. Every time I have gone there, I have found offerings: candles and flowers in the tomb of Christ, for instance, or a coin on Jesus' outstretched hand in the Last Supper scene. One day I was photographing the statues when a man dressed in a sweatsuit jogged along Congress Street and down the steps that in those days led to the park. He jogged up to the crucifix, fell on his knees, and remained there long enough to say a couple of "Our Fathers." Then he crossed himself, got up, and jogged off again.

There are negative reactions to the site as well. Vandalism seems to be a recurring problem in the Garden of Gethsemane. Every now and then visitors to the park will find that someone has come by with a sledgehammer and smashed Christ's face and outstretched hand in the Last Supper scene, for instance, or the Infant Jesus in the Holy Family group, or the feet of the crucified Saviour. In my experience it is always Jesus who is so treated. I have heard local speculation that these are the acts of those who are said to view the statues as idolatrous and evil. The damage is usually quietly repaired by one of a small group of volunteers who several years ago assumed that responsibility, along with the duty of keeping the site clean.

Such vandalism, by the way, is not confined to Felix Lucero Park. A ceramic statue of Santa Teresa honoring the memory of three school children who died in two separate accidents near a downtown school was similarly desecrated a few years ago. The statue was replaced with one by a local blacksmith, which so far has proved to be hammer-proof. The shrine is now being guarded by neighbors, and two older women have taken it upon themselves to

141

keep it neat and clean. Two eighteenth-century wooden lions flank-ing the main altar at San Xavier Mission were stolen and possibly burned in the early 1980s. These were replaced through the efforts of a local couple who located a family of woodcarvers in Puebla, Mexico, who were able and willing to take on the job of making copies. A mentally disturbed individual broke into St. Augustine's Cathedral in downtown Tucson in December 1987 and smashed several large plaster statues. A local artist undertook their restora-tion as a labor of love.[14]

In similar ways, the community responds to damages in the fab-ric of its visual religious heritage. I find it fascinating that in at least two cases I know about, the individuals who donated their time, money, and skills to make good damage done to local shrines were not members of the Catholic community at all, but rather concerned Tucsonans who felt strongly about the particular incidents. This seems to be similar to the ways in which Anglos have come to use el Tiradito, or the way in which O'odham, Yaquis, Mexicanos, and Americanos all have different traditions concerning San Francisco. The sites are acquiring new devotees who approach them in their own, culturally conditioned ways. For their traditional "owners," however, the shrines still appear to be as sacred as they were.

Hilltop Monuments

Many hilltops in the Pimería Alta are crowned with shrines. Often these will consist of one or three crosses. They may be wooden crosses, or they may be painted on a cliff face like the ones visible from Los Reales Road just to the west of Cardinal Avenue between San Xavier Mission and the New Pascua Yaqui community.

When my friend Richard Morales moved into the same general neighborhood, his was one of the first houses in the area. Even be-fore he built the house, he climbed to the top of the nearest hill with various family members and erected three white wooden crosses. They stayed up for about five years, he told me, until some neigh-borhood kids dismantled them and took the pieces down the hill. The purpose of the crosses seems to have been protective: they appear to have been intended to make the area a better place in which to live.

Similar crosses and other hilltop shrines dot our region. According to the information that I have been able to gather, most were erected by single individuals, often in full or partial payment of a manda or promise to do so. A case in point is the shrine on a low hill just north of the junction town of Santa Ana, Sonora, on Highway 15. On the crest of the hill are three pillars, each about ten feet tall. The left-hand column supports a statue of the Virgin, the center one, the Sacred Heart of Jesus, and the right-hand one, St. Jude. Attached to the central column is a plaque reading "Manda Cumplida/ Ofrecida por/Joaquin Espinosa Arnett/al Sagrado Corazón de Jesús/ Santa Ana, Sonora/Junio 12, 1962" (Vow fulfilled/offered by/Joaquín Espinosa Arnett/to the Sacred Heart of Jesus/Santa Ana, Sonora/June 12, 1962). Another plaque, dated June 24, 1989, attributes the entire assemblage of statues, columns, cement floor, and landscaping to a "group of friends" in Santa Ana.

One hilltop shrine in particular stands out in my memory. On a rocky hilltop just north of Pitiquito, Sonora, stands a life-size statue of the Sacred Heart of Jesus. No road or trail leads to the site, and it is quite a scramble to get up there. The statue is right at the top of the hill with a small, empty nicho a few yards below it, to the south. Candles and floral offerings at the base of the statue on the day I visited it were proof that visitors had come to this place. But others still had used the hill, centuries before. It was quite literally covered with petroglyphs—lines and figures pecked into the dark volcanic boulders that make up the surface of the knoll. There were parallel wavy lines, circles, mazes, and figures of mountain goats. A possible representation of a man on horseback suggested that some of the drawings, at least, were of comparatively recent date. The modern town of Pitiquito grew up around a Franciscan-built, colonial mission church. The mission was established because there was already a village on the same site. The hill was used by villagers long before Europeans established a presence in the region. The same places are used over the centuries, perhaps for similar purposes, and the continuities of our region's culture show themselves in yet another way.

Disasters Averted

There are a few places in the Pimería Alta where petitions are believed to have been answered in such a spectacular manner that the stories are still told over a century later. Entire communities have been miraculously delivered from impending doom, apparently by divine intervention. One such place is the mission community of Oquitoa, in Sonora's Altar Valley. In chapter 1 I told of Father Joaquín Olizarra saving the village from being destroyed by a *culebra de agua*. Oquitoans have preserved yet another tale of miraculous delivery. In the mid-nineteenth century, Oquitoa was under attack by a group of Indians from several different tribes. The villagers sought refuge in the church and prayed to its patron, San Antonio, for help. The attackers inexplicably melted away without pressing their attack home. Months later, a man who was known to have been in the attacking force was asked why they had left. He replied that the attackers left when they saw the relief column of horsemen approach the village, led by an officer wearing a blue cloak. No such column had been seen by the villagers, and no such column had been sent by the nearby military garrison at Altar. The assumption was—and is—that the officer in the blue cloak was San Antonio, protecting his church and village. The saint is often shown wearing blue, a common color of the Franciscan habit in colonial times (though not the color worn by the Franciscans who served in the Pimería Alta).

Another story of miraculous intervention takes us to Caborca, to the mission church of La Purísima Concepción—the Immaculate Conception. This church was also the scene of a siege in the mid-nineteenth century. On April 1, 1857, Caborca was attacked by a party of American adventurers under the command of Henry Alexander Crabb. After a preliminary battle, the Caborcans sought refuge in the mission church and its attached convent, with Crabb's forces occupying buildings across the road from the church. At one point the invaders stormed the convento and from this vantage point attempted to blow in one of the doors of the church with a barrel of gunpowder. This attempt failed, with considerable loss of life, and the attackers retreated to the buildings across the street.

144

Finally, Indians set the roofs of these houses on fire with flaming arrows, and the Crabb party surrendered on April 6. All were executed except for a sixteen-year-old lad named Charles Evans, who eventually escaped, returned to the United States, and wrote down his story of the unsuccessful expedition.[15]

So much for history. Living family traditions tell us more, however. According to a descendant of a mother and daughter who were among those seeking refuge inside the church, when Crabb's men tried to blow up the church door they rolled the powder keg into place, lit the fuse, and retired. When they had done so, a lady dressed in blue appeared and extinguished the fuse. They posted sharpshooters, among them young Charles Evans, and tried again. The same lady put out the fuse once more, despite the attempts of the Americans to shoot her. As often as they tried, she would foil their attempts, until they finally gave up.

The Virgin Mary traditionally wears a blue dress, and conventional wisdom would suggest that this is a story of how the Virgin saved her church. The woman in whose family the narrative is preserved, however, feels that there is another possible interpretation. While admitting that others attribute the deed to the Virgin Mary, my informant insists that there is a strong possibility that it was someone entirely different—Sister María de Agreda, the famous Lady in Blue who was believed to have teleported herself from Spain to preach to Indians in what is now New Mexico and Arizona in the early 1600s.

When Father Kino traveled to the junction of the Colorado and Gila Rivers in 1699, he and his companions were told by Indians that a woman dressed in blue and carrying a cross had preached to their grandparents in a strange language. Similar stories were told to the Franciscan missionaries who arrived in New Mexico in the 1620s: a Lady in Blue had visited the Indians a few years before, preaching Christianity. When the story got back to Spain, an explanation was ready and waiting: a well-known mystic nun, Sister María de Agreda, told of how she had been miraculously transported to the American deserts, where she had preached in her own language to the Indians. The tale gained considerable currency in its day and is still told as a part of the unexplained lore of the American

Southwest.[16] And, as my informant told me, if Sister María traveled from Spain to the Southwest in the 1600s while she was alive, there is no reason why she couldn't do so again in 1857, two hundred years after her death.

This story, which neatly connects the arrival of the Spaniards in the Pimería Alta with the arrival of the Americans, ends our discussion of places of petition. With this chapter, we have entered a transplanted European world, the world which Father Kino and his co-workers did much to introduce to the Sonoran Desert. There are a few traces of the older, O'odham universe, to be sure. As I mentioned in chapter 2, the Children's Shrine is also a place of petitions, especially during the ceremonies of renewal when the people ask for rain and crops. Petitions of some sort also seem to be involved with the rockpile shrines where passers-by pause, add a rock to the pile, and move on. But most of the stories told in this chapter have their equivalents all over the Catholic world. We have moved from the things of our region to imports that have been basically unchanged by their presence here. It is now time to examine the physical, artistic settings that are associated with many of the sites I have mentioned.

7. Art: Our Created Landscape

I visited the mission church of San Xavier del Bac on December 1, 1989. It was just before the patronal feast of Saint Francis Xavier, and the church was decorated for the occasion. The statue of the standing St. Francis had been brought down from behind the main altar and placed in a small, gauze-covered booth to the left of the altar railing, where the faithful could visit and touch him. Red and yellow ribbon roses had been pinned to the white cloth covering the sides and back of the booth, and the effect was quite lovely.

This statue consists of a carved and highly finished head and hands, mounted on a roughly finished wooden torso, which in turn is supported by a wooden framework. The torso is fashioned from one piece of wood, with a flaming heart carved in relief on its chest. This representation of San Xavier's heart is conventional and symbolizes the saint's missionary zeal.[1] The statue is normally dressed in a black cassock and white surplice, with a black biretta on its head. The head and hands were ordered from Mexico in 1759 by Father Alonzo Espinoza, S.J., to go in the church that preceded the one which stands today.[2] The body and the wooden framework were probably constructed at the mission. It is easy to see the rationale behind such a fragmentary statue; it had to be carried on the back of a pack animal from Central Mexico, and any reduction in bulk or weight would make the whole process a good deal easier.

A casual observer of Mission San Xavier's ornate interior on a typical day of the year might think that it was already decorated to the utmost. That person would be mistaken. For the occasion of the feast of St. Francis Xavier, several additions had been made. The soaring angels that flank the main altar were temporarily dressed in long, white gowns and crowned with white. In their hands were placed standards supporting red and white banners bearing the letters "SFX" done in gold rickrack. Smaller red and white banners hung from each of the pedestals along the walls of the nave, and from the cornice along the nave. These banners were held in place with large coffee cans that had been painted red and white. Strings of red and gold tinsel crossed over the length of the nave as well. The lily, in other words, had been successfully gilded.

The Baroque Style in Mexico

This is in perfect keeping with the artistic style in which the mission was built and decorated—a style which, directly or indirectly, informs much of the appearance of the places and sites we have been discussing in this book. This style is the baroque, or better, the Mexican baroque.

The baroque style originated in western Europe as a logical outgrowth of the art of the Renaissance. A product of the Age of Kings and of the Catholic Counter-Reformation, baroque art uses and adapts the classical principles rediscovered in the Renaissance to create artistic statements of great drama and intensity. When transplanted to Mexico via Spain, the baroque style of architecture took on new characteristics from the unique artistic traditions of the latter country. Spain had been occupied for over seven hundred years by followers of Islam, and Spanish architectural decoration absorbed many of the characteristics of Islamic art.[3] All these elements were recombined in Mexico to produce the distinctive style of architectural decoration called Mexican baroque.[4]

What role did Mexico's huge Indian population have in the formulation of this new style? The answers are complex and vary from region to region.[5] Some of the mural paintings and relief sculptures on the sixteenth-century churches in central and southern Mexico show a decided Indian influence. But the question remains as to how much of the nature of eighteenth-century baroque church decoration may be attributed to Indian tastes and ideas. Such a question can really only be answered on a case-by-case basis, dealing with individual churches and relating them to the traditions of specific Indian cultures. Later on, I will try to suggest some answers that apply to the churches of the Pimería Alta.

Although it is easy to get bogged down in a mass of detail when discussing baroque buildings in Mexico, the basic principles of the style are easily defined. They are: movement, contrast, and richness.

Little is quiet and peaceful in the world of eighteenth-century Mexican church decoration. Strong diagonals cause one's gaze to shoot off toward the horizon. Lines seldom move directly from point A to point B but rather jiggle up and down, in and out, in a complex series of angles and curves. Where there are statues, they, too, seem imbued with motion. Figures gesticulate and seem about to step off their pedestals. Even Christ is no exception to this rule. He flinches against his bonds, stumbles on the road up Calvary, seems to writhe rather than hang on his cross. The classical repose of the Renaissance has been exchanged for a physical activity that in turn seems to reflect emotional intensity and turmoil.

The second basic principle of the Mexican baroque decoration is contrast. Densely decorated surfaces are placed between large expanses of bare wall. Brilliantly lit areas alternate with dark shadows. Much of the exterior detail seems designed to catch shadows, accentuating the lines of the façade with black bands of deep shade.

Besides this there is richness, richness of material, with retablos covered with gold leaf and statues of Christ and the Virgin crowned with real gold and silver. There is richness of color as well, with deep reds, blues, and greens adding a sense of opulence to painted surfaces. Especially there is richness of detail, with each church being equipped with a multitude of paintings and statues, each one of which brings its own meaning to the ensemble.

149

San Xavier del Bac

Having touched on the major aesthetic principles that underlie most eighteenth-century Mexican baroque church decoration, we can now take another look at San Xavier del Bac, Southern Arizona's very own example of that rich and expressive style. The church we see today was not the first one at the site. An earlier church built in 1756 by Father Espinoza was located just to the west of the present mission. This was the church for which the standing statue of St. Francis Xavier was ordered. Only the foundations of the original mission remain. When the church that stands today was completed in the 1790s, the older church building was dismantled, moved around the corner, and reassembled as the *convento* wing that stretches to the east of San Xavier Mission.[6]

The present church was built in a campaign that began around 1783 and ended in 1797 or shortly thereafter. Fray Juan Bautista Velderrain was in charge of the project until his death in 1789 or 1790, and then Fray Juan Bautista Llorenz took over. The church was never really finished, the incomplete east tower being the most obvious indication of this. There are several traditional explanations for this fact, some of them dramatic; they include a fatal accident to one of the men working on the tower, an accident which effectively halted the project. There is no documentary evidence supporting this legend nor is there any basis to the widespread notion that no taxes had to be paid on an unfinished church. The most probable explanation of the unfinished tower is that the friars simply ran out of funds for the completion of such a huge project.[7]

Like most Mexican baroque churches, San Xavier is built on a simple cruciform plan, with a dome at the crossing. Two towers, which would be symmetrical if both were finished, flank the portal at the south end. The bare white surfaces of the tower bases set off the densely packed carving of the portal. The white paint is a twentieth-century addition to San Xavier, by the way. Photographs taken in the 1880s and 1890s show the towers as being of unplastered brick, and the rest of the church as covered with lime plaster, which was probably a tan color. The so-called "White Dove of the

The main retablo of San Xavier Mission. St. Francis Xavier
stands in the lower central niche. Above him is Our Lady of the
Immaculate Conception, and above her is God the Father. The
estípite columns and the overarching scallop motif discussed in
the text are clearly visible. Photo by John P. Schaefer.

San Xavier Mission from the southeast. Photo by
John P. Schaefer.

Desert" wasn't painted white until Bishop Henry Granjon's restoration campaign, completed in 1907. A restoration project underway
in 1990–91 is replacing the glaring white paint with a softer, cream-
colored lime plaster, which is then hand-burnished with smooth
stones.

The soft brown of the portal would have contrasted well with
the original lime plaster. Enough traces of red, yellow, and green
paint remain on the portal to show that it was once brilliantly colored. The portal is organized in three levels and is best thought of
as three classical temple facades stacked one on top of the other. In
the lower story, the doorway is flanked by two pairs of columns; in

152

the next level, it is a central window that is so flanked. There are only two columns in the top story. Cutting across each of these uppermost columns near its top is a curious diagonal element; this is all that remains of the triangular pediment that caps the facades of most classical temples. Vertical lines in high relief climb up the edges of the portal; these end in curved elements called *volutes*. A deeply scalloped line frames the top of the portal.

Within these vertical framing lines is a wild profusion of architectural and sculptural detail. Complex columns called *estípites*[8] support multi-layered lintels that move in and out as they cross the portal. Lintels and estípites join with the broken pediments and volutes to give the portal a sense of movement.

The portal contains five statues of saints. One, Saint Francis of Assisi, sits at the very top and has been reduced by time, weathering, and inept restoration to a truncated cone. The others occupy niches between the pairs of estípites on the lower two stories. Saints Barbara and Cecilia appear on the upper story, Saints Catherine and Lucy on the lower.[9] Saints Cecilia and Catherine are missing their heads; village tradition has it that these were roped and pulled off by Apaches during a nineteenth-century raid.[10] Drapery is carved in relief over the niches, topped by sprigs of foliage. More carved foliage is densely packed into the space above the main door. Over the second-story window is a scallop or cockle shell. The top story has neither niches nor statues. In its center is the coat of arms of the Franciscan Order; a cross bearing the naked arm of Christ and the clad arm of St. Francis of Assisi, the whole surmounted by coils of rope. The two arms refer to the mystical experience in which St. Francis received the stigmata or wounds of Christ on his hands and feet; the rope is the cord that Franciscans use to fasten their habits. On either side are smaller lozenges bearing the monograms of Jesus and Mary. Surrounding these are densely packed grapevines, carved in relief.

On the outer side of the estípites, two lions face outward, reared up on their hind legs. They support themselves with their front paws by holding onto carved sheaves of wheat that lean in turn against the volutes at the edge of the portal. Finally, a mouse sits atop the left-hand volute, while a cat crouches on the right-hand one.

While all these forms and shapes are highly decorative, they are something more than decoration. Each detail, no matter how bizarre or insignificant, may well carry its special meaning. Some are easily understood: St. Francis of Assisi and the Franciscan insignia occupy their central locations within the portal because the church was constructed under the direction of Franciscan missionaries. Saints Barbara, Cecilia, and Lucy were women in the early Christian church who were martyred for their faith. Their presence on the facade may have served as a reminder that a similar fate was always a possibility for Christian missionaries. St. Catherine of Siena lived between 1347 and 1380, a thousand years later than the other three. One of the great Christian mystics, St. Catherine of Siena also aided the sick and worked tirelessly for unity within the Catholic Church. Her presence on the portal is a bit harder to understand. However, her identification with the headless statue clutching a palm frond in the lower-right niche is only an educated guess.[11]

With the scallop shell over the window we are on safer, if still somewhat ambiguous, ground. This is the symbol of St. James the Greater, *Santiago de Compostela,* patron saint of Spain. He is the Apostle James, one of the twelve original followers of Jesus who, according to legend, preached in Spain before his martyrdom in Rome. The same legends have his body miraculously translated to Spain after his death, where it was buried in Compostela and became the focus of huge pilgrimages during the Middle Ages. Later legends tell of his returning to earth to help in the struggle against the Moors, with the result that Santiago became, in a sense, the patron of the militant expansion of Spanish Catholicism. It is assumed that this is the reason his scallop shell appears so often on the mission churches of the Pimería Alta.

The scallop was an ancient symbol in the Mediterranean world long before it became connected with Santiago. Associated with Venus, it symbolized the female reproductive organs, and by extension, birth and regeneration. In the Roman Empire it was used in funeral rites as a symbol of resurrection. This meaning it carried into early Christian art. Finally, the scallop shell, with its serrated edges and fluted surfaces, is a perfect baroque decorative motif. Simple in overall form, yet complex in detail, it suggests movement and catches shadows.[12]

This brings us to one more important characteristic of the baroque style in Mexico: ambiguity. While it is probable that the builders intended the scallop shells that appear both inside and outside the church to refer to Santiago, there is no guarantee that this is the case. The reference in some or all cases may be to another of the meanings of the shell, or there may have been some personal reason known to the designer of the building alone. For that matter, it may be that no meaning whatever was intended and that the designer simply thought the shell looked nice. This ambiguity is, perhaps, inevitable in any system that relies heavily upon the use of symbols for communication, and it may exist mainly in the eye and mind of the modern observer. But for me, ambiguity is a very real aspect of Mexican baroque decoration.

The carvings on the upper story have their meaning, too. The monograms of Jesus and Mary remind the worshiper of the basic characters of the Christian story. The grapes and the wheat sheaves refer to the bread and wine of the Last Supper and to the sacrament of the Mass. The lions appear to be the emblems of the Spanish royal house of León, and supporters of the Spanish coat of arms. There is food for thought—and even a sermon or two—on this portal, with its references to the basic persons and events of the Christian faith, to some of the early martyrs of the church, and to the Spanish crown. And it is good to remember that the sculptures may have been used for that very purpose. For this was designed and built as a mission church, a place where Indians were trained to become Christian subjects of the Spanish crown.

It is not as easy to explain the cat and mouse that crouch on the volutes. To be sure, many writers and speakers quote an "Indian legend" to the effect that when the cat catches the mouse, the end of the world will be upon us. In my own experience, this story is usually told by Anglos and attributed to Indians. It may, in fact, be of O'odham origin, or it may be another of the many "native legends" that have arisen in response to the need to tell something interesting to visitors.

Whatever it is, it seems to be an explanation for features that are already there rather than a reason why the figures were carved in the first place. Such a reason is, however, given in a story that was told to a group of tourists who visited San Xavier around 1940. According to an unidentified Anglo-American guide who showed them around the church, there had been friction, perhaps even open fighting, between the local Indians and the Spaniards. The church at San Xavier was built to signal an end to this friction by providing a church that would be specifically for the Indians. As a sign that this was being done, figures of a cat and mouse, natural enemies, were placed on opposite sides of the portal. The new state of peace would last until the cat caught the mouse.[13]

All I can add to the subject is that, having seen many eighteenth-century baroque Mexican churches in isolated communities such as San Xavier, I am not surprised to find the cat and mouse. They simply join the ranks of the many unusual and startling images I have observed in the course of looking at the churches of colonial Mexico. They were without a doubt put there for a reason but that reason seems at the moment to be lost beyond recall.

Inside the church, one is assailed by detail on all sides. Fifty statues of saints and members of the Holy Family adorn the walls; countless more angels and cherubs hold candlesticks, play musical instruments, or hover in mid-air. Decorative relief carvings on the walls include scallop shells, curtains, flowers, and vines. A relief representation of the knotted Franciscan cord surrounds the entire interior at the level of the cornice, some twenty feet above the floor.

Most of the interior was originally painted. Much of this painting has survived the ravages of time and moisture. The painting is concentrated in the crossing, transepts, and altarpieces with virtually every surface in these areas being covered with paint. The very domes overhead were once painted. Moisture has taken its sad toll here, and only in the sacristy (a room not open to the general public in 1991) can one get a notion of how the church ceiling may once have looked. In addition to this overall decoration, a series of murals with painted frames illustrate devotional subjects and New Testament scenes. Additional murals may be found in the sacristy, baptistry, and choir loft. There are even two wooden doors painted on the lower walls. One is on the east side of the nave, the other on the west side of the sanctuary. Each is directly opposite a real doorway, and each creates an illusion of symmetry, that element of design that is so important to the classically trained mind.

These false doors are not the only optical illusions painted onto San Xavier's interior. The cornice that runs around the church interior is painted to resemble marble. Furthermore, the lower portion of the interior walls is painted to resemble colored tiles, set in a pattern that suggests motion. These details add to the sense of ambiguity that I mentioned as yet another characteristic of the baroque style.

To get a notion of just how rich and complex the interior is, let's take a look at the *retablo mayor,* or main altarpiece. Itself the subject of an entire book, this is a wonderfully complex assembly.[14] God the Father watches over the entire scene from the top, flanked by small medallions containing busts of Cain and Abel. Below these figures, angels draw aside curtains to reveal the Virgin of the Immaculate Conception, who is supported by cherubs. Directly below the Virgin is the statue of Saint Francis Xavier I described at the beginning of this chapter. These central statues are flanked by four of the apostles: Saints Peter, Paul, Andrew, and either Simon or John. More cherubs hold candles, support the cherubs who hold candles, play musical instruments, and generally flutter about, observing the scene.

The saints' statues are separated by estípites, just as they are on the front portal of the church. In this case, however, the richly carved columns are covered with gold. A small lozenge on each estípite bears a symbolic painting: a ladder, a generalized tree, a cypress tree, and a tower. Each of these objects has layers of meaning in the language of Christian symbolism. For instance, the ladder can refer to a link between earth and heaven. It is also one of the instruments of the Passion, having been used to remove Christ from the cross. Finally, it can refer to Christ Himself, as a link between mankind and God. The other three symbols have similarly complex meanings.

Several scallop shells are carved in relief on the retablo, while much of its surface is richly painted with representations of vines. As we saw in the discussion of the portal, the vine is a reference to

157

the Last Supper and the sacrament of the Mass. It can also refer to the relationship between God and His People, as expressed in the phrase "I am the true vine, and my father is the husbandman. . . . I am the vine, ye are the branches" (John 15: 1–5).

The symbols and images of the retablo mayor were not assembled in a random fashion. A strong unifying theme runs through the whole work, from God the Father, through the consequences of Original Sin in Cain's murder of Abel, to the redeeming sacrifice of Christ on the cross. Redemption is further suggested by the Virgin Mary, conceived without sin according to Catholic belief, and by the presence of the four saints who labored to spread and interpret the Gospel. This theme of the relationship between sinful humans and a loving and forgiving God is echoed by the other symbols and representations on the retablo. In fact, the whole composition is a strong theological statement of the basic tenets of Christianity—a highly suitable theme for a mission church.[15]

There is much, much more. In fact, it would take a book just to describe and explain all of San Xavier del Bac's art and imagery. But this should be enough to suggest two of the ways in which a church such as this can be experienced: as a set of theological statements presented in a symbolic code, and as a representative of a specific art style proper to a certain place and time.

Buildings Between Two Cultures

San Xavier del Bac can also be viewed as a kind of frozen dialogue—in this instance, a fairly one-sided one—between two religious and philosophical systems. The church was built in a cooperative effort, with Fathers Velderrain and Llorenz directing the project. Under them were trained craftspeople, probably Spanish or mestizo in race and culture. These craftspeople were obviously working within the mainstream traditions of the Mexican baroque style, even though they were plying their trade on the far northwestern frontier of New Spain. For the moment they must remain anonymous, although two family names have come down to us in association with the task. One Pedro Bojorquez carved his name and the year 1797 on the east side of the door between the sanctuary and the sacristy. And oral tradition tells us that two brothers named Gaona were in charge of the project. Documentary research now underway may shed further light on this problem of identity. The laborers on the project were the O'odham. Many must have been residents of Bac. However, the true Desert People may have been involved in the construction as well. There is an oral O'odham tradition that the entire population of Tecolote village, southwest of present-day Sells, moved to San Xavier and stayed for four years, building the mission.[16]

Visitors to San Xavier sometimes ask about the role that local Indians may have played in the construction and decoration of the church. A common stereotype among people of European descent is that "primitive" peoples are attracted to bright colors. For many Americans, accustomed perhaps to the sober, classically influenced Protestant church architecture of the eastern United States, San Xavier can seem exotic and even garish. It would be only natural to wonder concerning the degree to which local Indian taste and traditions might have influenced its appearance.

The answer is almost completely in the negative. Almost all the details of San Xavier are well within the mainstream traditions of the Mexican baroque style. Actually, this is to be expected. After all, the church was built for the purpose of converting pagan Indians to Christianity and to civilization as defined by Europeans. There is little evidence to suggest that the eighteenth-century missionaries in the Pimería Alta were at all interested in native artistic or philosophical traditions. To the contrary, several missionary accounts describe cultural differences between Europeans and Indians in terms of error on the part of the natives.[17]

There is one set of details at San Xavier that has been suggested as a product of an "O'odham hand." I have mentioned that a cornice runs around the interior of the church, some twenty feet above floor level. This cornice is painted with great wavy bands of red, yellow, green, brown, and black speckles, which appear to be a very stylized imitation of the effect of marble or some other decorative stone. Diamond-shaped areas outlined in red may suggest some sort of inclusions in the rock. This is a perfectly normal baroque attempt at creating the illusion of richness of material; the interior cornice of the mission church at Tubutama, Sonora, is similarly treated. Within the area of the sanctuary, however, details have been added to this fake marble that make it unique. Snail shells outlined in red or black paint appear on the cornice, along with the wavy bands and the geometric shapes. So far, so good; one gets the impression that the artist has seen fossil-bearing rock and is striving for that effect. But there are also at least three rabbits depicted in outline, and the red outline of a man. Also discernible in outline is a snake and what looks like some sort of a cat. One explanation for these totally charming details is that the workmen were doodling at a time when they were not intensely supervised. It has also been pointed out that these workmen were probably O'odham. The figures certainly seem to fit in with today's O'odham sense of humor, which delights in the incongruous.

These tiny details are among the very few in the whole of San Xavier that might possibly reflect a specifically Indian touch. Another possibility involves the four busts of female saints on the top level of the west transept. These representations of Saints Gertrude, Theresa of Avila, Scholastica, and Collette have had their hands and faces overpainted with a dark brown pigment. Similar busts in the east transept have not been so treated. It is possible that this overpainting was the result of an attempt on somebody's part to make the figures look more "Indian."

However, these are pure speculations concerning small details in a complex church interior. It really appears that no matter how hard the O'odham worked on the church, and no matter how much a part of village life the church is today, Indian participation in its construction was confined to doing assigned tasks on a project that was almost entirely under European control. As I said earlier, this isn't surprising in view of the fact that the church was built specifically for the purpose of Europeanizing the O'odham villagers.

This does not mean that the O'odham passively accepted both the mission and the Spanish interpretation of its decoration. In the first place, many O'odham feel San Xavier to be their church. They built it, after all, and they kept it safe after the Franciscans left. Furthermore, there is evidence for the existence of a uniquely O'odham interpretation of many of the symbols on the facade and within the church. For example, a knotted cord, sculpted in plaster, runs around the whole interior of the church, just below the cornice I mentioned earlier in this section. For the Franciscans, it represents the cord with which each Franciscan belts his habit. For at least some O'odham, it is the great serpent that holds the church together. The scallop shells which I discussed earlier have their specifically O'odham meaning as well. They represent the sea, which figures in the lore and ritual of *O'odham himdag*. The church is visited regularly by O'odham ritualists who can see—and ritually remove—all sorts of dangerous presences of which the missionaries and others who use the building are blissfully unaware. In these and other ways, O'odham have developed a real ownership of this mission which was constructed by outsiders in order to bring about deep changes in the native culture.[18]

There is only one colonial mission church in the Pimería Alta whose decorations seem to show clear evidence of an Indian "hand" and Indian ideas. This is the church at Pitiquito, Sonora, a small ranching village just east of Caborca on International Highway 2. The church now standing at Pitiquito seems to have been completed by around 1780. It is a plain, massive building, very lovely in the afternoon sunlight. Inside, a series of paintings has been uncovered in the last fifteen years. The oldest group of these paintings, which was subsequently covered by coats of plaster about a quarter of an inch thick , appear to be frames for the Stations of the Cross. The Catholic Church recognizes fourteen such stations. They comprise a series of prayers and meditations on incidents that befell Christ on his way to his death.[19] Although only five of the painted frames in the Pitiquito church have been exposed, their position in the nave and the transepts makes it highly likely that they were intended for the Stations of the Cross. If one assumes the frames were arranged on the walls symmetrically, and if one completes the series implied by the five exposed frames, there are fourteen frames altogether— the proper number for Stations of the Cross. Interestingly enough, two of the painted frames on the walls of the nave have modern stations placed on top of them.

The frames are simple squares outlined with red pigment. Alternating red and white triangles point outward along the edges of the squares. Both the red and the white seem to be mineral pigments. One frame has two red triangles flanking one white triangle on each of its four edges. Three others have similar triangles on the top and sides and five white semicircles with red framing lines on the lower edge. The frame on the west wall of the south transept is more complex. It has five triangles on its upper and lower edges, with the outside and central triangles being red and the other two white. Four of the triangles on the top appear to have heads. Red dots seem to indicate eyes and mouth on the left-hand "head," which also has rays of red and white emanating from its top and sides. The central triangle has no "head" but rather a series of curving red lines issuing from its top. The sides of the square are framed with pairs of wavy red lines.

It is my opinion that these paintings are the work of an O'odham who possessed specialized ritual knowledge and used it in the making of the frames. The colors and the use of framing triangles are consistent with the colors and designs used in the few existing examples of O'odham ritual painting.[20] In many native traditions in the American Southwest, semicircles represent clouds, while triangles may represent clouds or mountains. This may be the case at Pitiquito. Most important, perhaps, the frames simply "feel" native rather than European, and do not have parallels in the mainstream baroque churches of Mexico, as do all the other motifs and designs I have seen in our region's colonial missions.

If these frames were, in fact, painted on the walls of the Pitiquito church by an O'odham—even by an O'odham religious specialist—the question remains why this was allowed. It is not easy to imagine any eighteenth-century Franciscan missionary permitting anything that looked like native ritual art inside his church. It is safest to assume that, if the frames are related in some way to traditional O'odham ritual, the priest was ignorant of the fact and simply thought of them as designs. Be that as it may, these frames are the only works of art in all the Spanish colonial missions of the Pimería Alta that appear to possess a specifically Indian content.

The Pitiquito murals were only discovered in 1966 when a young girl attending Mass with her mother noticed what appeared to be a huge human skeleton showing faintly through the whitewash of the wall near her. Frightened, she showed her mother what she had found. When they looked closely at the walls, the villagers found several other shadowy images: a hand clutching a pair of scales, a human face, and some written words. What they had discovered was a series of roughly executed murals that had been covered for well over a century by layers of whitewash. Their existence had been totally forgotten in the village. When some of the women had cleaned the walls of the church a short while before, the modern detergent they were using started to dissolve the whitewash, and the paintings became visible once more to the startled villagers.[21]

Later work by Mexican art experts uncovered several more images. In addition to the skeleton that frightened the little girl are a huge, dark, winged figure; a representation of the Virgin; the symbols of the four apostles; and other motifs. Some of the drawings may have been intended as educational aids in the teaching of Christian doctrine; others are more clearly decorative. Among these latter are sketches of neoclassic retablos on the walls behind the two side altars, and a series of floral motifs, also in the transepts. These paintings, along with others that are being uncovered in the spring of 1991, appear to date from around 1800. It was during the process of searching for more of them that the painted frames were discovered on a much earlier layer of plaster.

Macabre as some of the paintings may seem, they are understandable in terms of the Christian message that the Franciscans were trying to teach their congregations. The skeleton refers to death, which every person must experience; the scales to the judgment that follows death; paintings of the Virgin and a demon to unseen forces seeking to influence each individual in his or her conduct. I can imagine the priest in his gray Franciscan robes, armed with a saguaro rib pointer, moving from image to image as he addressed his class.

The twentieth-century mission churches on the Tohono O'odham Nation were also sites for a dialogue—in this case, between Franciscans and the followers of santo himdag, as was discussed in chapter 4. This dialogue has often been expressed through the decoration of the churches and chapels involved in the two systems.

A 1914 photograph in the Franciscan files at San Xavier Mission shows a small O'odham chapel at one of the villages of the western Papaguería. On either side of the doorway are four horizontal bands of painted geometric motifs, many of which are similar to ones traditionally used on O'odham pottery. A cornstalk and a long-legged bird, the latter partly effaced by peeling plaster, are visible on the side of the chapel facing the camera. This photograph, along with a 1913 diary reference to a painted chapel at what may be the same village, constitute the only early evidence I know of for the existence of paintings on O'odham chapels.[22]

Later on, probably in the 1930s, such motifs as squared frets and rows of opposing arrows begin to show up in photographs of mission church interiors. These decorations were probably viewed by the missionaries as an attempt to make the churches "Indian" in much the same way that the use of the Mission Revival style of architecture made them "Southwestern." This trend continued into the 1960s and 1970s, with its most dramatic example being at the church of St. Joseph at Pisinimo. The resident priest here in the 1960s was Father Camillus Cavagnaro. Father Camillus was interested in making the churches where he served look "Indian." He had previously been stationed in the mining town of Ajo, Arizona, where he transformed the mission church. He started using O'odham baskets and pottery in the Mass and commissioned a mural of the Crucifixion that included portraits of local people. Once in Pisinimo, he persuaded a local O'odham man to decorate the church inside and out with bold, painted designs taken from traditional Papago pottery and basket motifs. By the early 1970s, the church was a kind of Papago Reservation showcase.

Much of the exterior of the church as well as several school buildings were covered with brilliant yellow highway marking paint, making the village visible from afar. Pottery and basketry designs were painted on several exterior walls, and a row of saguaros leading up to the church door was fitted with metal crosses on their heads. In the center of each cross was a colored glass reflector.

Inside the church, the walls of the nave were painted with bold, diagonal basketry designs. A mural of the Last Supper in the sanctuary was the work of David Sine, an artist of Apache ancestry who was employed at the time in Sells. The nave was also decorated with a mobile of small round gourds, each of which was painted with a different pottery design. The mobile hung from a small O'odham basket plaque with a star design on it. The sisters who taught at the Pisinimo school had supervised the construction of this mobile, which represented the Milky Way with the Star of Bethlehem in the center. The entire assembly made a striking impression on visitors, many of whom went away feeling that they had seen a very "Indian" church. The only problem was that the whole project had been organized and directed by an outsider. According to a missionary who later served at the same church, the villagers, while they appreciated the fact that lots of people came to visit and admire their church, felt that basketry and pottery designs were more appropriate to baskets and pots than to churches.[23]

One design which seems to have been successfully transferred from baskets to churches is the Man in the Maze or I'itoi Ki (I'itoi's House). This complex basket design consists of a circular maze with a tiny human figure standing at its top. Within the past fifty years or so it has become a kind of symbol of Tohono O'odham identity. While it has been traditionally explained as a representation of a house that I'itoi built to keep his enemies from entering and finding him, the design has also been made into a kind of visual parable. The maze, it is said, represents the path that the figure at the top (which can symbolize an individual, the O'odham, or humankind) must travel in the course of life, or in quest of wisdom. In the 1970s, several mission churches utilized the I'itoi Ki in their interior decorations. Most notable of these was the church of the Sacred Heart at Covered Wells. Here a large I'itoi Ki was painted on the head wall, behind the main altar. Its shape was reflected in a circle containing a crucifix that was painted on the arch at the opening of the sanctuary, while a representation of the man from the I'itoi Ki was painted on the front of the tabernacle. This thoughtful recombination of O'odham designs and Catholic ideas was the work of a local villager named Felix James.

Several other mission churches are decorated with Indian designs of various kinds. Deserving special mention is the mission headquarters church at Topawa, near Sells. Here the nave is deco-

165

rated with painted circles, each of which contains a different basket design. On the wall opposite the altar is a realistic representation of Yaqui Matachin dancers, those "Soldiers of the Virgin" who can be seen doing their act of devotion at many Yaqui public ceremonies.

A similar process of mediation and accommodation can be seen in Franciscan missions in other parts of the American Southwest. In some places the process has gone much farther than it has here in the Pimería. The seventeenth-century mission church at the pueblo of Zuni in New Mexico was restored in the 1960s. Since then, a local Indian artist has executed a remarkable series of murals in the nave and sanctuary. These are done in a realistic style and represent figures and concepts from Zuni religion. Apparently, the work was done with the cooperation of Zuni religious traditionalists and contain many sacred details that cannot be explained to outsiders. No comparable statement of traditional O'odham religion has yet appeared on the walls of a Catholic church in our region.

Back to the Baroque

In following the threads of the dialogue between Europeans and Native Americans as it is expressed through church decoration, we have come a long way from our starting point, the baroque style as it exists in our region. It is now time to pick up that story once more and follow it to the present day. Although San Xavier del Bac is the most complete and important standing colonial church in our region, it is not the only one. La Purísima Concepción de Tumacácori, halfway between Tucson and Nogales and just east of Interstate 19, is the centerpiece of Tumacácori National Monument. Its rather sober portal, probably built in the 1820s, reflects the stylistic shift from the full baroque to the more dignified neoclassic. The broken pediment is the only truly baroque detail—a far cry from the luxuriance of San Xavier's portal. Featured in its excellent museum are exhibits and a film on daily mission life in the nineteenth century, as well as five saints' statues that were removed from Tumacácori when that settlement was abandoned and carried to San Xavier. They were only returned from the latter church in 1973.[24]

There are five standing colonial mission churches in the Sonoran

166

portion of the Pimería Alta. They are: San Ignacio on the Río Magdalena, Tubutama and Oquitoa on the Río Altar, and Pitiquito and Caborca on the Río Concepción. Each is well worth visiting as are the ruins of the church of Cocóspera farther to the east. In terms of baroque art, they are of particular interest for the following reasons: The church at Tubutama has a small wooden retablo dedicated to San José, which was undoubtedly brought there in sections on carts or pack animals. It also has two carved plaster retablos and an elaborately carved plaster portal. Its interior is painted and carved over most of its surface. The churches at Oquitoa, Pitiquito, and San Ignacio have eighteenth-century religious statuary in excellent condition. In addition, the Pitiquito church has the murals described earlier in this chapter. La Purísima Concepción de Caborca, which was modeled after San Xavier del Bac in the early nineteenth century, has a few recently uncovered mural paintings of architectural details on its interior walls. They resemble some of the Pitiquito murals. As of this writing, the Caborca mission church has been turned into a cultural center; all the other standing churches are still being used for their original purposes. While each site possesses some baroque art, none equals San Xavier in the richness and completeness of its exterior and interior decoration.[25]

The influence of the baroque style did not stop with the early nineteenth-century and the end of the Spanish Empire. This influence continues to the present day, and may be observed on several levels. The first of these is what art historians might call "neobaroque" art—objects which show details that are directly taken from baroque churches and other buildings. Examples of neobaroque structures would be the yard shrine mentioned in chapter 6, which is built as a miniature reproduction of a baroque church, or the shrine with the twisted columns described in the same chapter.

The Mission Revival style, so important to the appearance of the mission churches of the Papaguería, is a twentieth-century neobaroque style.[26] Most of its details were adapted from the missions of California. While some of these churches, notably those at San Francisco and Santa Barbara, were done in the neoclassic style that replaced the baroque in New Spain, few neoclassic details entered the Mission Revival. Some of the hallmarks of the revived style—tiled roofs, arcades, great expanses of bare white wall—were simply taken from the rustic architecture of the Mediterranean world as transplanted to North America. Other details, however, among them stepped bell towers, scalloped gable ends, and star-shaped windows, are quite baroque.

The Mission Revival style affected the O'odham chapels as well as the mission churches of the Papaguería. The gable at the chapel formerly at Shopishk was a copy of the gable on the church at Chui-chu a few miles away. It appears from photographs that the mission style started being used by O'odham for their chapels around 1920. Its popularity may have faded: the chapel erected at Shopishk in the late 1970s has a simple pitched gable over the door.

Some of the baroque details on O'odham chapels may have more direct sources in the Spanish colonial architecture of the Pimería Alta. When Father Theodore Williges was consulting with villagers at San Pedro Village in 1962 concerning what their proposed chapel should look like, the villagers handed him a postcard of the mission church at Caborca, Sonora. According to his account of the negotiations, Fr. Theodore said that he couldn't help them with anything that elaborate, but he did manage to get two domed bell towers flanking a façade which was equipped with a small shelf to hold a statue.[27]

I have already speculated that the arrangement of holy pictures and artificial flowers in vertical rows behind the altars of O'odham chapels might have been influenced by the baroque retablos remaining in such churches as those at Oquitoa, Tubutama, and San Xavier del Bac. And the brightly colored, glittering floral designs of the glass frames for the holy pictures must certainly appeal to a taste that has been conditioned by exposure to baroque art.

There is yet another way in which the baroque style makes itself felt in the religious art of our region. Many of the specific sites I have described in the course of this book seem to be somewhat similar to San Xavier del Bac in the complexity of their organization and detail. The shrines of St. Jude and El Señor de Los Milagros mentioned in the last chapter, for example, display a richness of materials and detail that would not be out of place in the eighteenth-century baroque church. Here are two more examples.

In a front yard in South Tucson, near the 39th Street Yaqui chapel of San Martín de Porres, is a large shrine. It was built on commission by a Yaqui man—a traditional musician and shrine maker—who wishes to remain anonymous. The shrine is built to resemble a wishing well—a phrase used by the builder. The base of the well is, in fact, a solid platform and not a well at all. It is made of bricks which have been painted alternately green and white. On this base sits a white plaster nicho containing a brilliantly painted Virgin. The nicho is edged with bits of red, blue, and black plastic tile. The upper edge of the nicho is scalloped, with a cross projecting upward from the center. In front of the nicho stand candles and small bunches of flowers.

The nicho is shaded by a pitched, gabled wooden roof, supported by four posts. The edges of the two forward posts are beveled to create an undulating outline. The forward edges of these posts are decorated with black and white cruciform plastic tiles. These tiles seem not to be real tiles, but plastic molds from which tiles might be cast. They have been cut from their matrix and painted, and used as though they were tiles in their own right. The roofline is painted green and white. In the center of the gable end stands a white wooden cross. It is overlaid with colored plastic tiles and bears a red plastic heart in its center. Immediately below it on the gable end is an automobile decal featuring Our Lady of Guadalupe and crossed Mexican and American flags. The boards of the gable end have their lower ends scalloped and are painted white. They are adorned with small tiles. The shrine is decorated with tiny, flashing colored lights; a string of larger lights appears on the eaves of the house directly behind it.

Here is another example, a Mexican-American grave marker in the Casa Grande cemetery. The entire grave is surrounded by a low cement curb. Within the curb, lying flat on the ground at the head of the grave, is a commercially sandblasted headstone bearing the name and dates of the deceased (a woman), along with an image of the Virgin of Guadalupe. Behind this conventional headstone is a low wall with a centrally located nicho. Inside the nicho is a small statue of the Virgin flanked by statues of angels and a small vase of artificial flowers. Statues of St. Anthony and St. Martin of Porres also appear inside the nicho. On the rear wall of the nicho is a painted architectural setting consisting of two columns flanked by vertical volutes.

A representation of the Last Supper is painted in the vertical space just below the nicho. Flanking the nicho are statues of the Virgin and the Sacred Heart of Jesus, a small holy water stoup, bunches of plastic flowers, a candle, a ceramic planter in the form of a cactus, and another ceramic planter containing a cactus.

This arrangement is by no means static over time. The description above was made from slides taken in 1984. These differed in a few details from other slides which had been taken two years previously. When I revisited the Casa Grande cemetery in 1987, the following changes had been made. The headstone had been raised to a slanting position and propped against the low wall at the head of the grave, covering the painting of the Last Supper. Inside the nicho, which had been stripped of its columns and volutes, were a picture and a statue of the Holy Child of Atocha, statues of St. Anthony and St. Martin of Porres, three angels (one wooden, one ceramic, and one a ceramic candle holder), a rosary and a palm leaf cross, a small glass jar for a votive candle, two pots of artificial flowers, and a stuffed toy mouse dressed in a sailor suit. Outside the nicho and flanking it were a ceramic statue of the Holy Child of Prague and eight arrangements of artificial flowers (one of which was made of sea shells).

The key to understanding what is going on artistically at both these sites seems to me to be the baroque concept of richness. Certainly there is richness of color. Richness of materials seems to be implied in the use of simulated tiles at the yard shrine and in the shell flowers at the gravesite. But most particularly there is richness of detail. Each site is assembled from a large number of individual objects, many of which have an independent meaning outside of the context in which they are brought together. Take, for example, the arrangement of the Casa Grande gravesite when I visited it in 1984. Two statues of the Virgin, an engraving of Our Lady of Guadalupe, a painting of the Last Supper, and statues of the Sacred Heart of Jesus, Saints Anthony and Martin, and a number of angels all shared the site with purely secular objects like the ceramic cactus-shaped planter. Each of the objects at the grave may well have had a specific meaning for the person who placed it there. Together, they form a dense and complex web of symbolically charged objects, just as do the decorations on the portal of San Xavier.

Like at least some of the symbols at San Xavier, these contemporary folk assemblages display a certain sense of ambiguity. The shrine near 39th Street is an excellent example of this. Built in the shape of a wishing well—a common object in secular mainstream American culture—it nevertheless lacks one basic feature common to wells—a hole of some kind.[28] Moreover, the shrine is not really a wishing well, but a shrine to the Virgin. On the other hand, it may be a place of petitions, just as a wishing well is. The tiles with which it is decorated are not really tiles but pieces of plastic that have been cut and painted to resemble ceramic tiles. The lights that decorate it are Christmas lights in mainstream society, but in this context they are used year-round.

More ambiguities crop up in other works done by the maker of this shrine. On several smaller shrines, as well as on one grave marker in the Tubac cemetery, he has carved wooden crosses that are at the same time large birds—"thunderbirds," he calls them—with their wings outstretched. In the case of the grave marker, a relief carving of the Sacred Heart of Jesus appears just under the bird and cross image.

This use of what appears to a baroque system of organization is not confined in our area to religious art. I have seen Low Rider car displays that seem to use precisely the same principles, with a greater emphasis on motion than is possible in the basically static displays I have been describing here. A strong case could be made that this same set of aesthetic rules is followed in the organization of social and religious events as well as of grave markers, shrines, altars, and car displays. The message is clear: two centuries after it was abandoned as a fashionable art style in Mexico City, the baroque remains a fact of life on what was once the frontier of New Spain.

8. Some Final Thoughts

In this book, I have attempted to describe the spiritual geography of the Pimería Alta—the various kinds of supernaturally sanctioned ties that have over the centuries been formed between members of the region's traditional cultures and specific places. These bonds in their turn have created sets of relationships between places within the Pimería Alta which cannot be seen on contemporary maps of the region.

In the first place, it is clear that the Pimería Alta is a single region, cutting across national boundaries. Within that area there are two patterns: one related to I'itoi and the older O'odham beliefs and the other related to Magdalena and regional Catholicism.

I'itoi lives on the west side of Baboquivari Mountain. From his cave, lines of narrative and belief stretch out to the various places where he went to help the People: to Quito Wa:k, to Pozo Verde and the Ho'ok's cave, to the ancient cities in Pima Country where he fought with Siwani. From the summit of Baboquivari one can easily see the broad Santa Rosa Valley, the traditional population center of the Papaguería. Here the great ceremony of the wi:gida took place through the 1930s, and here the Children's Shrine is located. Other invisible lines connect the Santa Rosa Valley with places farther away: the shores of the Sea of Cortez where the Desert People went on pilgrimage to obtain salt, the Gila and Santa Cruz rivers to the north and east where they went in time of drought, the Apache country far beyond the rivers where they went to wage war.

A more modern but equally important set of relationships connects each O'odham village with Magdalena. Before the 1940s, the lines of connection went south into Mexico and then angled south and east to Magdalena. Those were the old horse and wagon routes, now no longer used. They have been replaced by lines that follow the highways, crossing the border at Nogales and moving south along International Highway 15, now a divided highway from the border past Magdalena.

Magdalena is the center of the second and more recent of the Pimería's two major patterns of spiritual geography. A strong line of force connects Magdalena with San Xavier and with Chuwhiy Guwsk, homes of the other two important San Francisco statues. Other lines run from Magdalena to virtually every other human settlement within the Pimería Alta, to every place from which someone has gone on pilgrimage, to which someone has brought an image of San Francisco. Tucson may be the region's major commercial center, Nogales the major border crossing, and Caborca a vital agricultural center, but Magdalena is the spiritual hub of the Pimería Alta and has been so for at least a hundred fifty years. All roads lead there, and most O'odham, Mexicanos, and Yaquis will visit there at least once in their lives.

Embedded in the living traditional cultures of the Pimería Alta is a record of the region's contacts with the outside world. Earliest of all the arrivals on the scene may have been the water serpent. If archaeologist Charles Di Peso is correct, the cult of Quetzalcoatl was deliberately introduced to Paquime and thence to much of what is now the Southwest several hundred years before Columbus. Among the Pueblo Indians, Water Serpent is a powerful being to be propitiated; here in the Pimería Alta there are simply a number of connections between snakes and water. Some of these need outside information to make them meaningful. For instance, only in the light of Hopi parallels does the O'odham sacrifice of the Flood Children seem to be connected with the great Horned Serpent, which seems to be a descendant of Quetzalcoatl. The connections are more obvious in the case of Mexicano beliefs concerning la culebra de agua and especially la corúa.

La corúa seems to stand a bit apart from the rest of the book's subject matter. The huge serpent does not interact with people in any known way; it simply lives in its spring, "guarding" it. But la corúa appears to be a rather ineffective protector. Its only known response to human meddling is to die. Of course, when the corúa is killed, its spring dries up, but this seems more a response on the part of the spring than the result of any activity by the corúa. I'itoi, San Francisco, even el Tejano all influence human affairs in one way or another. La corúa simply exists. Alone of all the subjects of this book, it stands defiantly aboriginal in concept and behavior. Alone? But what of I'itoi? He has indeed been presented as remaining from the days before the missionaries came, from the time when Pimería Alta was simply that—O'odham country. Parts of his story, however, have been commented on by scholars as possibly revealing a reaction to the central event of the Christian universe: the death and resurrection of Jesus Christ.[1] So while I'itoi himself may have been with the O'odham for as long as they have been O'odham, the stories of his death and resurrection and the hopes for his eventual return in his guise of Montezuma may have been added since Father Kino's arrival in this land. Even I'itoi, who was called "the Papago Christ" by some very acculturated O'odham in the 1930s, may partake to some degree of the presence on the desert of Christian missionaries.[2]

The picture is much clearer for the rest of our subject matter. The San Francisco who resides in Magdalena is a direct result of Father Kino's work in the Pimería Alta and of the Jesuits' eventual expulsion and replacement by Franciscans. The legends concerning his statue take us from Father Kino's New Spain to the social and religious tensions and conflicts of modern Mexico. To learn about Magdalena and its composite saint is to learn the history of the Pimería Alta and its peoples.

Likewise, to gain some understanding of O'odham and Yaqui Christianities is to see the contact between European and Native American in a slightly different light than that afforded by written historical documents. These cultural traditions are in themselves documents. They are certainly difficult to interpret, and at times even to read, but they are there and provide insights that written texts produced by members of only one of the parties involved in the history of contact cannot give us. In many cases, the cultural documents can serve to clarify the written ones. For example, twentieth-century Franciscan letters complaining about the intransigence of the "Montezumas" are easier understood when one realizes the degree to which superficial similarities between Roman and O'odham Catholicism masked fundamental differences in the basic assumptions and purposes of the two religious systems.

With the material discussed in chapters 5 through 7—our region's dead, its places of petition, and the various permutations of the Baroque style—we are dealing with regional manifestations of traditional Mexican culture. To be sure, much of what exists in this region is unique, but unique in the way that individual works of art are unique while still belonging to recognizable schools or styles. There are, as we have seen, roadside death markers, victim intercessors, shrines of petition, and baroque churches in other parts of Mexico. The ones in the Pimería Alta do not assert its uniqueness. Rather, they reiterate its strong cultural and historic ties to Mexico and Hispanic America, ties which were forged in the seventeenth and eighteenth centuries. These ties remain important in the 1990s, despite the fact that for over a hundred years, the northern half of the Pimería Alta has been part of the English-speaking United States, with its centers of power far to the north and east.

In the Introduction I wrote that when I first came here, I thought of myself as living in the Southwest. By now it should be obvious that, while our region has been part of a very real Southwest for over a century, it has for much of its history been the Northwest. If Charles Di Peso is correct, it was the northwestern frontier of the high cultures of Mesoamerica for hundreds of years before Europeans arrived in the Americas. From the sixteenth until the nineteenth century, it was the far northwest of New Spain. For thirty years it was northwest Mexico, following that country's independence from Spain. Even though the region is now divided between Mexico and the United States, it is still the Northwest in many important ways.

175

But much of it is also in the Southwest, and the history of many of the ideas and customs discussed in this book reflects that fact. Major changes have been taking place with increasing frequency since the Gadsden Purchase split the Pimería Alta in 1853. The most important of these changes seem to have been stimulated by two things: technology and war. Technology in the form of railroads permitted the region's major lines of communication with the outside world to shift northward. This meant that a northern European Protestant culture replaced the older mestizo Catholic culture as the dominant influence in much of the Pimería Alta. Later developments of water-pumping and air-conditioning systems enabled the population explosion that has overtaken the region. As a result of all this, the cultures which once were in control of the region are now minorities.

War, too, has left a major impact on the Pimería Alta and its traditional cultures. The Apache wars of the eighteenth and nineteenth centuries ensured that major population centers did not develop east of the Santa Cruz Valley. Warfare between the Mexican government and the Yaquis resulted in the establishment of Arizona's Yaqui communities. The Mexican Revolution led to an influx of Mexican immigrants into Arizona, as well as to the religious conflict that resulted in the destruction of the San Francisco statue in Magdalena and the appearance of the statue at Chuwhiy Guwsk. The First and Second World Wars each caused dislocation and population shifts that have accelerated the rate of change in the Pimería Alta and elsewhere. Another war is being waged today between drug dealers and government forces over the control of the border. It, too, is influencing the traditional religions of the Pimería Alta. New kinds of printed prayers are sold in Magdalena. Problems along the border have led the Tohono O'odham to institute a "floating" fiesta of San Francisco, held each year at a different village on the reservation.[3] Lavish sums of drug profits are being spent on ostentatious religious displays along the highways.

Yet while traditional culture is changing in response to pressures from the world outside the Pimería, it is remaining remarkably stable. Tohono O'odham resisted the opening of Baboquivari to mineral exploration, not from abstract ecological principles, but because I'itoi lives on the mountain and should not be disturbed. Pilgrims still go to Magdalena in vast numbers and still show an intense devotion to San Francisco. Two hundred years after it fell from fashion in Mexico City, the baroque style of artistic organization informs the traditional arts of Mexican Americans. There is change, to be sure, but much of it occurs within the boundaries of tradition. Perhaps the most remarkable instance of persistence is the fact that, more than a century after it was divided between two modern nations, each with its own language and national culture, the Pimería Alta remains a cultural region in its own right.

The northern half of the Pimería is a part of the American Southwest, however, and the vast majority of residents of southern Arizona are English-speaking participants in contemporary American national culture. As we have seen, Americanos participate to a certain degree in some of the cultural patterns of the spiritual geography I have been discussing. They do so in their own way, from their own cultural perspectives. As the beliefs and traditions move to yet another culture, they change and are reinterpreted. For instance, some Anglo Americans seem to have created their own version of the story of the Flood Children—a version that fits better with traditional Anglo culture and values than does the O'odham version. Anglo use of El Tiradito, Anglo pilgrimages to Magdalena, and Anglo participation in restoration projects are likely to be motivated by different sets of values than are similar activities on the part of Mexicanos or Native Americans. This participation, in turn, causes the places themselves to change. El Tiradito is no longer simply a place of petitions with an attached legend cycle. It is also a National Historic Landmark, a destination for formal and informal tours of Tucson, and a symbol of the successful battle to stop the Butterfield Freeway. Magdalena is now visited by those who wish to learn about the region's traditions as well as by those who participate in those traditions. Many of the places and stories mentioned in this book have taken on new meanings in a similar fashion.

In addition, many Anglo Americans are developing their own spiritual geography of the region, a geography that contrasts in important ways with the subject matter of this book. With the exception of la corúa, the Pimería Alta's traditional spiritual geography is human oriented. I'itoi lives by himself, to be sure, but he came to the villages when his help was needed, and people still leave offerings at his cave. San Francisco's statue lies in the middle of downtown Magdalena, and the saint concerns himself in the affairs of mankind, as do all our other answerers of petitions. People, their stories, and their needs lie close to the core of the legends and beliefs that tie O'odham, Yaquis, and Mexicanos to the places of this region.

The new order of Anglo-American spiritual geography, however, focuses mostly on those places where people have no real presence. As our cities have become overcrowded, as human society is felt to be stifling rather than protective, we have forged spiritual links with the wilderness areas that still remain in our region. This new set of relationships has been celebrated by many noted writers of our century, from John Van Dyke to Joseph Wood Krutch and beyond.[4] It goes hand in hand with the growing ecological movement, bent on preserving as much of our rapidly changing natural world as possible from the ravages, intentional and otherwise, of modern technology and the demands of post-industrial civilization. These relationships may be destined to replace the traditional links between the people and places I have been discussing. However, this new order of spiritual geography, reflecting the pressures of the post-industrial world and an approach to nature that has been heavily conditioned by the Romantic period of the nineteenth century, lies beyond the scope of this book. It is fitting that the subject of ecology be raised, however, for what I have been describing in this book is a kind of human, cultural ecology of our region. This intricate set of stable, yet ever-changing, relationships between people and places in the Pimería Alta is as much a part of the reality of our region as is the complex interrelationship between saguaro cactuses, the bats that pollinate them, and the birds that spread their seeds.[5] It, too, can be easily threatened by the pressures of the late twentieth century. And if ever these relationships become things exclusively of the past, this part of the world will have lost much of its unique beauty and character.

I am not suggesting that we should all start making pilgrimages to Magdalena, praying at El Tiradito, or regarding I'itoi as our Creator and Elder Brother, though that option is open for those who need to take it. Nor am I contemplating the creation of a kind of reservation for traditionalists, where they can live uninfluenced by modern life. The participants in the cultural patterns I have been describing, the tellers of the legends, the carriers of the beliefs, all occupy precisely the same corner of the twentieth century as do the rest of us. They are as much a part of "modern life" as are today's headlines. But as the immense waves of immigrants from elsewhere in the world enter this region, each individual with his or her own sacred order of things and places, it would be good to approach our region's traditional cultures with the same three watchwords that should govern our relationship with the fragile Sonoran Desert: Learn. Respect. Walk Softly.[6]

I would like to end this book as I began it, on a note of personal reflection. As I thought about the various legends and beliefs that I was discussing, I kept being drawn back to la corúa, the oldest, most shadowy figure in our story. For me, the great snake whose only response to being molested is to die has become a potent symbol of nature in general and the Sonoran Desert in particular. Not made with humans in mind, the desert, like the corúa, exists in its own place, for its own purposes. As we tamper with the details of our fragile desert ecosystem, we are increasingly discovering that this tampering has results beyond our initial imaginings. We may not be going around killing huge legendary water snakes, but we are in the process of pumping groundwater faster than it can be replaced, dumping toxic chemicals where they can seep into the water table, and removing natural vegetation which checks erosion. Nature is not vindictive. It will not lash back at us, any more than the legendary corúa of the Pimería Alta retaliates against those who kill it. But it is reactive. As Richard Morales expressed it in 1983, kill the corúa and you lose your water rights.

Notes

Although this book is intended primarily for the general reader, I wish to make it useful to my professional colleagues as well. Therefore, these notes serve more than one purpose. They provide a wider context for the material treated in the text and give details which, though relevant to the subject at hand, would interrupt the flow of the main text. In addition, they give general sources and further reading for the topics I have discussed, as well as the sources for specific statements and quotations. In both cases, the citations are to the works listed in the References. The information for which sources are not given comes from my own experience and field journals.

Chapter 1 Meeting la Corúa

1. The exhibition was "Glittering Recuerdos: Reverse Painting on Glass from Magdalena, Sonora." It appeared at the Pimería Alta Historical Museum in Nogales, Sonora, from October, 1983, through March, 1984, and then traveled through Arizona and the Southwest courtesy of the Arizona Commission on the Arts. See also Griffith, 1982.

2. Sobarzo 1966: 81–82.

3. Sobarzo 1966: 11.

4. Vigil 1983.

5. Father Olizarra is a well-known figure in Oquitoa. Villagers still tell of the time he was summoned to attend a dying man in the mission community of Tubutama, several miles away. According to one version of the

legend, when he arrived at the ford to cross the river into town, he found the river to be impassible. He knelt on the river bank in full sight of his Indian companions and remained thus in prayer for a long time. He then returned to Oquitoa. According to the people in Tubutama, he was seen to arrive at the bedside of the dying man, administer the Last Rites of the Catholic church, and leave town. Another legend has it that when his cloak would get wet, he would dry it off by hanging it on a sunbeam. (Kieran McCarty, O.F.M., personal communication.)

6. Thomas Sheridan, personal communication, May 1990.

7. Saxton and Saxton 1973:316.

8. Mason 1957:206.

9. Giddings 1959:67.

10. Coolidge 1985:76.

11. Wood 1956:34.

12. Cather 1945.

13. Caso 1958:23–27.

14. Di Peso 1974.

15. Ibid., 290–95.

16. Ibid., 548–55.

17. Parsons 1939:184–85.

18. Ibid., 295n.

19. Ingham 1989:112.

20. Madsen 1960:113.

21. Parsons 1936:223.

22. Sahagún 1963, Book II:70.

Chapter 2 A Mountain and a Shrine

1. Granger 1983:42.

2. Pete Cowgill, personal statement.

3. My account of the conflict between I'itoi and Siwani is greatly condensed from that given in Saxton and Saxton 1973:147–68.

4. Parsons 1939:1078–79. For a discussion of the Montezuma legend, mostly as it appears in New Mexico, see Parmentier 1893. See also Weigle and White 1988:62–71.

5. Saxton and Saxton 1973:305–16.

6. Davis 1920:159–62.

7. Davis 1920; Underhill 1946:155.

8. Davis 1920:164; Ives 1950:322–23; also Nabhan, personal communication, 1990.

9. Thompson 1968:321–22.

10. Ramsey 1977:9–12.

11. Condensed and retold from Fontana 1981a:22–31.

12. The story of the hawk, as it is known by Tohono O'odham on the Mexican side of the border, is retold in Saxton and Saxton 1973:263–70.

13. Karnes 1954:105–6.

14. Russell 1975:254.

15. Nabhan 1982:14.

16. Ibid., 12–21.

17. Kreutz 1983.

18. Anonymous 1983a.

19. Anonymous 1983b.

20. Ellement 1983.

21. Lumholtz 1990:207–9. See also Ives 1950:323.

22. Hartmann 1989:136–42.

23. This version of the legend I have given was told by José Poncho of Quijotoa village and published in the *Arizona Daily Star* (Thomas 1963). The earliest printed version of the drought story that I have found was published in *The Desert Magazine* in March 1943 (Muench 1943a). The author learned the story from a state senator in Casa Grande and from the owner of a reservation trading post. Both men seem to have been Anglos (Muench 1943b). A version of the drought narrative in which four children were sacrificed was published in Casa Grande in 1990 (Woods 1990).

24. Photographs of the Children's Shrine taken by Julian Hayden in the 1930s and 1940s appear in Bernard-Shaw and Shaw 1989:464–65.

25. Underhill (1946:68–75) gives an account of the renewal ceremony as it was in the 1930s.

26. Parsons 1939:185.

27. A brief description and a photograph of the chelkona appears in Griffith 1988:69–70.

28. Descriptions of this dance as well as the song texts I have quoted are from Haefer 1980:250–56.

29. Granger 1983.

30. Saxton, Saxton, and Enos 1983:132–38.
31. Fontana 1981a:23.

Chapter 3 A Saint and His People

1. The annual Magdalena fiesta as it existed in the late 1940s is treated in some detail in a special issue of *The Kiva* 16 (1–2), October–November 1950. See also Fontana 1981b and Griffith 1988b.

2. Bartlett 1955:425–26.
3. Officer 1988:337, n.88.
4. Delany 1980:236–37.
5. Ahlborn 1974:78.

6. An excellent short biographical sketch of Kino may be found in Polzer 1982:1–19. For a longer treatment, see Bolton 1960.

7. Polzer 1982:58–64.
8. Delany 1980:234–35.
9. Walsh 1987:173–79.
10. Fontana 1961:15–16.
11. Officer 1987:337, n.88.
12. Joseph, Spicer, and Chesky 1949:85–86.
13. Holzapfel 1948.
14. Kieran McCarty, O.F.M., personal communication.

15. Pack Carnes, personal communication. The legend concerning the Papagos and San Francisco's body, retold later in this chapter, seems to relate to this belief.

16. O'Neill 1967.

17. For an account of a pilgrimage to Magdalena in the late 1940s by a teenaged participant, see Laguna 1950.

18. Fontana 1981b.
19. Seibold 1949:33 and Laguna 1950:17–18.
20. Seibold 1949:33–34.
21. Ibid., 34.
22. Arizona Folklore Archives.
23. Arizona Folklore Archives.
24. Jorge Olvera, personal communication.
25. Jorge Olvera, personal communication. Variants of this legend

which I have recently collected include the carreta carrying the statue becoming immobile at the church site (Santa Ana, Sonora, 1989) and the men who carried the statue setting it down for a rest and then being unable to lift it again (Tucson 1990). See Bartlett 1955:424 for the 1851 version of the same legend.

26. Arizona Folklore Archives.

27. Ahlborn 1974:78.

28. Duell 1919:87. Other early photographs are in the files of the Arizona Historical Society, and in the personal files of Bernard Fontana of Tucson.

29. Bleser 1989.

30. Robert K. Thomas, personal communication.

31. Nolan and Nolan 1989:257–66.

32. Capistran Hanlon, O.F.M., personal communication.

33. Examples of eighteenth-century *santo entierros* in the Pimería Alta may be seen in the mission church of San Ignacio and at Santa Ana Viejo.

34. Arizona Folklore Archives.

35. Williamson 1950:3–4.

36. Schweitzer and Thomas 1952:6.

37. Williamson 1950:4–8.

38. Gary Nabhan, personal communication. See also Nabhan 1991.

39. Interview with José Pomposo Sálazar Araisa, April 27, 1983. Arizona Folklore Archive 83-11/C-1.

40. For details of Posada's life and career, see Charlot 1979.

41. Conningham 1970:v–vii.

42. Taylor Museum catalogue number 867. A photograph of the print and its tin frame is published in Coulter and Dixon 1990:99 (Fig. 5.53).

43. Griffith 1982, 1988b.

44. Leight 1983.

45. Coulter and Dixon 1990:54–57; 122–24.

46. Celestin Chin, O.F.M., personal communication.

47. Daniel Matson, personal communication.

48. Gary Nabhan, personal communication.

49. Evers and Molina 1990.

50. This mixture of the sacred and the secular is also a characteristic of

many major European pilgrimage fiestas and has been since the Middle Ages (Nolan and Nolan 1989:46–49).

51. Arturo Carrillo Strong, personal communication.

Chapter 4 Native Christianities

1. Nabhan (1982) provides a good introduction to Papago flood-plain agriculture.

2. Fontana 1981b:45.

3. Fontana 1987.

4. My research on the history of the Catholic churches and chapels of the Papaguería is reported on more fully in Griffith 1973 and Griffith 1974. The former reference contains detailed historical information and descriptions of every church and chapel known to me on the Reservation.

5. A photograph of the Oquitoa retablo appears in Eckhart and Griffith 1975:31; a photograph of the altarpiece formerly at Anegam appears in Griffith 1973:258.

6. St. Anthony of Padua (1195–1231) was a Franciscan noted for the brilliance and effectiveness of his preaching. He is patron of the poor and oppressed, and is often invoked for help in finding lost articles. He is frequently represented wearing a blue Franciscan habit and holding the Infant Jesus (Delaney 1980:63).

7. A short biography of the Bessed Kateri may be found in Delany (1980:541–42); the devotion to her among O'odham Catholics is discussed briefly by Bahr (1988:163–64).

8. Representations of the Sacred Heart of Jesus refer to Jesus' love for mankind as evidenced in His Incarnation, Passion and death, and the institution of the Eucharist (Broderick 1976:535).

9. The Santo Niño de Atocha or Holy Child of Atocha is a purely Mexican devotion that originated in the town of Plateros, near Zacatecas, in Mexico's northern mining country. The Holy Child was originally part of a Mother-and-Child statue representing the Spanish Virgin of Atocha. At some point the statue of the child was removed from his mother's arms and became the object of a separate devotion. The Santo Niño is patron of miners and prisoners. His devotion is important all through the area that was once northern New Spain (Lange 1978).

10. Bahr 1988:163–64.

11. Descriptions of Tohono O'odham Catholicism may be found in Bahr (1988) and Griffith (1975).

12. The walled space around a church is called the *atrio* by Mexican art historians. I have borrowed the term.

13. The Virgin of Guadalupe is the Virgin Mary as she appeared in 1531 to the Indian Juan Diego on the outskirts of Mexico City. She is venerated as the Queen of the Mexicans, the Patroness of the Americas. Her devotion is dealt with more thoroughly in chapter 6.

14. St. Martin of Porres (1579–1639) was born in Peru as the illegitimate son of a Spanish knight and a freed Black Panamanian. He became a Dominican lay brother and was known for his humility and concern for the poor. He is shown wearing a black-and-white Dominican habit and often holding a broom. He is patron of social justice and people of mixed race (Delany 1980:477; Walsh 1987:304–6).

15. Griffith (1975) has a discussion of O'odham chapels.

16. Underhill 1973.

17. Griffith 1979.

18. Bahr 1988:151–53.

19. Pfefferkorn 1949:49.

20. Bahr 1988.

21. I have heard stories of misfortunes befalling incautious travelers who failed to add to rock-pile shrines. Julian Hayden, personal communication.

22. Fr. Lambert Fremdling, O.F.M., personal communication.

23. Ibid.

24. Spicer (1980) provides an excellent starting place for learning about Yaqui history. See also Sheridan (1988).

25. Painter (1976, 1986) presents Arizona Yaqui ceremonialism in great detail.

26. Evers and Molina (1987).

Chapter 5 *The Presence of the Dead*

1. A Jewish woman was hit by a truck and killed on December 7, 1989, on a busy Tucson street. The next day, her grown daughter found an orange near the site of the accident and placed it on the road median, where the woman was hit. Later she placed more objects there, including some dirt from the desert and a funeral wreath of artificial flowers. Her comment concerning the flowers was: "They won't die. But maybe they'll blow away" (Rawlinson 1989).

2. Dobie 1980:160–61.

3. McCarty 1983.

4. The story was collected in 1965 by Joe Goldmark. A note identifies it as being "told in camp."

5. Anonymous 1979. A man who delivered the South Main Street paper route in Tucson in the mid-1920s told me that in those days the shrine was on the west side of Main Street, just north of the corner of Main and Simpson and not far from the site of the old Elysian Grove amusement park. It consisted of a "pile of tin cans" that had been cut to serve as candle holders. Candles were almost always burning at the site, which he calls the Wishing Shrine (Randall Legler, personal communication). The oldest description of the site that I am aware of is in a 1909 diary. The shrine is described as being in a little thicket, near the entrance to the Elysian Grove. It consisted of a circular rim of earth filled with lighted candles. The murder it commemorated was described as having happened about five years previously, i.e., about 1904 (Berrell 1909:17).

6. Anonymous 1979; Perkins, n.d.

7. Tucson-Pima County Historical Commission 1979. See also Griffith 1987.

8. Father Celestin Chin, O.F.M., personal communication.

9. Wogoman 1972.

10. Alva Torres (1989) describes the process of placing El Tiradito on the National Register of Historic Places from the point of view of a participant.

11. A special use for El Tiradito by neighborhood children a generation or two ago is described in Allen (1989). When tourists approached the shrine, they would find a group of children there, throwing pennies at the wall "as though that was the tradition." The tourists would often follow suit but with coins of larger denominations. "After the tourists left, the kids would run up and gather up the coins and go to the store to buy candy."

12. Escobedo 1989:147.

13. Figgen 1989.

14. Griffith 1987.

15. Seibold 1949:25.

16. Ibid., 24–25.

17. Further discussion of Southern Arizona's Mexican American cemeteries may be found in Griffith 1988:34–41. The cemeteries of Nogales, Arizona, and Nogales, Sonora, are discussed in some detail in Griffith 1985.

18. Simmons and Turley 1980:166.

19. Joseph, Spicer, and Chesky 1949:88. An excellent recent discussion of O'odham beliefs concerning death may be found in Kozak 1990.

20. Seibold 1949:20.

21. Ibid., 20.

22. La Llorona as she is known in Arizona is treated by Leddy (1948, 1950) and Seibold (1949:8–10). For a glimpse of La Llorona as she was understood by teenaged girls in a Southern California juvenile detention hall, see Hawes (1968).

23. Seibold 1949:12, 18.

24. Roach 1968.

25. Duarte 1983.

Chapter 6 Places of Thanks and Petition

1. Griffith 1973:160–61.

2. Gentry suggests a precontact origin for rock-pile shrines in his delightful essay "Caminos of San Bernardo" (1942).

3. Kozak (1990:129–42) discusses these shrines, which he calls "shrine-chapels." He has discovered ten of them along different stretches of highway within the reservation. According to his informants, they have been built since the late 1960s, a time of increasing O'odham concern over the dangers of highway travel.

4. Piper 1988.

5. Ketchum 1988.

6. The story of the apparition of Our Lady of Guadalupe has been told many times. One accessible version is given in Toor (1947:172–74).

7. Conde and Conde (1981) present a profusely illustrated discussion of the artistic traditions associated with Our Lady of Guadalupe in Mexico. The illustrations concentrate on fine art material, but folk and popular art are represented as well.

8. Arturo Carrillo Strong, personal communication.

9. Anonymous, n.d.

10. Husband (1982) discusses Tucson's yard shrines from a geographer's perspective.

11. Stiles 1982. St. Joseph is another popular saint to ask for help in real-estate transactions. His assistance is usually asked for by the seller,

who may bury a small statue of him (sometimes upside down) in the yard and threaten to leave it there till the property is sold. This custom prevails among Catholics of several ethnic groups in many parts of the United States (Danielson 1986:50).

12. Duarte 1982.
13. Anonymous 1982; Weisman 1988.
14. Jordan 1988.
15. Forbes 1952.
16. Hartmann 1989:44–46.

Chapter 7 Art: Our Created Landscape

1. Lange 1975:476.
2. Fontana 1961:7. Fontana's booklet is still in print and is still the best discussion of San Xavier Mission.
3. Art Historian Jorge Olvera (1989) has written a provocative discussion of the Islamic architectural elements found at San Xavier. It must be emphasized that these elements are present, not because there were Muslims on New Spain's frontier, but because Muslim traditions had become a part of the Spanish architectural repertoire.
4. Many books discuss Mexico's baroque colonial architecture. Weismann's *Art and Time in Mexico* is profusely illustrated and thoughtfully written. Its bibliography provides an excellent starting place for further reading on this complex subject.
5. Two studies of the survival (or otherwise) of native artistic traditions in the earliest days of New Spain are found in Kubler (1961) and McAndrew (1965). Coming closer to home, Neuerberg (1975) identifies some paintings and graffiti in the California missions, which he feels reveal Indian minds and hands.
6. Bernard L. Fontana, personal communication. The Espinoza church was excavated by Fontana and others in the 1970s. The results of this work are presented in Cheek 1974.
7. Fontana 1961.
8. Ahlborn 1974:11,12. Estípites came to Mexico in 1711, when Jerónimo Balbás from Seville started work on the Altar of the Kings in Mexico City's Cathedral. They became *the* decorative column of eighteenth-century Mexico, falling from popularity in Mexico City by the 1770s but continuing to be used in the provinces until much later. The portal of the

mission church of La Purísima Concepción in Caborca, Sonora, dedicated in 1809, has estípites much like those at San Xavier (Baldonado 1959).

9. All the details concerning saints' statues at San Xavier are taken from Ahlborn (1974).

10. Robert K. Thomas, personal communication. According to a tradition encountered by Thomas in the 1940s, the villagers fled with their livestock to the top of Black Mountain, a hill to the southwest of San Xavier. Black Mountain's possibilities as a place of refuge were enhanced by the fact that it is a prehistoric *trincheras* site, with stone walls encircling its top. On the occasion of this particular raid, the Apaches were said to have mutilated the statues on the facade and stabled their horses in the church itself. However, Duell (1919:79) published a photograph of St. Cecilia showing her head in place.

11. Delany 1980:139–40.

12. Goss (1974:75–76) discusses the scallop shell motif as it appears at San Xavier.

13. Hilda Kimball, personal communication.

14. Goss 1974.

15. Ahlborn 1974:17–19; Goss 1974.

16. Robert K. Thomas, personal communication.

17. Pfefferkorn provides a dramatic, if extreme, example of how some missionaries came to view some of their Indian charges in a passage describing Sonoran Indians which begins: "Imagine a person who possesses all the customary qualities which make one disgusting, base, and contemptible" (Pfefferkorn 1949:166).

18. Robert K. Thomas, personal communication.

19. Broderick 1975:563.

20. A Tohono O'odham drypainting is illustrated in Wyman (1983: 233–42); the ritual equipment for the wi:gida is illustrated in Hayden (1987:324ff.)

21. Kuehlthau 1967; Thomas 1967.

22. Griffith 1973, illustration on p. 286.

23. Fr. Lambert Fremdling, O.F.M., personal communication.

24. Bleser (1989) has recently written a well-illustrated booklet on Tumacacori's history.

25. Illustrations of the mission churches of Sonora's Pimería Alta may be found in Polzer (1982:40–56) and in Eckhart and Griffith (1975). Further

information on the history of Sonora's missions may be found in Roca (1967).

26. Gebhard (1967) discusses the various Spanish architectural revivals in California.

27. Fr. Theodore Williges, O.F.M., personal communication.

28. The wishing well itself appears to have a complex history. Gribben (1990:6,7) suggests that wishing wells came into being in Western Europe (and especially in England) after the Protestant Revolution, in response to the enforced secularization of Catholic and pre-Christian holy wells. The secular wishing wells simply took the place of the holy wells as places of petition and sources of revenue for the communities where they were found.

Chapter 8 Some Final Thoughts

1. Bahr 1988:142.
2. Underhill 1949:315.
3. Nabhan 1991.
4. Van Dyke 1901; Krutch 1952.
5. McGregor, Alcorn, and Olin 1962.
6. Cultural conservation is receiving increasing attention from folklorists, anthropologists, and others, especially since the National Historic Preservation Act Amendment of 1980 made special mention of the need for preserving the intangible elements of our cultural heritage. For a good discussion of the early phases of the cultural conservation movement, see Loomis (1983).

References

Ahlborn, Richard E.
1974   *Saints of San Xavier.* Tucson: The Southwest Missions Research Center.

Allen, Paul
1990   "El Tiradito's Origins Shrouded in Haze of History," *Tucson Citizen,* January 13, 1990, section A, pp. 7,8.

Anonymous
n.d.   "Shrines along the Camino de los Padres." Three photocopied pages from an original in the Archives of Tucson Diocese. Additional type-written notes by E. Brownell, February 28, 1976.

1979   *El Tiradito—"The Wishing Shrine"* (leaflet). Tucson: Tucson-Pima County Historical Commission

1982   *Garden of Gethsemane/Felix Lucero Park* (leaflet). Tucson: Downtown Development Corporation.

1983a "Battle Over Baboquivari Peak is Beginning to Build." *The Papago Runner,* March 10, 1983, p. 7. Sells, Arizona.

1983b "Papago Tribal Council." *The Papago Runner,* March 10, 1983, p. 8. Sells, Arizona.

Bahr, Donald
1988   "Pima-Papago Christianity." *Journal of the Southwest* 30 (2): 133–67. Tucson: The University of Arizona Press and the Southwest Center.

Baldonado, Luis, O.F.M.

1959 "The Dedication of Caborca." *The Kiva* 24 (April, 1959): 25. Tucson: The Arizona Archaeological and Historical Society.

Bartlett, John Russell

1955 *Personal Narrative of Explorations and Incidents in Texas, New Mexico, California, Sonora, and Chihuahua, connected with the United States and Mexico Boundary Commission during the years 1850, '51, '52, and '53.* Chicago: The Rio Grande Press (reprint).

Bernard-Shaw, Mary, and Chet Shaw

1989 "Borderlands: Views of a Region by Julian Hayden." *Journal of the Southwest* 31 (4). Tucson: The University of Arizona Press and the Southwest Center.

Berrel, George

1909 *Diary*. Typescript on file at the Arizona Historical Society, Tucson.

Bleser, Nicholas J.

1989 *Tumacacori:. From Rancheria to National Monument.* Tucson: Southwest Parks and Monuments Association.

Bolton, Herbert Eugene

1960 *Rim of Christendom: A Biography of Eusebio Francisco Kino, Pacific Coast Pioneer.* New York: Russell and Russell.

Broderick, Robert C.

1976 *The Catholic Encyclopedia.* Nashville: Thomas Nelson.

Caso, Alfonso

1958 *The Aztecs, People of the Sun.* Trans. by Lowell Dunham. Norman: University of Oklahoma Press.

Cather, Willa

1945 *Death Comes for the Archbishop.* New York: A. A. Knopf.

Charlot, Jean

1979 "José Guadalupe Posada and His Successors." In *Posada's Mexico,* Ron Tyler, ed., pp. 29–57. Washington, D.C.: The Library of Congress in cooperation with the Amon Carter Center Museum of Western Art, Fort Worth, Texas.

Cheek, Annetta Lyman

1974 *The Evidence for Acculturation in Artifacts: Indians and Non-Indians at San Xavier del Bac, Arizona.* Unpublished M.A. thesis in anthropology. Tucson: The University of Arizona.

Conde, José Ignacio, and María Teresa Cervantes de Conde
1981   "Nuestra Señora de Guadalupe en el arte." In *Album conmemorativo del 450 aniversario de las apariciones de Nuestra Señora de Guadalupe.* Mexico: Ediciones Buena Nueva.

Conningham, Frederic Arthur
1970   *Currier and Ives Prints: An Illustrated Check List updated by Colin Simkin.* (Rev. ed.) New York: Crown Publishers.

Coolidge, Dane
1985   *Texas Cowboys.* (Reprint of 1937 edition). Tucson: University of Arizona Press.

Coulter, Lane, and Maurice Dixon, Jr.
1990   *New Mexican Tinwork, 1840–1940.* Albuquerque: University of New Mexico Press.

Danielson, Larry
1986   "Religious Folklore." In Elliott Oring, ed., *Folk Groups and Folklore Genres: An Introduction.* Logan: Utah State University Press.

Davis, Edward H.
1920   "The Papago Ceremony of the Vikita." *Indian Notes and Monographs,* 3 (4). New York: Museum of the American Indian, Heye Foundation.

Delany, John J.
1980   *Dictionary of Saints.* New York: Doubleday.

Di Peso, Charles C.
1974   *Casas Grandes: A Fallen Trading Center of the Gran Chichimeca.* vols. 1 and 2. Dragoon: The Amerind Foundation and Flagstaff: Northland Press.

Dobie, J. Frank
1980   *Tongues of the Monte.* Austin: University of Texas Press.

Dobyns, Henry F.
1960   *The Religious Festival.* Unpublished Ph.D. dissertation, Cornell University.

Duarte, Carmen
1982   "Westside family shares El Señor with all who need assistance." *The Arizona Daily Star,* Thursday, September 16, 1982, section H, p. 1. Tucson.
1983   "Cat Mountain has yet to yield treasure of El Tejano." *The Arizona Daily Star,* January 6, 1983, section H, p. 1. Tucson.

Duell, Prent
1919 *Mission Architecture as Exemplified in San Xavier del Bac.* Tucson: The Arizona Archaeological and Historical Society.

Eckhart, George B., and James S. Griffith
1975 "Temples in the Wilderness: The Spanish churches of Northern Sonora, their architecture, their past and present appearance, and how to reach them." *Historic Monograph* 3. Tucson: The Arizona Historical Society.

Ellement, John
1983 "Baboquivari Peak regains wilderness study status." *Arizona Daily Star,* Saturday, April 16, 1983, section B, p.1. Tucson.

Escobedo, Helen
1989 *Mexican Monuments: Strange Encounters.* Photographs by Paolo Gori. New York: Abbeville Press.

Evers, Larry, and Felipe S. Molina
1987 *Yaqui Deer Songs/Maso Bwikam: A Native American Poetry.* Sun Tracks Series, vol. 14. Tucson: The University of Arizona Press.
1990 *Wo'i Bwikam—Yaqui Coyote Songs.* Tucson: Chax Press.

Figgen, Kathleen L.
1989 "Antonio Gil: Folk Saint or Folk Subversive?" Unpublished paper read at the annual meetings of the American Folklore Society, Philadelphia, Pennsylvania, October, 1989.

Fontana, Bernard L.
1961 "Biography of a Desert Church: The Story of Mission San Xavier del Bac." *Smoke Signal,* no. 3, Tucson: The Tucson Corral of Westerners.
1981a *Of Earth and Little Rain.* Photographs by John P. Schaefer. Flagstaff: Northland Press.
1981b "Pilgrimage to Magdalena." *American West* 18 (5).
1987 "Santa Ana de Cuiquibúritac: Pimería Alta's Northernmost Mission." *Journal of the Southwest* 29 (2): 133–59. Tucson: The University of Arizona Press and the Southwest Center.

Forbes, Robert H.
1952 *Crabb's Filibustering Expedition into Sonora, 1857.* Tucson: Arizona Silhouettes.

Foster, Nancy H.
1984 *The Alamo and Other Texas Missions to Remember.* Houston: Lone Star Books.

Gebhard, David
1967 "The Spanish Colonial Revival in Southern California (1895–1930)." *Journal of the Society of Architectural History* 26 (2): 131–47.

Gentry, Howard Scott
1942 "Caminos de San Bernardo." *The Quarterly Review*, Winter 1942, pp. 152–57.

Giddings, Ruth Warner
1959 *Yaqui Myths and Legends.* Anthropological Papers of the University of Arizona, no. 2. Tucson: The University of Arizona Press.

Granger, Byrd Howell
1983 *Arizona's Names (X Marks the Place).* Tucson: Treasure Chest Publications.

Gribben, Arthur
1990 "Holy Wells, Wishing Wells, Evian and Perrier. Who Could Ask for Anything More?" Unpublished paper read at the Annual Meetings of the American Folklore Society, Oakland, California.

Griffith, James S.
1973 *The Catholic Religious Architecture of the Papago Reservation, Arizona.* Unpublished Ph.D. dissertation, the University of Arizona.
1974 "Franciscan Chapels on the Papaguería, 1912–1975." *The Smoke Signal*, no. 30. Tucson Corral of Westerners.
1975 "The Folk-Catholic Chapels of the Papaguería." *Pioneer America* 7 (2): 21–36. Falls Church: The Pioneer America Society.
1979 "*Waila*, the Social Dance Music of the Indians of Southern Arizona: An Introduction and Discography." *JEMF Quarterly* 15(56). Los Angeles: John Edwards Memorial Foundation at the University of California.
1982 "The Magdalena Holy Picture: Religious Folk Art in Two Cultures." *New York Folklore* 8 (2–4): 71–82.
1985 *Respect and Continuity: The Arts of Death in a Border Community.* Nogales and Tucson: The Pimería Alta Historical Society and the Southwest Folklore Center.
1987 "El Tiradito and Juan Soldado: Two Victim-Intercessors of the Western Borderlands." *International Folklore Review* 5:75–81. London: New Abbey Publications.
1988a *Southern Arizona Folk Arts.* Tucson: The University of Arizona Press.
1988b *Legends and Religious Arts of Magdalena de Kino.* Tucson: The Southwest Folklore Center.

References

Goss, Robert C.
1974 *The San Xavier Altarpiece*. Tucson: The University of Arizona Press.

Haefer, J. Richard
1980 "*O'odham Celkona*: The Papago Skipping Dance." In *Southwestern Indian Ritual Drama*, edited by Charlotte J. Frisbie, pp. 239–73. Albuquerque: The University of New Mexico Press.

Hartmann, William K.
1989 *Desert Heart: Chronicles of the Sonoran Desert*. Tucson: Fisher Books.

Hawes, Bess Lomax
1968 "La Llorona in Juvenile Hall." *Western Folklore* 27 (3): 153–69.

Hayden, Julian
1987 "The Vikita Ceremony of the Papago." *Journal of the Southwest* 29 (3). Tucson: The University of Arizona Press and the Southwest Center.

Holzapfel, Herbert, O.F.M.
1942 *The History of the Franciscan Order*. Translated by Antonine Tibesar, O.F.M., and Geruase Brinkmann, O.F.M. Teutopolis, Illinois: St. Joseph Seminary.

Husband, Eliza
1982 "Yard Shrines and Hispanic Culture in Tucson, Arizona: A Preliminary Survey." Unpublished term paper on file in the Southwest Folklore Center.

Ingham, John M.
1989 "Mary, Michael and Lucifer: Folk Catholicism in Central Mexico." *Latin American Monographs,* no. 69. Institute of Latin American Studies. Austin: University of Texas Press.

Ives, Ronald L.
1950 "The Sonoran 'Primer Montezuma' Legends." *Western Folklore* 9: 321–25.

Jordan, Jill
1988 "Satisfaction artist's only payment for recreating statues." *El Independiente*, April, 1988, p. 6. Tucson: The University of Arizona.

Joseph, Alice, Rosamund B. Spicer, and Jane Chesky
1949 *The Desert People: A Study of the Papago Indians*. Chicago: The University of Chicago Press.

Karnes, Harry J.
1954 *Unknown Arizona and Sonora, 1693–1721*. Tucson: Arizona Silhouettes.

Ketchum, Larry
1988 "Roadside shrine re-dedicated." *The Bisbee Observer*, Thursday, June 2, 1988, p. 4.

Kozak, David Lee
1990 *The Cult of the Dead: Neo-Colonialism, Violent Mortality and Religious Change.* Unpublished M.A. thesis in Liberal Arts, Arizona State University, Tempe.

Kreutz, Douglas
1983 "Peak not protected by law, but may be by Indian god." *The Tucson Citizen*, Friday, January 7, 1983, section A, p. 1. Tucson.

Krutch, Joseph Wood
1952 *The Desert Year.* New York: Sloane.

Kubler, George
1961 "On the Colonial Extinction of the Motifs of Pre-Columbian Art." In Samuel K. Lothrop, et. al., *Essays in Pre-Columbian Art and Archaeology.* Cambridge: Harvard University Press.

Kuehlthau, Margaret
1967 "Detergent Uncovers Ancient Frescos in Sonora." *Tucson Daily Citizen*, Thursday, January 19, 1967, p. 25.

Laguna, Angel
1950 "My Pilgrimage to Magdalena." *The Kiva* 16 (1–2): 14–18. Tucson: Arizona Historical and Archaeological Society.

Lange, Yvonne
1975 *Santos: The Household Wooden Saints of Puerto Rico.* Unpublished dissertation, the University of Pennsylvania.
1978 "Santo Niño de Atocha: A Mexican cult is transplanted to Spain." *El Palacio* 84 (4) Santa Fe: The Museum of New Mexico.

Leddy, Betty
1948 "La Llorona in Southern Arizona." *Western Folklore,* 7:272–77.
1950 "La Llorona Again." *Western Folklore* 9:363–65.

Leight, Edward
1983 "Tinsel Paintings." Exhibition catalogue. New York: Washburn Gallery.

Loomis, Ormond H.
1983 *Cultural Conservation: The Protection of Cultural Heritage in the United States.* Washington, D.C.: The American Folklife Center, Library of Congress.

Lumholtz, Carl
1990   *New Trails in Mexico*. Tucson: The University of Arizona Press.

Madsen, William
1960   *The Virgin's Children*. Austin: The University of Texas Press.

Mason, J. Alden
1957   "The Chief Singer of the Tepecanos." In Elsie Clews Parsons, ed., *American Indian Life*. Lincoln: Bison Books.

McAndrew, John
1965   *The Open-Air Churches of Sixteenth Century Mexico*. Cambridge: Harvard University Press.

McCarty, Kieran
1983   Translation of letter from Felipe de Neve to Pedro Corbalán. *SMRC Newsletter*, vol. 17, no. 54, p. 7. Tucson: The Southwest Missions Research Center.

McGregor, S.E., S.M. Alcorn, and G. Olin
1962   "Pollination and pollinating agents of the saguaro." *Ecology* 43: 259–67.

Muench, Joyce Rockwood
1943a   "Shrine of the Three Babies." *The Desert Magazine* 6 (5): 13–15.
1943b   "Author Gives Legend Source." *The Desert Magazine* 6 (8): 28.

Nabhan, Gary Paul
1982   *The Desert Smells Like Rain: A Naturalist in Papago Country*. San Francisco: North Point Press.
1991   "The Moveable O'odham Feast of San Francisco." *Native Peoples* 4(2): 28–34.

Neuerberg, Norman
1987   *The Decoration of the California Missions*. Santa Barbara: Bellerophon Books.

Nolan, Mary Lee, and Sidney Nolan
1989   *Christian Pilgrimage in Modern Western Europe*. Chapel Hill: The University of North Carolina Press.

Officer, James E.
1987   *Hispanic Arizona, 1536–1856*. Tucson: The University of Arizona Press.

Olvera, Jorge
1989   "San Xavier del Bac: Spanish Mission or Muslim Mosque?" In *Dove of the Desert; A Newsletter to the Friends of San Xavier Mission*. Tucson: San Xavier Mission.

O'Neill, C.
1967   "Saints." In *New Catholic Encyclopedia*, vol. 12, pp. 82–83. Washington, D.C.: The Catholic University of America.

Painter, Muriel Thayer
1976   *A Yaqui Easter*. Tucson: The University of Arizona Press.
1986   *With Good Heart: Yaqui Beliefs and Ceremonies in Pascua Village*. Tucson: The University of Arizona Press.

Parmentier, Richard J.
1983   "The Mythological Triangle: Poseyemy, Montezuma, and Jesus in the Pueblos." In *Handbook of North American Indians*, vol. 9. William Sturtevant, general editor, and Alfonso Ortiz, volume editor. Washington, D.C.: Smithsonian Institution Press.

Parsons, Elsie Clews
1936   *Mitla, Town of Souls*. Chicago: The University of Chicago Press.
1939   *Pueblo Indian Religion*. Chicago: The University of Chicago Press.

Perkins, Beverly
n.d.   "Tales of the Wishing Shrine." Unpublished paper on file at the Southwest Folklore Center of the University of Arizona.

Pfefferkorn, Ignaz
1949   "Sonora: A Description of the Province." Theodore Treutlein, trans. and ed. *Coronado Cuatro Centennial Publications*, vol. 3. Albuquerque: The University of New Mexico Press.

Piper, Posy
1988   "Family honors sons who served." *Pimería Alta Historical Society Newsletter,* December, 1988. Reprinted from *Nogales Weekly International*, November 30, 1988, Nogales, Arizona.

Polzer, Charles W., S.J.
1982   *Kino Guide II: his missions-his monuments*. Tucson: Southwestern Mission Research Center.

Ramsey, Jarold
1977   *Coyote Was Going There: Indian Literature of the Oregon Country*. Seattle: University of Washington Press.

Roach, Joyce Gibson
1968   "The Legends of El Tejano, the Texan Who Never Was." *Western Folklore* 17 (1): 33–43.

Roca, Paul M.
1967   *Paths of the Padres Through Sonora*. Tucson: Arizona Pioneers' Historical Society.

References

Russell, Frank
1975   *The Pima Indians*. Tucson: The University of Arizona Press.

Sahagún, Fray Bernardino de
1963   "General History of the Things of New Spain." Trans. from Aztec into English, with notes and illustrations, by Charles E. Dibble and Arthur O. Anderson. *Monographs of the School of American Research and the Museum of New Mexico*, no. 4, pt. 12. Santa Fe and Salt Lake City: The School of American Research and the University of Utah.

Saxton, Dean, and Lucille Saxton
1973   *O'othham Hoho'ok A'agitha/Legends and Lore of the Papago and Pima Indians*. Tucson: The University of Arizona Press.

Saxton, Dean, Lucille Saxton, and Susie Enos
1983   *Papago & Pima to English, English to Papago & Pima Dictionary*. Edited by Robert L. Cherry. Second edition, revised and expanded. Tucson: The University of Arizona Press.

Schweitzer, John, and Robert K. Thomas
1952   "Fiesta of St. Francis at San Francisquito, Sonora." *The Kiva* 18 (1–2): 1–8. Tucson: The Arizona Archaeological and Historical Society.

Seibold, Doris
1949   "Folk Tales from the Patagonia Area, Santa Cruz County, Arizona." *University of Arizona General Bulletin* 13. Tucson: The University of Arizona.

Sheridan, Thomas E.
1988   "How to Tell the Story of 'A People Without History'." *Journal of the Southwest* 30 (2): 168–89. Tucson: The University of Arizona Press and the Southwest Center.

Simmons, Marc, and Frank Turley
1980   *Southwestern Colonial Ironwork*. Santa Fe: The Museum of New Mexico Press.

Sobarzo, Horacio
1966   *Vocabulario Sonorense*. Mexico: Editorial Porrua.

Spicer, Edward H.
1980   *The Yaquis: A Cultural History*. Tucson: The University of Arizona Press.

Stiles, Edward
1982   "Shrines on a small, but important, scale." *Weekender, The Tucson Citizen Magazine*. Saturday, May 8, 1982, pp. 12–14.

Thomas, Bob
1963   "Papago 'Baby Shrine' Recalls Ancient Legend." *The Arizona Daily Star*, Sunday, July 7, 1963, section C, pp. 10, 11. Tucson.
1967   "Rare Mission Art Uncovered." *Arizona Republic*, Monday, March 6, p. 23. Phoenix.

Thompson, Stith
1968   *Tales of the North American Indians*. Bloomington: Indiana University Press.

Toor, Frances
1947   *Mexican Folkways*. New York: Crown Publishers.

Torres, Alva
1990   "Torres' living room is now a movie star." *Tucson Citizen,* Tuesday, January 23, 1990, section B, p. 2.

Underhill, Ruth
1946   *Papago Indian Religion*. New York: Columbia University Press.
1973   *Singing for Power: The Song Poetry of the Papago Indians*. New York: Ballentine Books.

Van Dyke, John C.
1901   *The Desert: Further Studies in Natural Appearances*. New York: Scribner.

Vigil, Maria
1983   "When it Storms, try wrapping the knives." *Tucson Citizen,* Friday, August 26, 1983, section B, p. 1.

Walsh, Michael, Ed.
1987   *Butler's Lives of Patron Saints*. San Francisco: Harper and Row.

Weigle, Marta, and Peter White
1988   *The Lore of New Mexico*. Albuquerque: University of New Mexico Press.

Weisman, Alan
1988   "Arizona's Shrine of St. Joseph." *Arizona Highways,* June 1988, pp. 32–37.

Weismann, Elizabeth Wilder
1985   *Art and Time in Mexico, from the Conquest to the Revolution*. Photographs by Judith Hancock Sandoval. Icon Edition. New York: Harper and Row.

References

Wogoman, Ronald
1972 "Collected Tales from Mexican-American Children: Tucson, Arizona." Unpublished manuscript in the Arizona Folklore Archives of the Southwest Folklore Center.

Wood, Elizabeth Lambert
1956 *Arizona Hoof Trails.* Portland: Binford and Mort.

Woods, Dan
1990 "Legend Says Children Sacrificed." *Tri-Valley Dispatch,* October 24 and 25, p. 3. Casa Grande, Arizona.

Wyman, Leland C.
1983 *Southwest Indian Drypainting.* Santa Fe: School of American Research. Albuquerque: The University of New Mexico Press.

Index

Abel, 157
Accidents: highway, 103–4
Acencio, 8
Acoatl, 12–13
Aduana, 63
Age of Kings, 148
Agreda, María de, 145–46
Agriculture: Tohono O'odham, 67–68
Ajo, 70
Akimel O'odham, 15, 20
Alicante, 5
Ali Chukson, 70, 90
All Soul's Day, 120, 121–22, 123–24
Altarpieces: at Anegam, 88–89. *See also* Retablos
Altar River Valley, 6, 14, 126, 167
Altars: in Tohono O'odham churches and chapels, 83, 88, 89–90, 92; in Yaqui ceremonies, 94, 96
Alto, 126

Americanos, xx, 177. *See also* Anglo Americans
"A" Mountain, 29
Andrew, Saint, 157
Anegam, 72, 88–89
Anglo Americans, xv, xvii, xx, 25, 28, 71, 109, 177, 178; at Fiesta de San Francisco, 32, 59; and San Francisco, 61–62
Anthony (Antonio) of Padua, Saint, 74, 144, 169, 170, 185–86 n.6
Apaches, 46, 101, 103, 190 n.10; war with, 173, 176
Archaeology: Hohokam, 86–87; at Magdalena, 36–37; at Paquimé, 10–11
Arches: processional, 75, 78–79
Architecture, 98, 166; baroque, 148–49, 167; church, 73, 190 n.8; of San Xavier, 150–54, 189 n.3; Tohono O'odham Catholic, 76–78, 84–85; Yaqui church, 94–95

Castillo, Pete, 4, 6, 126
Castillo Morales, Juan. *See* Soldado, Juan
Castro, Jesús, 8
Cat, at San Xavier del Bac, 153, 155, 156
Cather, Willa: *Death Comes for the Archbishop,* 8
Catherine of Siena, 153, 154
Catholicism, xix, 70–71, 172; folk, xviii, 76, 87; and Mexican Revolution, 50, 55; popular, 65, 66; Roman vs. folk, 78, 90, 98, 175; and souls, 114–15; Tohono O'odham, 68–69, 93; Yaqui, 93–99
Cat Mountain, 127
Cavagnaro, Camillus, 164
Caves, 18; Ho'ok's, 19, 20; I'itoi's, xviii, 16–17, 21, 178
Cayetano, San, 47
Cecilia, Saint, 153, 154, 190 n.10
Cemeteries, 111, 129, 138; cleaning of, 120–22; dangers of, 115–16; Mexican, 116–20; O'odham, 123–24
Cempazúchiles, 122
Central America, 125
Ceremonies, xviii; O'odham, 78–79, 99; Yaqui, 94, 95–96. *See also Chelkona;* Dances, dancers; *Wi:gida*
Cervecería Sonora, 50, 51, 55
Chanes, 7
Chapayekas, 95
Chapels, xiv, xviii, 84, 111, 134, 168; family, 91–92; feasting at, 78–82; features of, 76–78, 88; holy images in, 82–83;

in Papaguería, 51, 52–54, 68–69, 75–76, 89–90, 92, 93; purpose of, 85–86, 87; for Juan Soldado, 112, 113–14; Yaqui, 94, 98–99
Charity, 72
Chelkona, 26, 79; songs in, 27–28. *See also* Skipping and Scraping Dance
Cherubs, at San Xavier, 157
Chicago, 125
"Chicken Scratch." *See* Waila
Chihuahua: archaeology of, 10
Children: capture of, 19, 20, 125; dancing by, 26–27; sacrifice of, 24–25, 183 n.23
Children's Shrine, 172; changes at 84–85; offerings at, 25–26, 146; origin of, 22–24
Christ. *See* Jesus Christ
Christianity, 13; native, xviii, 76, 97–98, 174–75. *See also* Catholicism
Chuichu, 59, 69, 168; mission church at, 73–74, 83, 88
Chuk Shon, 29
Churches, 68, 85, 86, 175; colonial mission, 164–67; funds for, 71–72; mission, xviii, 36, 37, 70, 73–75, 83–84, 88–89, 93, 143; Mission Revival style, 167, 168; Yaqui, 94–95
Chuwhiy Guwsk, 52, 173, 176; pilgrimage to, 53–54; on San Francisco, 60–61
Cibuta, 29
Clark, Joe, 8
Clouds, 79
Cocóspera, 167

About the Author

Jim Griffith was born and raised in southern California but he has called the Pimería Alta home since the early 1960s. He lives with his wife Loma within earshot of the bells of San Xavier Mission, just south of Tucson, and is director of the Southwest Folklore Center of the University of Arizona Library. His previous book, *Southern Arizona Folk Arts*, was also published by the University of Arizona Press.